Critical Events in Psychotherapy Supervision

Critical Events in Psychotherapy Supervision

AN INTERPERSONAL APPROACH

Nicholas Ladany, Myrna L. Friedlander,
and Mary Lee Nelson

American Psychological Association • Washington, DC

Fourth Printing, December 2010

Published by
American Psychological Association
750 First Street, NE
Washington, DC 20002
www.apa.org

To order   Tel: (800) 374-2721, Direct: (202) 336-5510
APA Order Department   Fax: (202) 336-5502, TDD/TTY: (202) 336-6123
P.O. Box 92984   Online: www.apa.org/books/
Washington, DC 20090-2984   E-mail: order@apa.org

In the U.K., Europe, Africa, and the Middle East, copies may be ordered from
American Psychological Association
3 Henrietta Street
Covent Garden, London
WC2E 8LU England

Typeset in Goudy by NOVA Graphic Services, Jamison, PA

Printer: Sheridan Books, Ann Arbor, MI
Cover Designer: Naylor Design, Washington, DC
Project Manager: NOVA Graphic Services, Jamison, PA

The opinions and statements published are the responsibility of the authors, and such opinions and statements do not necessarily represent the policies of the American Psychological Association.

Library of Congress Cataloging-in-Publication Data

Ladany, Nicholas.
   Critical events in psychotherapy supervision : an interpersonal approach / Nicholas Ladany, Myrna L. Friedlander, and Mary Lee Nelson.
      p. cm.
   Includes bibliographical references and index.
   ISBN 1-59147-206-7 (alk. paper)
1. Psychotherapists—Supervision of.   2. Psychotherapists—Training of.
3. Psychotherapy—Study and teaching.   I. Friedlander, Myrna L.   II. Nelson, Mary Lee.
III. Title.
   RC459.L33   2005
   616.89'14—dc22
2004016378

British Library Cataloguing-in-Publication Data
A CIP record is available from the British Library.

Printed in the United States of America
First Edition

CONTENTS

PREFACE

Critical Events in Psychotherapy Supervision: An Interpersonal Approach is a guidebook for supervisors of mental health practitioners as well as a text for supervisors in training and the faculty who train them. Our audience includes academic and clinical supervisors in counseling and guidance, counseling psychology, clinical psychology, school psychology, social work, psychiatry, and psychiatric nursing in public and private colleges and universities, agencies, and hospitals.

Essentially, *Critical Events in Psychotherapy Supervision* will help supervisors understand and handle the most frequently encountered dilemmas in psychotherapy supervision. We selected dilemmas that, in our experience, frequently challenge supervisors regardless of their discipline or the settings in which they work. These include handling supervisees' role conflict and ambiguity, cultural- and gender-related misunderstandings, sexual attraction to clients, countertransference and projective identification, skill difficulties and deficits, and problematic attitudes and behavior.

Though this book will be useful in a practical sense, it is also theoretically and empirically informed. The models presented apply to supervision from all theoretical persuasions, and the relationships and processes depicted reflect an interpersonal or relational approach to supervision (Frawley-O'Dea & Sarnat, 2001; Gill, 2001). In this approach, based on contemporary psychoanalytic and humanistic writings (Bromberg, 1982; DeYoung, 2003; Mitchell, 1988; Orange, 1995), supervisory relationships are considered the centralized vehicle for professional growth and development (Skovholt & Rønnestad, 1992). Moreover, the quality of these relationships is a reflection of, and an interaction between, the working interpersonal models of client, supervisee, and supervisor (Bromberg, 1982; Frawley-O'Dea & Sarnat, 2001; Gill, 2001).

From this perspective, in supervision as in therapy, the cognitions, emotions, and behaviors of one interactional partner constrain, and thus influence, the cognitive, emotional, and behavioral reactions of the other partner. In therapy relationships, the client is not a passive recipient of the therapist's wisdom but, rather, an active participant in constructing meaning in the therapeutic relationship. The therapist, also an active participant, is in some ways knowing and in other ways not knowing—neither an expert nor a neutral witness. Thus, the therapeutic process reflects not only the client's relational models as expressed with the therapist but also the therapist's relationally determined reactions to those expressions.

In interpersonal therapy, a strong emphasis is placed on moving through relational impasses to the resolution of therapeutic ruptures (DeYoung, 2003; Safran & Muran, 1996). In our view, the supervisory relationship is key for "working through" challenging and conflictual events, and we provide verbatim illustrations of how focusing on interpersonal processes can liberate both supervisee and supervisor from their sometimes confusing gridlock.

As a final thought, despite emphasis on the supervisory relationship, we discourage psychotherapy with supervisees. In our case examples, we illustrate how boundaries of relational work can be defined within supervision and when supervisory challenges should prompt supervisors to recommend psychotherapy as a follow-up to the work done in supervision.

OVERVIEW OF THE BOOK

The first chapter introduces the task-analytic paradigm on which the book is based, along with a history and description of this events-based paradigm as it has been applied to psychotherapy. The premise is that the resolution of challenging interpersonal dilemmas represents an important change mechanism in supervision, as it does in psychotherapy. Throughout the book, we emphasize the centrality of the supervisory relationship and the importance of collaboration and trust to the successful resolution of the critical events we present.

Although numerous tasks need accomplishment in the supervisory process, we target events or episodes in which there is a critical task to be worked through, such as addressing a supervisee's crisis in confidence or sexual attraction to a client. The specific events we target include (a) remediating skill difficulties and deficits; (b) heightening multicultural awareness; (c) negotiating role conflicts; (d) working through countertransference; (e) managing sexual attraction; (f) repairing gender-related misunderstandings; and (g) addressing supervisees' problematic thoughts, feelings, and behaviors.

The first chapter presents a generic model, or template, for the various process models further explicated in subsequent chapters. Each chapter begins with a review of the available theoretical and empirical literature relevant to the critical event and continues with the basic elements of the model: the Marker, which signals which "task" is to be worked through, the Task Environment, and the Resolution. In the heart of each process model, the Task Environment represents specific stages, or selected interactional sequences (e.g., *exploration of feelings, a focus on self-efficacy, attention to parallel processes*), that we believe can lead to a successful "resolution," or integration, of the original point of concern. For illustrative purposes, case examples with annotated dialogue explicate the processes leading to successful, partially successful, or unsuccessful resolutions of the various critical incidents presented. Some case examples are hypothetical, whereas others are based on actual, yet disguised, supervisory sessions from our own professional work. Each chapter concludes by discussing additional, relevant issues for the reader's consideration.

The final chapter offers further thoughts on our model, theoretical as well as practical, and discusses a context for the reader's application of it in diverse clinical settings. Although the book is designed to be of practical use for supervisors and supervisors in training, the 11 sequences identified and defined and the process models for addressing different critical events, lend themselves to empirical testing, as recommended in the concluding chapter of the book.

ACKNOWLEDGMENTS

We are grateful for the feedback, insight, and guidance provided to us by Clyde Beverly, Amy Centofante, Jennifer Crall, Lia Pate-Carolan, Laura Deihl, Mary Donahue, Eric Frey, Michael Groat, Julie Hau, Pamela Lehman, Abby Russin, John Thibodeau, and Jessica Walker. We further thank Sandra Banks for her technical and citation assistance. We also extend our appreciation to Susan Reynolds for her laudable editorial assistance throughout the process of putting this book together.

Critical Events in
Psychotherapy Supervision

1

TOWARD AN EVENTS-BASED UNDERSTANDING OF THE SUPERVISORY PROCESS

Hold every moment sacred. Give each clarity and meaning, each the weight of thine awareness, each its true and due fulfillment.
—Thomas Mann, *The Beloved Returns*, 1939

Lia, a beginning therapist, has her very first session with a client. Coming from the interview, she is exhilarated but exhausted—the task facing her seems daunting. After the client presented a series of problems, there was a silence, and Lia felt pressed to provide *the answer*, or at least guidance toward the answer.

It is easy to see how a novice would feel overwhelmed. In the initial interview, she is bombarded with what seem like many individual, unrelated bits of information that do not form a coherent whole. Nor do they suggest a pathway for achieving Lia's primary goal, *solving the client's problem*.

With time, as Lia gains an understanding of her client, the process seems more manageable, and she relaxes. She and the client together are creating a miniculture, an island apart, with a regular pace and emotional tone; one with implicit rules and mutual expectations. The "we're both in this together" feeling comes about in part as Lia begins to see her role differently. In sessions, she focuses less on the ultimate outcome, solving the problem, and more on definable tasks, such as encouraging the client to look at her, express feelings, or see something differently.

To illustrate, Yoshi, Lia's client, needs to make an important decision in his life but is consumed with anxiety. Lia's first task is to lower his anxiety so that he can participate productively in the session. The next task is to explore the nature of his dilemma, its context and history, and his feelings about it. In doing so, Lia realizes that Yoshi is not at all in touch with his emotions and has very little self-understanding. Increasing his ability to be introspective becomes an intermediate goal, and the therapeutic dialogue in this phase of treatment revolves around self-exploration, rather than the client's original concerns. As Yoshi becomes more self-aware, together he and Lia reconsider the problem from a different, new perspective. At this point, Yoshi's presenting dilemma is reinterpreted in light of what they have since learned about him, unless another issue becomes more pressing.

Our novice therapist is no longer overwhelmed after interviewing a new client. She has seen that therapy is a sequential process composed of different tasks, and she is beginning to develop a style of her own, partly *me-as-professional* and partly *me-as-a-person*. Of course, this change is largely due to receiving support and guidance in supervision, being less anxious, and seeing that her work is valuable and appreciated.

There is, however, another important reason for Lia's increased comfort—she has a greater understanding of the therapeutic process and how it "works." *How to solve the problem* no longer daunts her because she knows that there are meaningful steps along the way to a problem's solution; steps that she can anticipate and plan for. She also realizes that several (or many) therapy sessions may be needed to achieve a single therapeutic objective, and that within a session, more than one task can be worked on and more than one objective can be addressed.

In other words, over time and with experience, our therapist begins to think about the therapy process in chunks—phases, if you will—rather than seeing it as an uncohesive blur of facts and suppositions. She feels the rhythm of a session as well as the rhythm of change. She can see herself working on something specific within each session and over time. And she learns that occasionally, an event within a session can be incredibly powerful—the "aha" of an insight or a poignant moment of intimacy, propelling the therapy forward in new and unexpected ways.

Perceiving the therapeutic process as a sequence of events occurs naturally with time, experience, and supervision. Perhaps unknowingly, supervisors help novice therapists start to think about each session, or portion of a session, as an episode in a story; each episode having a specific "task" to be accomplished. It is simply unrealistic to work any other way.

Just as therapists need proximal, intermediate, and distal goals for their clients, so do their supervisors. Like the therapeutic process, the supervisory process can be considered a series of episodes, like chapters in a book. As an illustration, consider working with the beginner we just described. The primary goal of supervision, to *learn how to do therapy*, is not addressed globally in any individual session. Rather, there are minigoals in the process, such as to *learn to apply theory to practice* or to *enhance self-awareness*. To achieve each goal, there are proximal (within-session) and intermediate (across-session) tasks. Take the goal, learn to apply theory to practice, for example. In one supervisory session, the task might be to formulate a theoretical conceptualization of the client. In another session, the task might be to consider the client from various theoretical perspectives, to discuss the literature in relation to the client's problems, or to role-play a session using different approaches.

From this perspective, the portion of a session devoted to a given objective is an *event* or *episode*. Like an event in a film, the supervisory event has a definable beginning, middle, and end, during which a *task* or *series of tasks* is addressed. The identification of, working through, and accomplishment of a specific task is essentially what defines the event. For example, in a sexual attraction event, the task would be to help the supervisee *manage sexual attraction feelings*. Events are common and predictable, just as they are in therapy. For example, when the supervisory relationship begins, the event typically involves developing the supervisory alliance, with the associated tasks of *getting to know the supervisee, clarifying the roles and expectations for supervision,* and *reviewing agency policies*.

Some supervision texts describe methods for accomplishing these common tasks, but in this book, we focus specifically on *critical events* in supervision; events that are particularly challenging for both supervisee and supervisor. Each chapter offers guidance in the form of a process model for resolving a different dilemma in supervision. To introduce our perspective, the next sections provide a more detailed description of the events paradigm and a discussion of common critical events addressed in supervision.

THE EVENTS PARADIGM: A CONTEXTUAL APPROACH

Since the 1970s, interest in the supervisory process has increased dramatically in all mental health disciplines. Unfortunately, however, supervision theory and research have not provided the kind of knowledge that practitioners need for their actual, day-to-day work with supervisees. It is generally understood that supervision helps trainees learn how to form relationships with clients, diagnose clients' problems, develop treatment plans, and explore their personal contributions to the therapeutic relationships they engage in, and so forth. Yet supervision theory and research have not focused on how and under what conditions these objectives are best accomplished.

Although we know little about how supervisors get from point A to point B in a session, we do have some general knowledge about effective and ineffective supervision, broadly construed. Research has shown, for example, that role conflict can be detrimental to the supervisory relationship

(Ladany & Friedlander, 1995) and that supervisees especially value working with "interpersonally sensitive" supervisors (Friedlander & Ward, 1984, p. 541). More pertinent questions remain unanswered, however: How do effective supervisors avoid or reduce role conflict, and how do they enhance the supervisory relationship? How do interpersonally sensitive supervisors behave when their supervisees have personal difficulties?

We can address questions like these by considering supervisory processes in context. Interpersonal sensitivity should mean behaving differently with a beginning supervisee who is "in over her or his head" versus with an experienced one in the same situation. It should mean behaving differently with a supervisee who made a serious ethical error versus with one who is experiencing a personal crisis. It should mean considering carefully whether a supervisee has or has not consciously been seductive in reaction to a client who makes sexually explicit comments.

As humans, we naturally make decisions and behave according to our appraisals of the contexts we encounter. As supervisors, we need a wealth of information—about the culture, the setting, the client, the supervisee, and more—to inform our actions. To make effective decisions about how to handle challenging supervisory situations, such as working with an unethical or impaired supervisee, supervisors need a rubric to evaluate the dilemma and choose their behavior accordingly.

The events paradigm we introduce in this book aims to do just that. This paradigm addresses not only what is specifically discussed in supervision (the content) but also the types of sequential, interpersonal behaviors that can effect change. By segmenting the supervisory process into meaningful chunks (i.e., events with specific, definable tasks), we offer readers a conceptual model for facilitating supervisees' growth and development.

TASK ANALYSES OF PSYCHOTHERAPY

Prior to discussing our model of supervision, we turn our attention to the origins of the task-analytic approach. Over the past 15 to 20 years, the events paradigm for studying interactional behavior in context has taken hold in the psychotherapy literature. Although there are various approaches to studying meaningful therapy events, the most common is task analysis. Extrapolating from industrial psychologists' approaches to defining, studying, and measuring task accomplishment in the workplace, psychotherapy researchers (e.g., Greenberg, 1986; Greenberg & Pinsof, 1986; Rice & Greenberg, 1984) have used the task-analytic method to study various critical incidents in both individual (e.g., Clarke, 1990; Greenberg, 1983; Rice & Saperia, 1984; Safran, Crocker, McMain, & Murray, 1990) and family (e.g., Coulehan, Friedlander, & Heatherington, 1998; Friedlander, Heatherington, Johnson, & Skowron, 1994) therapy. Essentially, task analysis is a rational–empirical method for using theory and clinical wisdom to develop a valid model of interaction that results in a specifiable, in-session outcome.

There are several underlying assumptions in this paradigm. The first is that therapy consists of tasks to be accomplished or dilemmas to be resolved, and the cumulative process of accomplishing these tasks within a warm, accepting therapeutic relationship results in good treatment outcomes. To illustrate, therapy discussions often center on a client's "problematic reaction" (Rice & Saperia, 1984, p. 29) to something that has occurred in her or his life or on the "creation of meaning" from confusion (Clarke, 1990, p. 139) or from dreams (Diemer, Lobell, Vivino, & Hill, 1996). In many instances, therapists and clients consider how to resolve intrapsychic conflict (Greenberg, 1983) or complete unfinished business (Greenberg & Foerster, 1996). In other words, we can identify a number of important tasks regularly addressed in therapy because they are what therapy is about.

A second, related assumption is that some tasks are common for virtually all clients and therapists, regardless of the setting or the issues being discussed. Different therapists and clients, in different circumstances, and with different agendas, might need to clear up a misunderstanding (Rhodes, Hill, Thompson, & Elliott, 1994) or repair a break in their relationship (Safran et al., 1990; Safran & Muran, 1996), for example. Although a given task may not be approached in the same way in different therapeutic systems, many therapy tasks are universal.

Third, even though some tasks are universal, therapists with different orientations approach them differently. A common task in individual therapy is discussing termination, for instance. A cognitive–behavioral therapist addresses termination much differently than a psychoanalyst, even though termination events are meaningful for both. Indeed, most task analyses are closely linked to theory. One analysis (Coulehan et al., 1998), having to do with transforming family members' cognitive constructions of their presenting problems, was based on Sluzki's (1992) narrative treatment approach. As other examples, Clarke's (1990) task analysis of the creation of meaning and Rice and Saperia's (1984) task analysis of working through problematic reactions were based in humanistic–experiential theory.

Fourth, within a given theoretical approach, successful events—those in which the task is accomplished—are assumed to proceed similarly, yet the differences in the process that do occur have important clinical implications. This is another point in which context comes into play. Consider the investigation of "sustaining engagement" events in family problem solving (Friedlander et al., 1994). In all the unsuccessful events, but none of the successful events, the families were headed by single parents. This observation suggests that the authors' task-analytic model may only be valid for intact families; different steps may be needed to sustain engagement in single-parent families.

Finally, the accomplishment of therapy tasks is dependent on the quality of the therapeutic relationship. How a therapist proceeds with a given task depends on the stage of the relationship and the degree to which the working alliance is solid. Because the change mechanisms inherent in therapy tasks often involve challenge, clients need to see therapy as a place to take risks and the therapist as a safe person to witness these risks.

How, then, are task analyses conceived and studied? Typically, investigators begin by identifying an event (e.g., a misunderstanding between therapist and client) and its related task (e.g., resolving the misunderstanding). The event and associated task should occur commonly and also be of theoretical importance because they can effect therapeutic change. Friedlander et al. (1994) studied how families move from disengagement to engagement based on structural theory, in which observable, in-session changes are said to alter maladaptive family structures (Minuchin, 1974). As another example, Safran et al. (1990) argued, from the perspective of interpersonal theory, that "ruptures in the therapeutic alliance" are common events in all therapeutic dyads and that the task of "repairing" them is essential to provide the client with an important, new emotional experience and get the treatment back on track (p. 154).

Once a common event and its related task are identified, available theory and research are reviewed for suggestions about how best to approach the task. Typically, the literature has little to offer in the way of guidance other than to provide a general sense of what therapists should do in various situations. For example, from the Gestalt perspective, intrapsychic conflict can be addressed using an empty chair, "top dog/underdog" technique. In the Gestalt literature, however, there are few details defining how to actually accomplish this technique. Therefore, to begin an investigation of internal conflict events, Greenberg (1983) developed a preliminary process model from his own experience using the empty chair technique.

The next step in a task analysis is to undertake an empirical investigation to test the initial clinical–rational model with a few carefully selected events. In a program of research, typically both qualitative and quantitative, the task-analytic model is repeatedly subjected to verification tests so that it can be refined with different samples (Greenberg, 1986). Successful and unsuccessful events are contrasted in a search for regularities and distinguishing elements to account for as many individual differences and contextual factors as possible.

Task-analytic models have three basic components: Marker, Task Environment, and Resolution (Greenberg, 1986). The Marker, at the beginning of the event, is the client's statement or behavior that signals the specific task or dilemma to be addressed as well as a readiness for change. The Marker may be a single statement (e.g., "Why do I always act that way when I don't mean to?") or a segment of discourse lasting several minutes. In sustaining engagement events, the Marker was defined as three unsuccessful attempts by the therapist to get family members to engage with each other in solving a specific problem (Friedlander et al., 1994). Next, the Task Environment includes the "client performances" and the "therapist operations" (Greenberg, 1986), or interventions undertaken to address the task. These performances and operations are essentially the steps on the road toward accomplishment of the task (e.g., reducing internal conflict, sustaining engagement, or repairing a rupture in the alliance). Finally, the Resolution, at the end of the event, is the successful outcome or task accomplishment. Successful events result in a new understanding, an integration of conflict, a plan for action, and so forth. Unsuccessful events, by definition, have no Resolution. Rather, the Task Environment lasts until either the focus changes or the session ends.

The following is an extended illustration of a task analysis in individual psychotherapy. Safran et al. (1990), taking an interpersonal perspective on the therapeutic process, began with the argument that ruptures in the therapeutic alliance are not only meaningful events because they can lead to premature termination, but they also provide an opportunity for the client to experience a healthy resolution of interpersonal conflict. In order to "repair" a rupture, the therapist needs to behave in a manner that contradicts the client's classic response to conflict, such as denial, passive avoidance, withdrawal, or overt hostility.

From both the literature and their own clinical experience, Safran et al. (1990) identified seven potential Markers of a break in the alliance: "overt expression of negative sentiments," "indirect communication of negative sentiments or hostility," "disagreement about the goals or tasks of therapy," "compliance," "avoidance maneuvers," "self-esteem-enhancing operations," and "nonresponsiveness to intervention" (pp. 157–159). A preliminary model of the Task Environment was constructed, and a qualitative analysis of rupture events in a small, select sample of cases guided the authors' initial refinement of the model. Subsequently, the Markers were categorized as either confrontation, direct expression of negative feelings to the therapist or, more commonly, withdrawal (distancing or disengagement; Safran & Muran, 1996). In a more extensive study, empirical tests with confirmatory sequential analyses of observational data (Safran & Muran, 1996) resulted in a rational–empirical model of the successfully resolved withdrawal event. This model shows that in the Task Environment, the therapist focuses on the client's here-and-now experience, explores the meaning of the Marker with the client, and encourages the client to express any negative feelings about the therapy or the therapist directly. The stages of the process include (a) attending to the rupture marker, (b) exploration of the rupture experience, and (c) exploration of the client's avoidance. In the Resolution phase of the event, the client assertively discusses her or his role in the problem and the extent to which this behavior generalizes other interpersonal relationships. In successfully resolved events, the client's "evoked feelings . . . deepen his or her awareness of the avoided experience" (p. 452).

As discussed earlier, theory and research in supervision have unfortunately not progressed to the point at which important events have been identified or task analyses have been conceived and tested empirically. To move the field forward in this direction, we offer readers conceptual process models, developed from our own experience as supervisors, for working through challenging supervision events. As background, the next section presents our perspective on events-based supervision.

AN EVENTS-BASED MODEL OF SUPERVISION

Although supervision has many commonalities with therapy, it can be distinguished in three major ways: It is evaluative, typically involuntary, and explicitly educative (Ladany, in press). Because supervision has a unique set of interpersonal interactions and dynamics, specific elements in the supervisory process look different than those in the therapy process. Hence, events-based models of supervision should be qualitatively different from those that were created for therapy.

Our events-based perspective on supervision integrates supervision theory and research with our clinical experiences as supervisors. Our approach is intended to be heuristically appealing, meaningful, and practical for supervisors, and we anticipate that researchers can use the paradigm to begin investigating change mechanisms in the supervisory process. In essence, the basic process model is a template for identifying and studying critical events in supervision. The specific events discussed in this book (e.g., role conflict, gender-based misunderstandings) were selected because they are common, challenging, and frequently occurring, but other kinds of supervision events could well be identified, conceptualized, and studied using a similar task-analytic template.

Prior to describing specifics of the model, we discuss our assumptions. First, our process models are intended to be pantheoretical in nature. As such, a supervisor working with a supervisee to develop skills in cognitive–behavioral therapy can use the model as readily as a supervisor working within a psychoanalytic framework. Similarly, the model is applicable to the supervision of counseling and psychotherapy within any professional discipline—psychology, psychiatry, social work, counseling, school guidance, or nursing. Second, the model is interpersonal rather than focused solely on the supervisee's development. We see relational aspects as key for working through critical events in supervision. Third, we emphasize the supervisee's learning, growth, and development over case management. We do not see case review as the sole, or even primary, purpose for supervision. Nor do we consider the supervisor to be a surrogate therapist where the supervisor's primary role is to rigidly direct the therapist's approach, as may be the case when implementing and adhering to a manualized treatment. Fourth, as described earlier, we view the supervisory process as a series of events or episodes, each with a definable beginning, middle, and end. Although many events begin and are completed within one session, some may stretch over two or more sessions. Finally, we assume that the *critical events* discussed in this book are particularly salient for supervision outcomes. By this we mean that working through these events to a successful Resolution is the salient mechanism for growth to occur in supervision. Support for this last assumption awaits an empirical test of our models, of course.

Figure 1.1 illustrates the events-based process model of supervision. To reiterate, we identified specific *critical events* because of their common occurrence and importance to supervision outcome, and we use the term *task* to indicate what the supervisor attempts to accomplish in each kind of event. For example, the event may be a portion of a supervisory session devoted to discussing a gender-based misunderstanding, and the task would be to *resolve* the misunderstanding. As detailed in Figure 1.1, the Marker, Task Environment, and Resolution—the three phases in the process model—are embedded within a relationship context; the supervisory working alliance.

Supervisory Working Alliance

The working alliance, one of the most frequently studied variables in the literature, is arguably the foundation for effective supervision. Research indicates that a strong supervisory alliance predicts enhanced supervisee competency with multicultural issues (Ladany, Brittan-Powell, & Pannu, 1997); an effective evaluation approach (Lehrman-Waterman & Ladany, 2001); a flexible balance of collegial, interpersonally sensitive, and task-oriented supervisory styles (Ladany, Walker, & Melincoff, 2001); super-visees' self-disclosure (Ladany et al., 1997; Walker, Ladany, & Pate-Carolan, 2003); and attraction to the supervisor (Melincoff, 2001; Melincoff, Ladany, Walker, Tyson, & Muse-Burke, 2003), self-efficacy (Efstation, Patton, & Kardash, 1990), and satisfaction with supervision (Ladany, Ellis, & Friedlander, 1999). Alternatively, a weak alliance is associated with supervisees' role ambiguity and conflict (Ladany & Friedlander, 1995), nondisclosure in supervision (Ladany, Hill, Corbett, & Nutt, 1996), and vicarious traumatization (Fama, 2003). Supervisees who report a relatively weak alliance are also more likely to view their supervisors' behavior as unethical (Ladany, Lehrman-Waterman, Molinaro, & Wolgast, 1999) and to report counterproductive incidents in supervision (Gray, Ladany, Walker, & Ancis, 2001).

According to Bordin (1983), the supervisory alliance consists of three components: (a) the supervisor and supervisee's agreement on the goals of supervision (e.g., mastering specific therapeutic skills, expanding

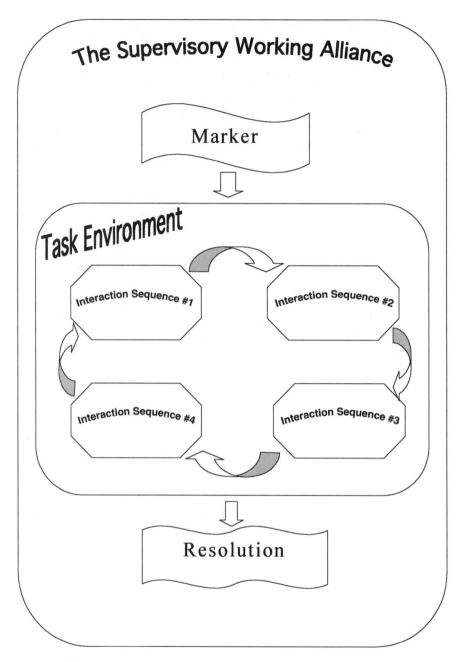

Figure 1.1. Prototypical critical event in supervision.

conceptualization ability, and increasing awareness of how feelings toward a client influence the therapeutic process); (b) an agreement on the tasks of supervision (e.g., focusing on countertransference); and (c) a strong emotional bond. For the alliance to strengthen over time, supervisors and supervisees need to negotiate, implicitly and explicitly, what should happen in supervision and to what end. For example, if one goal is to enhance the supervisee's understanding of family systems theory, the supervisor and supervisee must agree that this goal is meaningful and on ways to accomplish it, such as creating a genogram of the supervisee's own family. Naturally, many different tasks could be chosen to expand the supervisee's understanding of family systems, but the extent of supervisee–supervisor agreement on what should take place (and when) is the rate-limiting step in the successful accomplishment of the goal. Stuck points in supervision usually reflect implicit or explicit disagreements about a goal or task, and these disagreements often signal the critical events described in this book.

At times, however, the problem originates in the quality of the emotional bond. The bond is the keystone of the supervisory alliance, just as it is of the therapeutic alliance. A strong bond is characterized by mutual caring, liking, trust, and respect between the supervisor and supervisee. Indeed, the quality of the bond determines the extent to which the supervisor can suggest or impose goals and tasks that challenge the supervisee. Because the bond is strengthened when the supervisor demonstrates understanding and empathy for the supervisee's struggles, the use of empathy cannot be understated. Ironically, supervisors may be quite empathic with their own clients but fail to demonstrate the same level of caring concern for their supervisees, especially when they give critical feedback. In many cases, a supervisor's zeal to "cause insight" can lead her or him to overlook the supervisee's vulnerability and need for support and reassurance to hear and eventually assimilate the feedback. It is daunting for a supervisee to feel disdain coming from the supervisor when that same supervisor talks about clients with compassion.

In our model, the moment-to-moment relevance of the alliance in working through critical events is construed as figure versus ground. In other words, at times, the alliance is the focus of attention (the figure), whereas at other times, it is the backdrop (the ground) against which the client-focused, technical aspects of supervision take place. Typically, the alliance is in the foreground when it is actively being developed in the initial supervisory sessions. The alliance also should be attended to when conflicts—or ruptures—occur in the relationship. At other times, a strong alliance alternates between being a secure base or a catalyst, with movement back and forth, depending on the nature of the event at hand. When the alliance is strong, for example, the supervisor is in a good position to challenge his supervisee's behavior with clients or to consider alternative theoretical or skill-based perspectives. Moreover, in the context of a strong alliance, the supervisee is likely to be receptive to these types of challenging interactions. If the supervisee becomes overwhelmed or upset by what is occurring during the discussion of a client, the supervisor needs to "check in" about the alliance before proceeding further. Repeatedly failing to do so could irreparably damage the foundation for the supervisory work.

Marker

In a task-analytic model, the Marker is the supervisee's statement, series of statements, or behavior signaling the need for a specific kind of help. Just as the Marker in a therapy event informs the therapist that a particular task needs to be accomplished (e.g., working through resistance) at a given point in time, the supervision Marker informs the supervisor of the need to initiate action and the nature of the action to be taken.

At times, supervisees explicitly ask their supervisors for direction with a particular client, a professional concern, or a skill implementation. In other cases, the Marker is more subtle—not so much what the supervisee says or does as much as what he or she does not do or express. Examples include chronically arriving late to a supervisory session, coming unprepared, or avoiding discussing a particular client. In a group supervision context, the Marker might be a consistent lack of participation or behaving defensively following another supervisee's comments. The Marker may also involve something the supervisor observes in the supervisee's sessions with clients, some attitude or behavior that suggests a need for guidance or corrective feedback. Of course, the supervisor must proceed cautiously when the supervisee does not clearly communicate receptivity to feedback. Thus the Marker signals the initiation of a specific kind of event and the nature of the supervisee's difficulty, informing the supervisor what to do next.

Although different Markers suggest similar problems, different problems can manifest themselves with similar Markers. As an example, role conflict (see chap. 4) can be marked by prolonged silence or missed appointments. These same Markers might also reflect the supervisee's crisis in confidence (see chap. 8). As illustrated in the chapters that follow, the Marker phase of the event continues until it is clear to the supervisor precisely what needs addressing.

Task Environment

After the Marker is understood, the event moves to the Task Environment. Essentially, when broken down into its elemental parts, the Task Environment (see Figure 1.1) is a series of stages, which we call *interaction sequences*, comprised of various supervisor operations (interventions or strategies) and supervisee performances or reactions (cf. Greenberg, 1986). Although Task Environments differ depending on the nature of the event at hand, as well as the supervisee's readiness and developmental level, they generally contain sequences of exploration, clarification, and working through. In a countertransference event (see chap. 5), for example, the interactional sequences include exploring the therapy relationship, focusing on the countertransference (clarification), followed by interpreting the parallel process (working through).

Table 1.1 lists and defines 11 interactional sequences that can characterize the various stages in any given Task Environment. Of course, these sequences are not mutually exclusive, nor is the list exhaustive. Other interactional sequences characterize events not under consideration in this book, such as *case review* and *discussing expectations for supervision*. Our attention is geared to the interaction sequences that occur most commonly in working through the various critical events discussed in each chapter.

TABLE 1.1
Common Interactional Sequences in the Task Environments of
Critical Events

Sequence	Explanation
Focus on the supervisory alliance	Discussion of aspects of the relationship related to agreement on the tasks and goals of supervision (including evaluation), as well as to the emotional bond between supervisor and supervisee. May either be a "checking in" about the alliance or an explicit discussion about what is taking place or should take place in supervision, including a focus on the supervisee's or the supervisor's feelings about their relationship.
Focus on the therapeutic process	A discussion about what is taking place between the supervisee and client (i.e., the kinds of interactions that occur, the strength of the therapeutic alliance, and how the client sees the supervisee's behavior in relation to self and vice versa).
Exploration of feelings	Typically, but not exclusively, a here-and-now focus. Feelings can be expressed about the client, the therapeutic relationship or process, about the supervisee's progress in training, or about personal issues.
Focus on countertransference	Discussion of how and why the supervisee's feelings and/or personal issues are "triggered" by a client's behavior or attitude.
Attend to parallel processes	A discussion that draws attention to similarities between a specific therapeutic interaction and the supervisory interaction. Parallel processes may originate in either interaction and be mirrored in the other.
Focus on self-efficacy	A discussion of the supervisee's sense of confidence in his or her therapeutic skills (either specifically or globally), sense of self as a professional, or ability to function in various roles (e.g., as therapist, student, supervisee, colleague).

continued

TABLE 1.1 (*Continued*)

Sequence	Explanation
Normalizing experience	A discussion of how the supervisee's experience, (either as a therapist, colleague, or supervisee), is typical and developmentally expected or appropriate.
Focus on skill	Discussion of the how, when, where, and why of conceptual, technical, and interpersonal skills. May include role-playing or a discussion of how to apply theory to specific therapy interventions.
Assessing knowledge	Evaluating the degree to which the supervisee is knowledgeable in areas relevant to the case(s) under discussion. Knowledge bases include ethics, research, and theory as applied to practice.
Focus on multicultural awareness	Discussion of the supervisee's self-awareness in relation to individuals who are similar and different from them in terms of gender, race, ethnicity, age, sexual orientation, religion, disability, family structure, or socioeconomic status.
Focus on evaluation	Discussion of the supervisee's performance in therapy, in supervision, and as a professional. May involve a discussion of feedback, critical and positive, either summative or formative.

Various interventions can be used within each interaction sequence. When exploring the therapy relationship, for example, the supervisor might ask about the supervisee's feelings during a silence with a client or ask the supervisee to describe how the client behaved toward the supervisee in recent weeks. When focusing on the countertransference, the supervisor might ask if the supervisee ever felt similarly with other clients or what the emotional reactions bring to mind. In a gender misunderstanding event (see chap. 7), while focusing on assessing knowledge, the supervisor might ask the male supervisee to take a feminist perspective on his client's life story. As yet another example, during a skill deficit event (see chap. 2), the focus on skills might involve demonstrating an intervention technique, asking the supervisee to give the rationale for an intervention, or conceptualizing the client's problems from a different perspective (Neufeldt, 1999).

It should be noted that the stages or sequences in a Task Environment are not altogether discrete, and at times, the process is recursive. Nonetheless, a continual forward movement toward some kind of "working through," can in turn lead to a Resolution. For example, in Figure 1.2, the Marker in a managing sexual attraction event is the supervisee's report of being attracted to a client. Once the Marker is recognized, the Task Environment proceeds through four stages: (a) *exploration of feelings,*

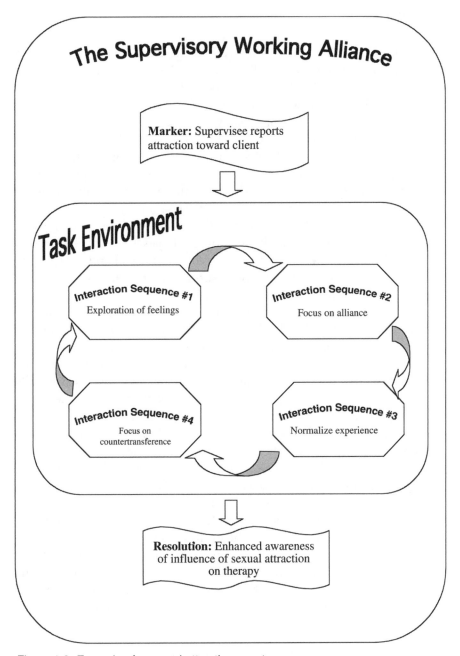

Figure 1.2. Example of a sexual attraction event.

(b) *focus on the supervisory alliance*, (c) *normalizing experience*, and (d) *exploration of countertransference*. Again, for illustrative purposes, Figure 1.2 depicts a linear progression of stages, but in actuality, the order—and even the nature—of these sequences may differ, depending on the complex interaction of supervisee, supervisor, client, setting, and so forth.

Resolution

The final component of the event is the Resolution, which is—in effect—the outcome or accomplishment of a particular supervisory task. Generally speaking, Resolutions can be thought of in four broad categories: an enhancement of or decline in (a) self-awareness, (b) knowledge, (c) skills, or (d) the supervisory alliance. Self-awareness refers to the supervisee's ability to understand how personal biases, feelings, behaviors, and beliefs influence the ability to work with clients. Knowledge includes theoretical, empirical, and practical understanding gained through training and experience. Skills, as discussed in chapter 2, can be interpersonal, technical, or conceptual and range from microskills (response modes like asking open-ended questions, making reflections, or confrontations) to complex therapeutic strategies (e.g., two-chair dialogues). The alliance refers to enhancing the emotional bond, negotiating an agreement on goals and tasks, or repairing a rupture in the supervisory working relationship.

On a more specific level, the nature of the Resolution is intricately linked with the task at hand. Thus, a Resolution might involve insight or planning for action. Essentially, the Resolution is a revisiting of the original concern or point of entry into the event. Successfully resolved events are those in which the task is accomplished. In the case of a successfully resolved countertransference event (see chap. 5), for example, the supervisee comes to understand the basis for personal feelings, thoughts, and reactions to the client and plans how to work with that client in light of this new understanding. Interaction sequences, or stages, along the way toward this successful resolution include *focus on the therapy relationship*, *focus on countertransference*, and *interpretation of parallel processes*.

Partially resolved and unsuccessfully resolved events lack closure. In the worst scenario, the session ends with a tense break in the supervisory alliance. In other cases, the end of the event is more obscure, such as when the supervisee pays lip service to the supervisor's suggestions without a real commitment to change or when the supervisor gives advice, and sensing resistance, abruptly shifts to another topic. Unresolved supervisory events can be as unsettling and damaging as unresolved therapy events.

IDENTIFYING CRITICAL EVENTS

Although there is no task-analytic research per se in supervision, there is some relevant literature on supervisory issues and critical incidents (Chen & Bernstein, 2000; Ellis, 1991; Gray et al., 2001; Heppner & Roehlke, 1984; Loganbill, Hardy, & Delworth, 1982; Rabinowitz, Heppner, & Roehlke,

1986; Sansbury, 1982). Taken together, results from this line of research, although limited, suggest important recurring themes and events in psychotherapy supervision, many of which are universal and linked to supervisees' development.

From this literature, as well as our own supervisory experience, we identified seven critical events, described in subsequent chapters of this book. The tasks addressed in these seven events are remediating skill difficulties and deficits (chap. 2), heightening multicultural awareness (chap. 3), negotiating role conflicts (chap. 4), working through countertransference (chap. 5), managing sexual attraction (chap. 6), repairing gender-related misunderstandings (chap. 7), and addressing problematic attitudes and behavior (chap. 8). Although this list is by no means exhaustive, it represents the most common and challenging incidents that arise in psychotherapy supervision, such as when a client is seductive toward a supervisee, when a supervisee experiences secondary traumatization, or when countertransference threatens either the therapeutic or the supervisory alliance. Finally, as discussed in chapter 9, events may at times occur within events, such as when a skill deficit event becomes a role conflict event or when a multicultural awareness event turns into a problematic attitude event.

Although we occasionally refer to supervision of couples/family therapy or to group supervision, in this book, we focus primarily on the individual supervision of therapists engaged in individual psychotherapy. Each chapter begins with research and theory relevant to the critical event. We then present a model for addressing the event, in which the supervisory task is articulated and "marked" by the supervisee's behavior or comments. Each process model contains a Marker, Task Environment (with suggested interactional sequences), and Resolution, as described earlier. We follow the description of each model with annotated transcripts that illustrate various degrees of successful or unsuccessful Resolutions. In these transcripts, process comments illuminate the supervisor's perceptions of and reactions to the supervisee as the event unfolds. Toward the end of each chapter, we offer special considerations that illustrate unique issues in the event identified that are noteworthy but not included in the annotated transcripts.

FINAL THOUGHTS BEFORE VENTURING FORWARD

Critical supervisory events do not occur in a vacuum. Supervisors and supervisees bring with them personal experiences and issues that create an exciting, albeit at times nonstraightforward, process of supervision. To capture the complexity of these dynamics, throughout the book, we vary the characteristics of supervisors and supervisees, settings, and formats of therapy and supervision to demonstrate the wide application of our models and encourage the reader to think about the diversity of supervision practices.

It is generally expected that supervisees come to supervision with openness to the supervisory process as well as with at least rudimentary skills, knowledge of psychotherapy processes, and self-awareness. However, many supervisees fall short of these expectations. It behooves the supervisor to recognize these shortcomings as early as possible and attend to them responsively and responsibly.

Because beginning and even more advanced supervisees often misunderstand or are threatened by the personal/emotional aspect of supervision, an important aspect of supervision is clarification of expectations. Such clarification can circumvent role conflict or ruptures in the supervisory alliance if, from the outset, the supervisee understands that if a personal concern becomes a focus of the supervisory process, the discussion of this concern may have a therapeutic value for him or her. However, the goal of the discussion is not to modify the supervisee's core personality or resolve personal problems. Rather, it is to work through specific personal barriers that impede work with clients or participation in individual or group supervision.

A discussion of professional behaviors cannot be conducted without consideration and delineation of both professional and unprofessional behaviors. Although our book is not intended as an ethics casebook, the discussions and hypothetical cases put forth will likely address ethical guidelines under which supervisors operate. Hence, supervisor practitioners are encouraged to consider the variety of professional ethical codes and guidelines for supervisor conduct. These codes and guidelines include, but are not limited to, those from the American Association of Marriage and Family Therapy (2001), American Counseling Association (1995), American Psychiatric Association (1995), American Psychological Association (2002), Association of State Provincial Psychology Boards (1991), Association for Counselor Education and Supervision (1995), and the National Association of Social Workers (1999).

Finally, we want to mention our terminology and intention to be inclusive. This book is intended for supervisors of mental health practitioners, including counselors, psychiatrists, psychologists, nurses, and social workers. Supervision literature spans many disciplines. It would thus be imprudent to write a book on supervision without acknowledging the contributions made by authors from all these professional specialties. Moreover, we recognize that good supervision of good therapeutic work is good supervision of good therapeutic work, no matter who is driving and regardless of whether you call it *counseling*, *therapy*, *psychotherapy*, or *Fred*. To that end, we use the term *supervisee* rather than *trainee* to include postdegreed clinicians who may be receiving supervision. Further, although we believe that the differentiation of counseling from therapy is neither precise nor meaningful, we use the term *therapy* as shorthand for *psychotherapy,* which (broadly defined) involves one person helping someone else therapeutically by using psychological principles. Ultimately, we acknowledge the richness of the many disciplines that have contributed to this field and that, together, provided us with a complex (but hopefully enlightened) perspective on the supervision of psychotherapists.

2

REMEDIATING SKILL DIFFICULTIES AND DEFICITS: IT'S MORE THAN JUST TEACHING

Force has no place where there is need of skill.
—Histories, III, 127, Herodotus, 485–425 B.C.

Legend has it that after the ancient Japanese samurai warriors were trained, they were forbidden to touch their weapons for a year. On return, their handling of the sword was no longer stiff and clumsy, but rather refined and fluid, as if an extension of themselves. So, too, the awkwardness felt by novice therapists dissolves with time, and their professional demeanor and clinical skills begin to feel more like a part of themselves.

Because novices are keenly aware of the differences between a therapeutic relationship and other relationships, their initial experience of themselves as therapists resembles a "false self." During the earliest phase of their development, supervisees are exquisitely sensitive to their supervisor's feedback (Bernard & Goodyear, 1998) and can either welcome criticism or see it as a personal indictment. If they had prior training in interviewing skills (e.g., Hill & O'Brien, 1999), they may expect their supervisors to examine each intervention they make microscopically. In the absence of experience with actual clients, it is difficult for the novice to understand how techniques, strategies, case conceptualizations, treatment models, and therapeutic relationship development fit together to define their clinical skills.

Indeed, clinical skills cover a vast territory, from communicating empathy to interpreting transference to following a case-sensitive treatment strategy.

When supervisors work with beginners, supervision focuses in large part on skill *improvement*. Although experienced supervisees also need and want to improve their skills, skill *deficits* can be more problematic. For this reason, recognizing and correcting skill deficits can be far more difficult with experienced supervisees than with novices. Advanced supervisees may not only be less aware of their deficiencies but also may be less willing to recognize them or to accept supervision to overcome them (Bernard & Goodyear, 1998).

Because many frontline therapists receive little or no supervision on their work, a supervisee may see clients for several years without knowing that something is awry. Supervisors often encounter this situation when a master's level clinician returns to school for more training, particularly if he or she receives interpersonally oriented supervision for the first time. It takes strength and maturity to allow one's work to be scrutinized closely after having worked independently for a long time. For this reason, when supervisors assume a didactic role with advanced supervisees, it is particularly important to be sensitive to the supervisory relationship. As illustrated in this book (e.g., chap. 4 on role conflict and chap. 7 on gender misunderstandings), giving feedback clumsily can jeopardize the supervisory alliance and harm the supervisee.

In this chapter, we consider how to work with supervisees' skill deficits in three broad areas: interpersonal skills, technical skills, and conceptual skills. Although there is far more research on interpersonal skills than the other two (Lambert & Ogles, 1997), surprisingly little is known about how supervision affects skill development. Most studies have focused on deliberate skill training (e.g., as in a prepracticum course) rather than on supervision of actual clinical work (Sansbury, 1982). For our purposes, interpersonal skills refer to establishing rapport and communicating empathy, responding with sensitivity—basically creating a warm, inviting climate for clients to explore themselves and their lives. Technical skills refer not only to making accurate, quality interventions but also to negotiating the goals and tasks of therapy, implementing a treatment plan, handling resistance and transference, and carrying out effective referrals and terminations. Finally, conceptual skills refer to psychodiagnostic assessment, case conceptualization and management, and the development and modification of theoretically driven treatment plans. Although these skill classes overlap, we discuss them separately in the following section to provide a framework for the process model that follows.

THREE CLASSES OF CLINICAL SKILLS

Interpersonal Skills

Before Harry Stack Sullivan's (1953) *The Psychiatric Interview*, psychoanalysts had little understanding of how paying close attention to the interpersonal aspects of treatment—observing the client in the unfolding interaction with the therapist—could facilitate diagnosis and treatment. Likewise, beginning therapists discover the power of their relations with clients.

When the focus in supervision is turned to the personal capacity to connect, respond with sensitivity, and contain strong emotions, many novice supervisees become highly anxious. Understandably, they fear being evaluated by the supervisor in this arena when they realize that they, as individuals, figure prominently in the therapeutic equation. Although many people are drawn to the field because they feel comfortable in a caretaker role with friends and family members, this is not the case for all supervisees. The person who views a therapist's work as primarily intellectual—figuring out diagnoses, developing and applying treatment protocols, writing reports—may suffer tremendously when told that he or she lacks some basic interpersonal skills.

Skill development presents many challenges for beginning therapists. Although most training programs offer some kind of prepracticum that systematically teaches relationship skills (Lambert & Ogles, 1997), many supervisees need to revisit these skills once they begin seeing clients. Demonstrating good interpersonal skills in a clinical context when a client's welfare is at stake is far more complex than practicing them in brief role-plays. Relying on skills they have used all their lives is a start, but novices soon learn that "being a good listener" is not enough. To develop and sustain an emotional bond that can weather the ups and downs of therapeutic work, an effective therapist needs to pay close attention to the client's comfort level and respond with caring concern, regardless of personal feelings, the topic, or the client's level of disturbance and sense of urgency. Therapists need to strike a balance between being fully themselves (e.g., self-disclosing, laughing, or crying spontaneously) and being therapeutic. This balance is not easily understood or achieved. It takes skill, for example, to stay silent for long periods of time, waiting for a client to fully experience whatever is needed in the moment. It is not uncommon for a beginner to rush to fill the silence or to smile along with clients who laugh derisively at themselves, as they might naturally do in a social situation. Another common hurdle is learning to use body language (leaning forward, maintaining eye contact, etc.) appropriately, being culturally sensitive, and respecting a client's boundaries in this area. Yet another skill is sensing when to push and when to back off, when to follow through with one's plan for the session, and when to shift gears because the client simply "isn't there yet." For many supervisees, the greatest challenge in their training—particularly when the therapy session is being observed or taped—is to learn to focus on the client rather than on their own performance anxiety. Sustaining attention on the client's needs from moment to moment cannot be done effectively, however, if supervisees cannot rely on solid interpersonal skills to carry them through.

Complex interpersonal skills are, of course, more difficult to address and remediate in supervision. Some supervisees are consistently unresponsive to strong affect from clients, especially when there is a hint of anger toward themselves. Therapists need to stand firm in the face of clients' hostility without retaliating. Managing boundaries (e.g., ending a session skillfully when a client is crying or gently, but firmly, declining a client's social invitation) can be challenging, even for seasoned therapists. To manage these kinds of situations effectively, therapists need to know themselves well, personal strengths and weaknesses, and know when to ask for help from a supervisor or colleague.

Research suggests that supervisors who demonstrate empathy, genuineness, and positive regard are likely to enhance their supervisees' behavior in these areas (Neufeldt, Beutler, & Banchero, 1997). This modeling effect is not a given, of course, and addressing supervisees' interpersonal skill deficits can be particularly troubling for supervisors. Remediation in this area is essential because the quality of the therapeutic relationship plays a greater role in the success or failure of treatment than does the specific theoretical approach taken by the therapist (Wampold, 2001). Whereas some supervisees may simply need to be shown where their anxiety interferes with the therapy relationship or be given permission to be more or less active in their sessions, other supervisees may so lack basic social skills that there is little a supervisor can do to make a significant difference. If interpersonal skills are so poor that a supervisee is unable to relate emotionally with clients or sustain a positive relationship, the supervisor should consider whether or not the supervisee is indeed suited for the profession (see chap. 8 on problematic attitudes and behavior).

Supervision is like a double bind in that the supervisee must simultaneously demonstrate competence and expose areas of weakness (Ward, Friedlander, Schoen, & Klein, 1985). The individual who is able to move fluidly from a superordinate role as therapist to a subordinate role as supervisee (Holloway, 1984) without overwhelming anxiety or defensiveness most likely has the requisite social skills to be an empathic therapist.

Technical Skills

There is no clear boundary between technical and interpersonal skills, for the reason that the person of the therapist is in large measure the agent of change. Although the relationship is the melody, so to speak, one also needs to know the lyrics. When supervisees are first learning, they are less aware of the relationship dynamics and more concerned with what to say next, what kinds of questions to ask and how to phrase them, if and when self-disclosure is appropriate, how to obtain the right background information, how to confront and interpret effectively, and so forth. If a supervisee has no interpersonal deficits, addressing these kinds of skills can be fairly straightforward. Through reading, didactic discussion, observation, and modeling in supervision, supervisees learn techniques. With beginners, a task-oriented supervisory style (Friedlander & Ward, 1984) is effective for developing and improving these skills. Indeed, it is common for an entire supervisory session to be technique focused if the relationship is strong.

A problem can arise, however, when addressing a technical skill demands that the supervisee exhibit a high level of self-awareness and a willingness to explore personal issues with the supervisor. Concerned with what to say when, the supervisee may not be aware that finding the answers can come from within. One example is recognizing transference difficulties as they occur in the therapy session and responding in a way that facilitates the client's insight. Because this is an advanced level of technical skill, supervision in this area can be complex, involving shifts in focus from the therapy relationship to the supervisory relationship and back again to the therapy relationship.

Naturally, techniques are not effective when simply applied like a string of formulas. At the beginning of their training, supervisees tend not to understand this point. Thus, supervisees commonly ask questions such as, "Is it okay to give advice?" Once a supervisee understands that techniques are selected based on a case conceptualization and in response to the client's emotional state, level of insight, stage of therapy, time elapsed in the session, and the quality of the therapeutic relationship, questions to a supervisor sound more like, "Would it have been better to let the client change the topic at this point or to have pushed for more feelings?" In other words, supervisees who have a good handle on technical skills will think like Paul (1967), who defined successful therapy as knowing which approach to use with which client under which conditions.

Because addressing basic technical skills with a beginning supervisee is fairly straightforward, deficiencies in this area are to be expected. When a beginner continually misses the client's affect or does little else but ask questions, simply drawing the supervisee's attention to the problem and discussing or role-playing a different approach may be all that is needed. Problems can arise, however, when a supervisee has technical problems that the supervisor does not expect. Seeing the supervisor's surprise that a particular skill has not yet been mastered, a supervisee is apt to become anxious, possibly defensive, because the evaluative aspect of supervision has now come into the foreground.

Conceptual Skills

Conceptual skills refer not only to making diagnoses but also to interviewing for important background information, assessing risk (e.g., suicide, homicide, child abuse), determining if and when to use standardized assessment tools, using a theoretical model to conceptualize a client's complaints in relation to personal history, writing integrative reports, and considering whether or not any form of treatment is likely to be successful for a given client. Treatment planning, also in this class of skills, refers to using assessment information to develop a case-sensitive plan that takes into account the clinical setting; the treatment format (individual, couples, family, or group therapy); the client's motivation, immediate needs, and resources; and the therapist requirements (background, skills, experience) to carry out the treatment. Treatment planning skills also involve identifying implementation barriers and the ability to revise the plan as needed (Linehan, 1980, 1993). Although the assessment and treatment plan should be congruent, the plan may not directly address all the client's difficulties due to any number of personal or environmental constraints. The skilled supervisee knows to take these factors into account and can make a case for doing so.

How one assesses a client is, of course, largely dependent on one's theoretical approach. Some training programs teach a single model of therapy, often with the help of a treatment manual, and supervisees learn the types of clinical material to look for to form an adequate assessment and treatment plan using that approach. In other training programs, supervisees are encouraged to try different theoretical models, selecting them based both on their clients' needs and their own developing style. Regardless of the supervisor's training philosophy, addressing conceptual skills is fundamental because supervisees cannot see how to take their clients from point A to point B without some theoretical understanding of the client's needs, strengths, and capacity for entering into a therapeutic relationship.

To conceptualize a case competently, the supervisee must have not only the ability to elicit and recognize important facts from the client's history, but also a basic understanding of normal development, psychopathology, and how a client's in-session behavior can inform the case conceptualization. Often, when asked for an assessment, beginning supervisees fail to make clinical inferences, instead paraphrasing the client's presenting concern as, for example, "She can't make a decision about leaving her husband," or "He's got family problems." At the next stage of their development, supervisees might say, "She has low self-esteem," without being able to articulate why. Because therapists' cognitive and implementation skills may develop independently (Avis & Sprenkle, 1990), a supervisee may well be able to conceptualize a client's difficulties but have little sense of how to carry through a treatment plan. Conversely, supervisees might feel "in their bones" what clients need at a given moment but not be able to articulate a cogent rationale for their interventions.

Deficits in this skill area may be simply due to the supervisee's lack of knowledge or experience or to anxiety. A more serious deficit is an inability to organize, synthesize, and integrate clinical material in a coherent, meaningful manner. Because the consequences of poor assessment and treatment planning can be dangerous, working with supervisees on this aspect of their skills is critical. Supervision as case management focuses on assessment and treatment planning in a strictly client-focused way, whereas an interpersonal approach to supervision also focuses on the trainee. As a starting point for drawing inferences about the client, supervisees may be asked to describe and then conceptualize personal reactions to the client's presentation. The supervisee's willingness to be supervised in this way depends on her or his openness as a person as well as on her or his expectations about what should take place in supervision.

PROCESS MODEL

Successfully carried out skill deficit events have as their goal not only to identify and remedy a problem but also to deepen the supervisee's understanding of and contribution to the therapeutic process. In general, the event begins with a Marker and proceeds in the Task Environment with some or all of the following interactional sequences: *focus on skill, focus on evaluation, attend to the parallel process, focus on the self-efficacy, focus on the therapeutic process,* and *focus on the supervisory alliance.* Typically, the supervisory relationship is in the foreground for both the Marker and Resolution (in this case, skill integration), whereas in the middle steps, it is in the background.

Marker

The Marker of a skill event can begin either with supervisees expressing concern about what they are or are not doing therapeutically or by supervisors becoming aware, through observation or discussion of the case, of a problem that needs addressing in supervision. If, as illustrated in the following excerpt, the supervisee knows that something in the therapy is not working, but the initial concern is vague, the Marker lasts until the supervisor has a clear sense of the skill(s) to be focused on in the supervisory episode. In other cases, a supervisee could be vaguely aware of her or his needs for skill improvement, commenting to the supervisor, for example, "I need another way to respond when my client keeps asking me for my opinion." Still more aware is the supervisee who, seeing a pattern in his or her behavior across clients, says, "I know I'm comfortable with confronting, but I worry that I push too hard, and maybe I'm not picking up the signals about when to quit or back off with my clients."

Markers like these reflect a skill *difficulty.* In more challenging situations, Markers that the supervisee is unaware of, tend to reflect skill *deficits.* Watching a videotape or listening to an audiotape, a supervisor takes note of many areas for improvement. The frequency of a behavior can suggest a deficiency (e.g., the supervisee who continually smiles anxiously when clients discuss painful feelings or the supervisee who only uses questions, never varying his or her technique). Deficits in relationship skills are often discovered by observation rather than by discussion because supervisees tend to be unaware of deficiencies in this area. An example might be under- or overactivity on the supervisee's part, with the client appearing more subdued or frustrated as the therapy session progresses. Observation may also reveal an error in judgment, signaling a skill deficiency, such as the supervisee's failure to assess for risk (e.g., child abuse, suicide) when it seems probable.

In the Marker, if the supervisee brings up a skill difficulty for discussion, the concern may be expressed neutrally or with a great deal of emotion if he or she is feeling overwhelmed or inadequate. Sometimes the emotion is so strong that the supervisor fails to see the Marker as involving skill enhancement, such as the novice supervisee who says, "I don't think I'll ever be good at this!" or (a more advanced supervisee), "I'm feeling very shaky right now and don't know why!" Clearly, with these kinds of Markers, the supervisor needs to attend to the supervisee's feelings, but it is also necessary to explore whether or not there is a skill deficit underlying the anxiety. Experienced supervisees may at times feel completely at sea, not realizing that insecurity is natural when therapists are on the brink of moving their skills to a new level.

Task Environment and Resolution

After the Marker, the task of addressing a skill deficit usually proceeds by focusing on the skill—relationship, technical, conceptual, or a combination of these. If more than one type of skill is involved, there may be a sequence in the event for each, as illustrated in the following transcript. The focus on skill sequence can proceed in a number of ways—by discussing the skill independently of any specific case, observing a tape of a session together, role-playing, and so forth. In the case of interpersonal skills, attending to parallel processes can be a useful way to demonstrate empathic attunement, as shown in the second case that follows. In some events, there may also be a focus on evaluation, a stage in the Task Environment in which the supervisor offers feedback about the supervisee's in-session behavior.

Once the supervisee has a better understanding of her or his difficulty and how to overcome it, the event moves to the next stage, focus on the therapeutic process. Here the supervisor aims to expand the supervisee's understanding of the skill in the context of a specific case. At this point, the "it depends" aspects of the skill are discussed (i.e., under what circumstances and with what goal in mind). For example, if the skill under discussion is interpretation, the supervisor and supervisee might consider how interpretations facilitate a client's insight and lead to behavior change, when they are indicated or contraindicated, how the supervisee could determine if the client is receptive to an interpretation, and so on. These topics might begin

with one client and be explored later for other clients with whom the supervisee is working.

Usually, at some point in the event focusing on self-efficacy, the supervisor returns to the original concern to check in. This checking in may be
about the supervisee's comfort level with the new skill, knowledge of when
and where to apply it, its relation to other skills, or its relation to the treatment plan with one or more clients.

A successfully resolved skill event is signaled by some expression of
understanding, relief, or confidence on the part of the supervisee as well as
a new understanding of the skill in question. In the sections that follow, we
present two very different skill events, a simple skill difficulty event with a
novice supervisee and a more complex deficit event with a highly experienced supervisee.

A SUCCESSFULLY RESOLVED SKILL DIFFICULTY EVENT
WITH A NOVICE SUPERVISEE

In this illustration, John, a 23-year-old novice supervisee in practicum
at an outpatient clinic of a private psychiatric hospital, is working with Ted,
his first client, whose compulsive sexual acting out has compromised his
marriage. The task in this episode involves a focus on John's skill difficulties
in two areas, technical and conceptual.

This episode begins when John expresses a common concern of neophyte supervisees: Am I meeting my client's needs and expectations? A latent,
more fundamental concern is, Am I doing what I am supposed to be doing
with this client? Because this worry is so general, the supervisor first needs to
determine where the supervisee's anxiety is coming from. It may be that John
is searching for feedback, feeling unsure about how the supervisor views his
work. Alternatively, it may be that John is communicating a felt need to focus
on and improve his interpersonal, technical, and/or conceptual skills.

Marker

John: . . . Some things that have come up for me are just, "Okay, I'm into talking
with him [Ted] and listening and reflecting feelings and stuff," but again, is it
enough? I guess the question comes up, "Where do I take it?" in the sense that . . .
And his view of therapy is, you know, to be able to talk with someone, and you
know, maybe they'll point out certain things, like questions or something that . . .

Supervisor: Is he kind of looking for answers? Or is he just looking for someone to
help him explore?
wants to ascertain the client's agenda

John: I think a little bit of both, but I don't think it's like, "Tell me the answer."
He doesn't expect that.

Supervisor: Mmhmm.

John: But it's like, "Maybe, by what you're asking me to reflect on, boom, an answer will come out." Or something will come out. So it's kind of like looking for some conclusions or something to grasp on to deal with those . . .

Supervisor: It sounds kind of collaborative, like you're going to . . .
reflects John's description of the therapeutic alliance

John: Right.

Supervisor: . . . experience together, and you may have some insight, and you may . . .

John: Right.

Supervisor: . . . have some things to contribute.

John: Right. And, so I guess for me, the thing that comes up now is, "Yeah, it's going good, but how do I keep this . . ." because I want to work with him on this, and I don't want him to be just where he feels like every session I come in and ask him questions, and you know, we'll talk about some stuff, but he doesn't really feel like he's getting anything.
worries that he may be disappointing the client

Because the initial sequence in this episode was so vague, the supervisor began by trying to ascertain the basis for John's concern. If there had been a rupture in the therapeutic alliance with Ted, it may be because John was not emotionally connected with his client or because he and the client had not reached a mutual understanding about the goals and tasks of therapy. If rapport was there and the alliance was intact, on the other hand, the problem may be due to John's restricted repertoire of techniques or to a fundamental lack of understanding on his part about the client's problems and how to develop a plan for treating them.

Supervisor: You're kind of worried that he won't be getting enough to keep coming in?
reflects

John: Mmm.

Supervisor: What evidence do you have so far that what you're giving him isn't enough? I mean, are you . . . is he invested, or are you feeling like he's, "Yeah, well maybe I'll see you next time and maybe I won't?"
seeks clarification in terms of behavior

John: No. There's a few . . . He . . . he seems, in a sense, to just want to deal with what's going on because he knows he's hurting right now. Um, he doesn't give me any problems about making appointments. And he's very open. When I ask him questions, he'll be open, not necessarily in the sense that he hasn't dealt with these things before, but he won't hide things from me. Like, if he went out cruising and wound up sleeping with a stranger, he'll tell me he slept with a stranger.
shows an awareness of the client's pain

John's description of his client's behavior leads the supervisor to conclude that there is no reason to suspect that either the supervisory or the therapeutic alliance is in trouble. Rather, as the Marker progresses, it became clear to John and to the supervisor that John's fear about the client's dissatisfaction is a projection of his own insecurity. With skillful questioning, the supervisor recognized that the general supervision theme is to enhance John's sense of efficacy with this client by providing him with a clearer understanding of how to work and how the therapeutic process can meet the client's needs.

Supervisor: Uhhuh. So the evidence that you're fearing you're not giving him enough is coming more from you than from anything you're getting from him?
questions whether John's concern may be a projection

John: Oh, definitely. I think it's more from me than from anything he's giving me right now. I guess what really got me started is, in the end, I said, "How was this for you?" And he kind of said, "You know, it's all right, okay, you know. I like that I can come somewhere, and I can speak my head off without being told to shut up or . . ." And, so I'm thinking that's what I want to do but yet, you know, is that going to be enough for this person? So I totally think it's me more than anything.
expands on his projection

The Marker, in this episode, began with John's stated worry and ends at this point, when it became apparent to the supervisor that John was either missing or avoiding his client's anger. When John said he feels he's not providing his client anything beyond what the client himself understands, the supervisor realized that John is only tuning into the client on a cognitive level. The Marker is now complete because the supervisor sees that John's skills need improving in two areas, technical (i.e., responding to client anger) and conceptual (i.e., learning that exploring a client's feelings can promote insight and change).

At this point, because John was not able to articulate clearly the source of his anxiety, the supervisor turns to the videotape to evaluate what skills John might be lacking or where he is floundering in his work with the client.

Focus on Evaluation

Supervisor: Uhhuh. (*pause*) Let's take a look at the tape together, shall we, to see if we can get a perspective on what's happening for him?

John: Okay.

Supervisor: (*listening to the tape*) Is this his wife he's talking about?

John: Yeah.

Supervisor: He's pretty insightful.
offers an inference

John: Yeah, that's right. I'm saying these things, but he's pretty insightful on his own.
suggests that he has little to offer conceptually

Supervisor: (*listening for a few more minutes*) Did you reflect that anger?
notes a missed opportunity

John: (*anxiously*) Yikes, no. I, I, I got . . . I don't know why I didn't reflect that. I knew it was there.

Supervisor: Uhhuh. You missed it.
direct feedback

Because the skills that John needs to improve are in two overlapping areas, the supervisor begins working with one (technical), bringing in the other (conceptual) at appropriate times. In the next stage of the Task Environment, the supervisor begins by exploring John's phenomenological experience of his client during the anger episode in the therapy. From the beginning of this next sequence, John shows a willingness to consider his own part in the problem they have identified. As the excerpt illustrates, it is not that John failed to recognize his client's anger.

Focus on Skill (Technical)

John: (*listening, then anxiously*) I said that instead. I think that was a little safer.
open

Supervisor: But it was a reframe you offered him.
reassures John that the intervention was appropriate

John: Yes, but I thought at the time that he was totally angry. (*pause*) Maybe I wasn't ready to deal with that right then—I didn't feel comfortable.

Supervisor: Well, what do you think was happening?
explores John's understanding of the process

John: For me or for him?

Supervisor: For you.

John: I was there for him.
recognizes his connection to the client

Supervisor: And you knew that was anger.
points out John's accurate recognition of the client's felt state

John: Yeah. I knew he was angry.

Supervisor: But what was that about resisting saying, "You sound angry?"
asks John to consider what blocked his natural response

John: I don't know because . . . I really didn't . . . I don't feel that it would have been threatening for me to make that statement.

Supervisor: Uhhuh. (*gently*) Well, how comfortable are you with anger in your own life?
explores a bit deeper

John: (*laughing*) I think that's one area where I *don't* have any trouble!

Supervisor: (*laughing along with him*) Okay. So then when Ted . . .
accepts his response and refocuses on the therapy

John: I guess, I mean it's like he already knows he's angry about it. But maybe I should have said it, because maybe he really doesn't realize he's angry.
begins to question his view of the client

Supervisor: Was there anything in there . . .

John: Oh, I know . . . A little before that he said, you know, "I'm still angry," or he said something like, "I'm still hurt and angry" or something like it.

Supervisor: So he'd already said it, and you didn't want to be redundant, or do you think you wanted to put a cap on it? And not stir it up, you know, and have him disclose too . . .
explores John's motivation to avoid the anger

John: I wanted his feelings to come out, and they kind of did, but the only thing that I worried about was how would I react when I'm in there, feeling these feelings that he's having in the sense that . . . really feel like I'm there with him, genuine with him, or if I'm just on the outside watching, you know?
recalls his concern of appearing false

Supervisor: Mmhmm.

John: And I don't want to be that type of person who's just calculating and watching.

Supervisor: So if you said, (*with feeling*) "Boy, Ted, that sounds like you're angry!"—that would feel like you were on the outside being calculating?
reflects and models

John: No. I think depending on how I said it, and if it seemed, wow, you know, like it touched me or like it's . . . then I think it would have happened. But if I had gone back and said, you know, "Well, you sound pretty angry about that," it would have been more like analytical in a sense, I guess.
recognizes a missed opportunity

Supervisor: Yeah. So, to you it makes a difference if it comes from your heart, like joining with him, like, "Wow!"
acknowledges John's understanding of empathic attunement

John: Yeah.

Supervisor: (*pause*) Let's go back to his anger. (*listening to the tape*) See how angry he is at this point? Maybe he doesn't think you . . .
points out that the client is not feeling heard

John: I think I'm taking it too cognitive. A lot of it's cognitive. I'm not making process statements. I knew he was angry from the voice. (*listening*) See, here I think he knows I'm engaged in what he's saying.
acknowledges the problem

Supervisor: Right.

John: But I don't know if he knows that I'm there with him at the level he is with his anger.
considers that his error may have been perceived by the client

When John said he doesn't fear the anger, the supervisor switched the focus to John himself, cautiously exploring John's ability to express anger in his own life. When John quickly and lightheartedly joked that anger is not a problem for him personally, the supervisor accepted this at face value and switched the focus back to the therapy process. This stage in the event ends when it became clear that John, not recognizing his difficulty, did not understand the importance of validating the client's anger and feared sounding false and mechanical if he were to do so.

Here was a choice point, however, because the supervisor could well have probed further into John's comfort level with anger. The supervisor opted instead to see whether John can work with his client's anger. Early in a supervisee's training, it is preferable to maintain a focus on skill difficulties unless countertransference threatens the therapeutic relationship (see chap. 5). In the present case, the supervisor concluded (in the Marker) that John's problem was more likely due his anxiety as a novice, inasmuch as the client seemed more comfortable with the process than John.

At this point, the supervisor is assured that John recognizes the need to express his emotional involvement with his client. John's mention of "the cognitive" was a cue that he is ready to discuss the conceptualization, specifically how Ted's anger relates to his problems and how it can be used therapeutically. In this next sequence, the supervisor is more didactic, offering guidelines for John to see the therapeutic process from a theoretical perspective—in this case, a psychoanalytic perspective.

Focus on Skill (Conceptual)

Supervisor: But while you're being cognitive, you're learning a lot about Ted, too. You're learning that he gets depressed when he remembers how little love and nurturance he got as a child. Then he goes out looking for sex so as not to be depressed.
reassures John that he was nonetheless pursuing an important path

John: Yes, and in the last session, he told me he got no love there from his parents. (*listening*) But again he's felt love and support from his wife, but now she's away from him. And it's compounded, you know what I mean? He hasn't gotten enough.
begins to see connections

Supervisor: Right. And then he gets too depressed to think about it, so he goes cruising to shut it off.
points out the pattern

John: Yeah. It strikes me . . . he said, "First I got laid, and then I was sad, and then I was pissed."
sees the pattern clearly

Supervisor: So what's his presenting affect? Lots of anger. And underneath it, you can bet there's a ton of pain. Coupling that up with the anger.
points out the importance of the client's anger

John: He sure feels something, the whole thing about defense mechanisms. I read someone, somewhere, who said that they're great because they *do* something for you.

Supervisor: Yes. I think there's a lot of ways he's defending against the stuff that hurts. (*listening*) And I think, here's a guy who's still in denial. He thinks he's in control and it's not a problem, like he thinks he can stop going out and picking up women. But he's not going to stop, even if his wife *does* leave him.
offers a perspective on the client

Having sketched out the possible dynamics related to the client's expression of anger, John and the supervisor now consider the plan for future sessions. In this next stage of the event, the technical and conceptual skills focused on earlier are brought to bear in an integrated manner. As illustrated in the following sequence, John does not quite see the link, and the supervisor consequently becomes more didactic and directive. Because such a shift in the supervisory role can cause defensiveness, the supervisor then checks in with John (focus on self-efficacy) to assess his comfort level with both the therapeutic plan and the supervisory process to this point.

Focus on the Therapeutic Process

John: Yeah. (*feeling inadequate*) But this is where I get confused. I don't know how equipped I am to deal with these kinds of issues for him, his cruising, I mean.

Supervisor: Well, it seems like he's not ready to give it up yet. And yet, he's having consequences in his life. You might just explore that, you know. He's angry with his wife for leaving, and yet, he does the very thing that's pushed her away.
suggests a strategy

John: (*slowly*) Yeah, so you mean, I guess, just keep exploring . . . what . . . ?
confused

Supervisor: Exploring his patterns. He's not convinced that he has to stop.

John: But is that my job? To convince him?
unsure

Supervisor: That's a good question. Some directive approaches would say, "yes." But from the dynamic approach we're using with him, I'd say, "No, it's your job to explore."
teaches

John: Well, there are some real overt things that I think he needs to get cleaned up in his life, but that's my own . . .
recognizes that he should not push his own agenda

Supervisor: . . . view.

John: Yeah, that's my own view.

Supervisor: Well, do you feel you will have accomplished anything if you help him explore and help him see patterns and help him see what cruising is doing to his life and how . . .
questions John's agreement with the suggested plan

John: I think if he owns it. I think if he owns that these things come out as patterns and what it's done to his marriage. And, you know, if he takes responsibility for it, I think I can feel I've helped accomplish it.
explains his understanding of how the plan relates to treatment outcome

Focus on Self-Efficacy

Supervisor: Yes, exactly! Are you okay with this plan?
checking in

John: Oh, yes! I see it now!
[*a few minutes of discussion on John's comfort level in working with Ted*]

Although events like this one often end with a discussion of the therapeutic action plan, it is desirable to bring the supervisory process back into the foreground by returning to the supervisee's concern as expressed in the Marker. In this case, the original concern was John's fear that he wasn't providing enough for the client. Skillfully, the supervisor revisits this concern to see whether or not John has a better sense of what initially troubled him. Thus, the focus will now switch back to the therapy relationship, as the event concludes with John demonstrating an integration of the technical and conceptual skills focused on earlier.

Resolution

Supervisor: When we started off talking about Ted, you said you were worried that you weren't offering him what he was expecting.

John: Right.

Supervisor: How do you see this now?
assess skill integration

John: Well, it's come together for me or . . . as we've talked about it. I knew he was angry and that he knows what he's angry about. But because *I* didn't see how exploring that anger deeper could lead to anything new, I wound up missing it. I think maybe . . . well, maybe he got a bit angrier since I was missing it and . . .
recognizes his own contribution

Supervisor: Mmhmm!

John: . . . and that's when I started feeling like, "What am I doing here," you know, "I can't tell him anything he doesn't already . . . he hasn't already figured out."

Supervisor: He knows, and then again he *doesn't* know.
reminds John of the client's defenses

John: Right. (*assertively*) I have to keep pushing it, the feeling, the anger, exploring . . .

Supervisor: . . . so he can see his patterns.
links technique to outcome

John: (*simultaneously*) . . . help him figure it out.

Supervisor: Yes, and you can't make his wife come back to him, and you can't make him stop cruising. All you can do is be there for him, *be* there, and he'll . . . hopefully, as you examine them together, he'll see how these patterns are self-defeating . . .
reminds John that therapy has limits and reinforces the need for empathic attunement

John: . . . and stop.
links insight and behavior change

Supervisor: . . . and stop, yes! Well, that's the hope!

John: Got it! (*laughs, relieved*)

Supervisor: Okay! (*smiling*)

As shown here, John demonstrates his understanding of how technique (in this case, working with anger) relates to his conceptual understanding of his client and the therapeutic strategy he's following. More importantly, perhaps, John shows an understanding of a complex process dynamic—when he felt frustrated and unsure of his own role in the therapeutic work, John became convinced that his client was frustrated with him, which resulted in his emotional distancing from the client and further uncertainty about the therapeutic strategy he should pursue.

In this illustration, initial questioning led the supervisor to believe that John's difficulty was from not understanding how to work therapeutically with anger—*not* a fear of strong negative emotions in others. Thus, the supervisor decided to focus on a skill difficulty in John's therapeutic repertoire rather than probe for a personal deficiency. If, however, John is not able to follow through with the therapeutic strategy just negotiated, the supervisor will need to reconsider the possibility of countertransference. On the other hand, if subsequent therapy sessions show a strengthening of John's therapeutic alliance with Ted and an increase in John's self-efficacy, this process would confirm the supervisor's present decision to focus only on technical and conceptual skills.

A SUCCESSFULLY RESOLVED SKILL DEFICIT EVENT WITH AN EXPERIENCED SUPERVISEE

In this next case, an interpersonal skill deficit is addressed when a 43-year-old supervisee, Tanya, fails to see a problem between her and her client, despite the supervisor's repeated attempts to point it out. The supervisor, a 54-year-old woman with over 25 years of therapy and supervision experience, is working with Tanya in a university counseling center.

Tanya's interpersonal deficiency is all the more striking because she has a fair amount of clinical experience (i.e., she is in her internship year and had eight years of therapy experience before entering graduate school) and is readily able to conceptualize her client's problems from various theoretical perspectives. As shown in this next session example, discussion of the deficit arouses so much anxiety for Tanya that a shift in focus on evaluation in the supervisory relationship becomes necessary. Thus, in this complex event, there are several recursive stages in the Task Environment: focus on skill (*interpersonal* and *conceptual*), focus on the therapeutic process, attend to parallel processes, focus on evaluation, and focus on the supervisory alliance. As in the previous example, the event ends with skill integration.

The Marker begins when Tanya reports an incident with a new client, Eleanor, whom she's only seen twice. At first, it is not clear to the supervisor what is going on in the therapy or what Tanya needs from her in supervision. For this reason, the supervisor suggests reviewing the videotape from Tanya's session with Eleanor.

Marker

Tanya: Eleanor called this morning to cancel.

Supervisor: Oh?

Tanya: She said her car broke down.

Supervisor: Hmm . . . what do you make of that?

T: I think it's probably an excuse.
shows an understanding of resistance

Supervisor: So then, do you think she's uncomfortable with something going on here?
probes for a more specific hypothesis

Tanya: (*reluctant*) I don't know really. Possibly.

Supervisor: Rather than just speculate, why don't we listen to the tape of last week's session together? Maybe we'll get some hints that way.
sensing Tanya's reticence, decides not to push her to talk about it

Tanya: Okay.
[*videotape review for several minutes*]

Observing the session, the supervisor immediately becomes aware of Tanya's extreme passivity and the client's clear discomfort (fidgeting, looking away, clutching her purse). Because Tanya was unable to label the problem earlier, the supervisor decides to see if she can do so after having seen the tape.

Supervisor: What do you see here? (*stopping the tape*)

Tanya: Well, she's talking about various things . . . tragedies in her life, her father's death, her sister's suicide, her mother's depression. She was hospitalized, oh I don't know, four times in the two years after her father died. That was 10 years ago, I think.
repeats the content of the session, adding some history

Supervisor: Whew! That's quite a load to carry around.
seeks Tanya's emotional reaction

Tanya: She's not . . . amazingly not depressed.

Supervisor: No? You've seen her, what, twice so far?

Tanya: (*quickly*) This one was the second. And she's seemed not depressed to me either time.

Supervisor: Not flat, not empty?
focuses on client's emotional state

Tanya: No. (*anxiously*) She denies all vegetative signs. No sleep disturbance, suicidal ideation, nothing.
remains cognitive

Noting that Tanya is comfortable discussing Eleanor as a "case," the supervisor asked about the client's mental status not only for information but also to reduce Tanya's increasing anxiety. However, when Tanya consistently avoids discussing the client's feelings, the Marker continues as the supervisor brings out what she suspects might be the problem, Tanya's lack of emotional connection with Eleanor. If, from what Tanya will reveal next, poor attunement is indeed the problem, the supervisor will know that there is an interpersonal skill deficiency to address.

Supervisor: So, watching the part of the tape we just saw, what do you see her asking of you? She's not depressed, but she's telling you about a lot of depressing events in her life. Only 24 and she's seen more of tragedy than most people have at 50.

synthesizes client's experience and probes for Tanya's understanding of her role in the process

Tanya: (*confused, uncertain*) I . . . I don't know what you mean.

Supervisor: Well, you said she's not depressed. But I hear her asking you for something anyhow. Any sense of what that is?
repeats, tying the question to Tanya's prior inference about the client

Tanya: (*silence, then quietly*) I guess not.
feeling threatened

Supervisor: Let's watch this last part again, shall we?
takes the heat off and tries to have Tanya discover the problem

Tanya: Okay. (*observing*) I think she wants to tell her story. (*stops the tape*)
continues not to see herself as part of the process

Supervisor: Yes, a witness, you to be a witness. What else?
transforms Tanya's statement (more interpersonal)

Tanya: (*tentatively*) I'm not sure. Maybe for me to hear it?

Supervisor: Yes! (*listening*) She's telling her story, but also I hear her asking you something here, actually pretty directly asking you, in fact.
more directive yet reassuring

Tanya: (*pause*) Oh, you mean when she asked if she should be in therapy?
sees the event for herself

Supervisor: Yes! (*pause*)
gives Tanya space to reflect

Tanya: Oh! (*silence, then quietly*) I missed it, didn't I? Wow, I don't even remember thinking about that question. I guess I was just wrapped up in her story.

Supervisor: Yes, you were quite attentive. It's some story!
reassuring

At this point, the Marker ends. The supervisor has enough information to recognize an interpersonal skill deficit, although it is not clear whether Tanya's difficulty is anxiety or a basic deficiency in relating to her client on an emotional level. For the sake of illustration, let's assume that this session takes place early in the supervisory relationship. Had it occurred later in the relationship and the supervisor knew that Tanya could easily connect with other clients, the supervisor might decide that the problem with this client was due to countertransference. In this case, because Tanya was unaware of her own passivity with Eleanor, the supervisor decides instead to focus on empathic relating.

Focus on Skill (Interpersonal)

Supervisor: Let's replay the tape here again.
wanting Tanya to observe for herself

Tanya: (*listening*) She sounds annoyed.
sees the client's reaction to her passivity

Supervisor: Yes, yes, I think she may be.
gives Tanya space

Tanya: (*pause, overwhelmed*) Boy! (*silence*)

Supervisor: (*after a minute, gently*) Where have your thoughts gone, Tanya?

Tanya: (*reluctant*) I guess I'm just thinking about what you said.

Supervisor: (*gently*) And feeling?
tries to draw Tanya out

Tanya: Well, surprised and feeling a bit embarrassed . . .
more open

Supervisor: . . . because . . . ?

Tanya: . . . because it's obvious! It's so obvious!
describes her feelings cognitively

Supervisor: (*pause*) What are your thoughts or feelings about it?

Tanya: (*softly*) I'm wondering what you think of me . . . For someone who's been a therapist as long as I . . .
worried but open to discussing her skills

Here Tanya has shifted the focus to the supervisory relationship, concerned that the supervisor thinks poorly of her because of her failure to recognize Eleanor's annoyance. This shift marks the beginning of the next stage in the event.

Focus on the Evaluation *and* Focus on the Supervisory Alliance

Supervisor: You're saying . . . What I think is that you see now that Eleanor was asking you for something, and you were quiet, not answering her, she was getting upset. And you think you *should've* seen it, answered her, whatever . . .
ties the problematic therapy event to Tanya's experience in supervision

Tanya: Yes.

Supervisor: . . . and you feel I may be judging you because you didn't do that?
probes for Tanya's perception

Tanya: (*quietly*) Well, maybe not "judging," but you're maybe *wondering* or *worrying* or . . .

Supervisor: You're right. I *am* "wondering," but I'm not "worrying" because I figure what we're talking about is something . . . maybe something new, or this discussion has touched something in you in a new way?
answers clearly, reassuring Tanya that this is a learning experience

Tanya: Mm (*silence*).

At this point, the supervisor recognizes that, by remaining uncomfortably silent, Tanya is too anxious to focus on their relationship, even though she was the first to mention it. Backing off, the supervisor shifts the discussion back to the cognitive, as this arena is most comfortable for Tanya. The supervisor's last question set the stage for a discussion of countertransference, but Tanya's silence suggested that the problem is more basic and general. To reduce Tanya's anxiety, the supervisor leads the discussion to a more cognitive level.

Focus on Skill (Conceptual)

Supervisor: What are your thoughts about where to go from here with Eleanor?
searches for Tanya's understanding of how to correct the problem

Tanya: (*bewildered*) But . . . I'm . . . how can I answer her now . . . now that I haven't in two sessions?

Supervisor: Well, let's think together. What do you see her needing?
models collaboration but more directive

Tanya: She needs to make a decision.
stays cognitive

Supervisor: . . . about . . . ?

Tanya: About whether to get into all this stuff or not.

Supervisor: Right. And the answer to that will help her decide if she wants therapy. You say she says there's no real problem of any sort in her life right now, no depression, she's going along . . .
expands Tanya's response

Tanya: . . . just fine, really.

Supervisor: Yes. So what does she need from you to get there, to the answer, I mean?
focuses on the interpersonal process

Tanya: I guess I've never thought . . . someone who could get something out of therapy, but then again it might open up old wounds in an overwhelming way, devastate her again. She thinks that because she's going to be a therapist herself, she has to have it all together, all resolved, all neatly tied up in a package.
sees the client's experience in therapy

Supervisor: (*laughs*) As if *we* all have it all together!
light-hearted diversion

Tanya: (*laughs along, a bit relieved*) Yeah, right!

Tanya's lightening up at this point reassures the supervisor that their alliance is not in jeopardy, and she decides to help Tanya see what may be missing in her relation with Eleanor. To do this, she tries to elicit Tanya's empathy for her client by using Tanya's own life experience as a parallel.

Attend to the Parallel Process

Supervisor: Well, how have you resolved "either/or" questions for yourself when you've been on the fence about something?

Tanya: Well, I know at least I don't go asking *someone else* to decide. I mull it over and over until I find my own answer by myself . . . oh! (*silence*)
realizes that she was expecting her client to be like herself

Supervisor: (*gently*) You thought that if you and Eleanor just went along, getting into therapy, as she goes along, that she'd see her way clear to decide? Just like you do when you have a problem?

Tanya: (*still unsure*) I guess. Maybe she can't do it on her own?

Tanya has now shown that she is able to separate her own experience from that of her client. Because the issue of feeling judged is still dangling, the supervisor decides to "check in" and in doing so, models for Tanya how to be more emotionally attuned in relationships. In other words, the supervisor leads Tanya to discover the parallel between the empathy she is experiencing in supervision and the empathy she needs to provide for her client.

Supervisor: I want to switch gears here for a minute. When we first started talking about this, you said you were embarrassed and wondered what I thought, wondered was I worried.

Tanya: Yeah.

Supervisor: How did I respond to *your* worry about that?
guides toward a here-and-now focus

Tanya: You answered . . . you said you weren't worried, just wondering what was going on for me.

Supervisor: Yes. And how did that feel? Then. And how does it feel now?
models a focus on feelings

Tanya: Good, good. (*assertively*)

Supervisor: Well, you just said I answered you.

Tanya: (*silence*) Oh!
insight

Supervisor: Oh?

Tanya: I get it, I think. Eleanor needs more of a direct answer from me.
makes the connection

Supervisor: I think so, yes. Why do you suppose?
probes, to expand Tanya's understanding

Tanya: (*less anxious*) Well, I'm the "so-called" expert here (*laughs*). I suppose maybe she needs some reassurance or support.

Supervisor: Like you did?
points out the parallel

Tanya: Like I did, yeah.

Supervisor: Well, I think she has a legitimate question, just like you had a legitimate question of me. Therapy *would* open up old wounds for her, I don't see how it can't. And she's not suffering now, but she thinks she *should* . . . she *ought* to suffer and work it through. So what does she need from you?
implies that Tanya needs to be more active

Tanya: You mean apart from reassuring her?

Supervisor: Yes.

Tanya: She needs me to deal with the question straight. Tell her what I think.

Supervisor: Not let her flounder, wondering . . .

Tanya: . . . wondering, yeah, if I'm judging her.

With this remark, Tanya demonstrates that she understands the parallel process. This awareness signals that the event can move forward to refocus on the therapeutic relationship and Tanya's part in it.

Focus on the Therapeutic Process

Supervisor: Right! So let's see how you could proceed with it. If we were to think about how to proceed . . . You could start with reassurance that her question is a good one, and then . . .
shows Tanya how to be more active

Tanya: . . . (*quickly*) and then ask her for her thoughts, pro and con.
considers a strategy

Supervisor: Yes! Good! And then take it from there.
supportive
[*further discussion about possible interventions, with the supervisor suggesting ways Tanya could be more active and responsive to her client*]

* * *

Tanya: But what about her not coming in today?
open to discussing the client's resistance

Supervisor: Yeah. What about it? (*smiling*)
suggests that Tanya can figure it out

Tanya: Probably she's mad, you know, that I . . .
recognizes the interpersonal

Supervisor: Or maybe not "mad," maybe disappointed, confused, frustrated . . .
points out the need for tentativeness

Tanya: Any of these, yes.

Supervisor: Any ideas about how to approach her when she comes in next week?
guides Tanya toward developing a plan

Tanya: Well, I need to somehow get to her question, her question about needing therapy.
sees only one piece

Supervisor: Yes, but first see where she's at before you jump in with that.
suggests more responsiveness

Tanya: (*uncertain*) You mean, wait for her to bring it up?

Supervisor: That would be great, but she may not. She may avoid it altogether. In that case, I think you'd best bring up the issue of "what we are doing in therapy," you know, "what do you want to get out of it?" and see where that leads. But do it in a collaborative, "we're putting our heads together about this" way. You need to be extremely sensitive about when and how to bring that up.
teaches, underscoring the need for activity and sensitivity

Tanya: . . . because she canceled this week.
shows understanding

Supervisor: Yes, right. She may be skittish. But I don't think you can afford avoiding it, and if she ties it into canceling today's session, all the better.

Tanya: But not confront her about it?
needs more clarity

Supervisor: "Confront," no, I wouldn't. You might lose her.
responds with direction
[*further discussion on ways to approach the client*]

* * *

Supervisor: Now let's talk about what to do if she cancels again or no shows next week. Any ideas?
guides Tanya to form an alternate plan
[*more discussion about handling the client's resistance*]

Now that many suggestions have been made and alternatives considered for Tanya's work with Eleanor, the next step is to generalize this learning. Because Tanya has strong conceptual skills, the supervisor decides to consolidate Tanya's new understanding of the importance of empathic attunement through a discussion of the therapeutic alliance. Thus, the Resolution of this event proceeds with an integration of skills and theory.

Resolution

Supervisor: We need to get back, I think, to what this was about in the first place. Have you read much about the therapeutic alliance?

Tanya: Bordin, you mean?
refers to Bordin (1979)

Supervisor: Yes, Bordin and others. There are various components to the alliance. (*continues teaching*)
ties the event to theory

Tanya: (*uncertain*) But which one was *this* one?

Supervisor: My question to you! Which one was this?
suggests faith in Tanya's ability to figure it out

Tanya: (*still uncertain*) Well, a little bit of all of them, I think.

Supervisor: I agree! You and Eleanor weren't together clear about the goals for therapy, that's the alliance part. Then there are other aspects of the overall therapy relationship such as the "real relationship" . . .
refers to Gelso and Carter (1985)

Tanya: . . . her realistic question of "do I need therapy?"

Supervisor: Yes, and the transference part, where you are someone important in her life that she's . . .

Tanya: (*eagerly, more confident*) . . . *projecting* onto.

Supervisor: Yes, precisely. We're not going to be able to get into that now because of time, but that's an excellent thing . . . food for thought, for you to think about. Given what you know about her, who are you in a transference way for her? Eventually, you may be able to do some interpreting around that, if your discussion with Eleanor leads in that direction.
suggests an avenue for Tanya's development

Tanya: Mmhmm.

Supervisor: But in the time we have, let's go back to the beginning here, her canceling the session today.
begins checking in

Tanya: I think I know why now. Of course, maybe her car *did* break down.
shows more understanding

Supervisor: Yeah, it might be. But she might've been able to get here another way, too.
offers her opinion that the client was resistant

Tanya: Hmm. But one way or another, my alliance with her wasn't all that good.
understands the problem behind the resistance

Supervisor: Well, the part about the goals for therapy wasn't clear. And I think you also need to . . .

Tanya: . . . to pay better attention to what my client is wanting from me.
generalizes

Supervisor: . . . be more active, tuned in, more responsive.
expands

Tanya: Right.

Supervisor: We went through a lot today. How're you . . .
checking in

Tanya: Good, good. I need this!

Tanya's eagerness to contribute to this last discussion about applying theory to practice suggests that her anxiety is substantially reduced. In this event, she had a new experience in supervision, working through a problem with an empathic supervisor who did not overwhelm her emotionally. Another supervisee may have been more able and willing to explore feelings of being judged or criticized by the supervisor, but Tanya's relational limitations precluded such frank exploration. The fact that Tanya was able to bring up her discomfort at all speaks to her willingness to take risks and to the underlying solidity of the supervisory alliance: two good signs for her continued personal growth and professional development.

SPECIAL CONSIDERATIONS

Of course, the distinction between a skill *difficulty* and a skill *deficit* is largely in the eye of the beholder. Although level of experience plays a part, supervisors who forge ahead, making assumptions without specific knowledge of their supervisees' skills, risk damaging the relationship, perhaps irreparably (Nelson & Friedlander, 2001). Novices who are held accountable for knowing technical or conceptual skills to which they had never been exposed, for example, can feel criticized, shamed, or misunderstood. Skilled supervisees who are offered basic information about relationship building can feel belittled, patronized, and angry.

How, then, is one to distinguish a difficulty from a deficiency? Although it would be reasonable to distinguish the two based solely on level of training, fallacious judgments could result. As a start, the supervisor should consider the supervisee's experience in relation to the skill in question. The lack of basic relational skills—attending, listening attentively, making eye contact—can be considered a deficiency for novices as well as advanced supervisees, but other interpersonal skills—such as staying calm but engaged in the face of a client's rage—are difficult for therapists at any level of experience. Trouble in this situation should not be considered a deficit.

Technical skills may readily be classified as basic or advanced. One rarely finds a novice who can make sophisticated interpersonal process interpretations or who can track a latent theme through a client's stories. On the other hand, it is reasonable to expect an advanced supervisee to address a client's suicidal ideation thoroughly, professionally, and appropriately. Not doing so would suggest a deficit, particularly if the supervisee had considerable prior experience with depressed clients.

Problems with conceptual skills may be due to a lack of knowledge or experience or to difficulties synthesizing and integrating disparate pieces of information. Supervisees who have had ample coursework and a fair amount of exposure to clients should be able to abstract the salient features of a case, draw conclusions, consider alternatives, and make hypotheses, inferences, and prognoses—essentially, to develop an integrative case conceptualization that goes well beyond the client's presenting complaint. Even novices should be able to think divergently about the possible effects of different intervention strategies. Deficits (rather than difficulties) should be suspected for supervisees at any level of training who can only discuss the therapeutic process in concrete terms or who are consistently unable to take an "observing ego" perspective on their own behavior. In extreme cases, conceptual deficits may indicate that the supervisee is unsuited for the profession.

What may seem like a deficit, however, may only be a difficulty if the supervisee is experiencing intense anxiety, vicarious traumatization, burnout, or a crisis in confidence (see chap. 8). Considering whether a problem is a deficiency also depends on how novel the setting, clientele, or treatment modality is for the supervisee (Ladany, Marotta, & Muse-Burke, 2001). Those who have only treated motivated, self-referred outpatients, for example, can be expected to have difficulties when they begin working in a partial hospital setting with seriously disturbed patients. Likewise, supervisees with extensive experience in individual psychotherapy can be expected to encounter technical and conceptual difficulties when they begin working with groups or families, and the more astute supervisees will also recognize the need for new interpersonal skills in these situations.

Although supervisees want and expect feedback on their skills, supervisors must tread gently in this area to avoid arousing undue defensiveness or a severe crisis in confidence. Defensiveness cannot always be avoided, of course, in evaluative relationships like supervision. Indeed, evaluation plus vulnerability is a basic recipe for defensiveness. To respond to defensive behavior, supervisors need to switch from a teaching to a therapeutic mode, paying attention to and eliciting the supervisee's reactions to what is being discussed. Defensiveness can be reduced if the supervisor communicates an understanding of the supervisee's embarrassment or fear of being criticized. Such empowering metaconversations are only likely to occur, however, when the norm has been set from the beginning so that the supervisee understands that talking about feelings and reactions is an important part of learning in supervision.

CONCLUSION

Skills are at the core of supervision and training. Because in the profession itself there is controversy about acceptable practices, there is no standard of excellence that applies to all supervisees in all clinical situations, and skills that come naturally to some people are alien territory for others. Indeed, the theoretical and technical differences in our field are so vast that what one supervisor considers an important, basic skill may not even figure in the repertoire of another supervisor.

The interpersonal perspective on supervision presented in this book reflects our emphasis on interpersonal processes in psychotherapy. This is not to say that we eschew training in empirically supported treatments (ESTs). Rather, we concur with Norcross (2001), who noted, "The EST lists and most practice guidelines depict disembodied therapists performing procedures on Axis I disorders. This stands in marked contrast to the clinician's experience of psychotherapy as an intensely interpersonal and deeply emotional experience" (p. 346). That is, it is our belief that supervisors who promote evidence-based treatments and ignore the overwhelming evidence about the importance of interpersonal skills do a disservice to their supervisees—and ultimately, to clients. According to the American Psychological Association's Division 29 (Psychotherapy) Task Force on Empirically Supported Therapy Relationships:

- The therapy relationship . . . makes substantial and consistent contributions to psychotherapy outcome independent of the specific type of treatment.
- Practice and treatment guidelines should explicitly address therapist behaviors and qualities that promote a facilitative therapy relationship.
- Efforts to promulgate practice guidelines or evidence-based lists of effective psychotherapy without including the therapy relationship are seriously incomplete and potentially misleading on both clinical and empirical grounds. (Steering Committee, 2001, p. 495)

In training, supervisees need to be knowledgeable, think critically and creatively, behave responsibly, and develop a unique, caring therapeutic style of their own. Effective supervisors keep these training outcomes in mind when addressing skill development with supervisees at all levels of experience.

3

HEIGHTENING MULTICULTURAL AWARENESS: IT'S NEVER BEEN ABOUT POLITICAL CORRECTNESS

Silence = Death.
—Anonymous

Economic globalization, ease of international travel, and the explosion of telecommunications and technological knowledge—are all reasons for heightening the multicultural competence of therapists in training (e.g., Ponterotto, 1988). But these generalizations, distant from the consultation rooms in which we work, are not as compelling as other, more proximal realities. People in the United States are far more attuned than they were even a decade ago to issues of gender, sexual orientation, religious differences, socioeconomic challenges, and the unique problems of nontraditional families and people with disabilities. In terms of race and ethnicity within families, more people are self-identifying as biracial and multiracial, and every year, more White parents adopt children trans-racially and internationally. Suburban, as well as urban communities are increasingly diverse, with immigrants arriving from all over the globe, many from economically depressed and war-torn countries, needing assistance to navigate the unfamiliar and often hostile environments in which they find themselves. Their acculturation difficulties and those of the increasing numbers of students of color in predominantly White colleges and universities demand multicultural knowledge and skills on the part of counselors and their supervisors. Indeed, students of color, as well as members of virtually every other socially oppressed group, have become more vocal regarding their experiences in U.S. society and their right to medical and mental health treatment by providers who are knowledgeable about, and sensitive to, their unique concerns.

How can we help our supervisees develop competencies to work with diverse clients if we, their supervisors, have never had multiculturally informed coursework and training? Not surprisingly, many supervisees find themselves more multiculturally adept than their supervisors (Constantine, 1997), especially supervisors trained prior to the mid-1990s. The need to catch up poses a major challenge for these supervisors as they try to assimilate the relevant and quickly evolving multicultural literature (Leong & Wagner, 1994; Sue, Arredondo, & McDavis, 1992; Sue et al., 1998). Toward this end, this chapter offers a process model for working through multicultural awareness events in supervision.

The changing demographic makeup of the United States has brought recognition of the importance of integrating multicultural issues in psychotherapeutic work (Ridley, Mendoza, Kanitz, Angermeier, & Zenk, 1994; Sue et al., 1998). This recognition has produced a series of models addressing different aspects of multiculturally competent therapy (Ponterotto, Fuertes, & Chen, 2000) and supervision (Ancis & Ladany, 2001). Recently, the American Psychological Association (APA, 2003) published "Guidelines on Multicultural Education, Training, Research, Practice, and Organizational Change for Psychologists" in an effort to consolidate resources and stimulate action relevant to multicultural work for educators, researchers, and clinicians.

To date, only a handful of empirical studies on multicultural supervision and training have been conducted (Constantine, 2001; Constantine, Ladany, Inman, & Ponterotto, 1996), most of which focus either on gender (e.g., Goodyear, 1990; Nelson & Holloway, 1990; Petty & Odewahn, 1983; Schiavone & Jessell, 1988; Stenack & Dye, 1983; Worthington & Stern, 1985) or race (e.g., Constantine et al., 1996; Cook & Helms, 1988; Fukuyama, 1994; Hilton, Russell, & Salmi, 1995; Ladany, Brittan-Powell, & Pannu, 1997; Thompson & Jenal, 1994; Vander Kolk, 1974). Some studies show no clear empirical support for matching supervisors and supervisees on gender or race (e.g., Ellis & Ladany, 1997). Other results suggest that many supervisees lack knowledge, have limited self-awareness in terms of multicultural issues (Ancis & Sanchez-Hucles, 2000; Johnson, Searight, Handal, & Gibbons, 1993), and tend to inflate their perceived multicultural competencies (Constantine & Ladany, 2000; Ladany, Inman, Constantine, & Hofheinz, 1997). Although supervisees of color view multicultural issues as particularly salient (Fukuyama, 1994), findings suggest that many supervisors are not sensitive to these concerns with either supervisees or clients (Fukuyama, 1994; Ladany, Lehrman-Waterman, Molinaro, & Wolgast, 1999). Indeed, supervisors that lack personal multicultural development may also limit their supervisee's development (Ladany, Brittan-Powell, & Pannu, 1997).

In our discussion of multicultural challenges in supervision, we define multiculturalism broadly to include gender, race, ethnicity, sexual orientation, disability, socioeconomic status, age, religion, and family structure. Further, we conceptualize multicultural supervision as incorporating three theoretical structures: supervisees' multicultural competence as therapists, client–supervisee–supervisor cultural identity interactions, and supervisors' multicultural competence. In the following sections, we delineate each of these components.

SUPERVISEES' MULTICULTURAL THERAPY COMPETENCIES

Constantine and Ladany's (2001) framework for conceptualizing supervisees' multicultural therapy competence presents six dimensions. First, *self-awareness* refers to supervisees' ability, through personal exploration, to understand their own multicultural identities as well as biases associated with their personal socialization. Second, *general knowledge about multicultural issues* refers to knowledge derived from various theoretical, empirical, and clinical sources about multicultural issues relevant to different cultural groups. Third, *multicultural psychotherapy self-efficacy* refers to supervisees' self-confidence about the effectiveness of their multicultural therapy skills. Fourth, *understanding of unique client variables* refers to specific cultural issues (e.g., cultural group membership, personality traits, values, willingness to self-disclose, motivation to change) presented by clients. Fifth, the *effective working alliance*, derived in large part from Bordin's (1979) model of the alliance, refers to supervisees' ability to develop an emotional bond with clients and engage in multiculturally sensitive discussions when negotiating the goals (e.g., multicultural identity change) and tasks of therapy (e.g., the extent to which multicultural issues will be discussed). Finally, *multicultural psychotherapy skills* refers to supervisees' proficiency in working with multicultural issues in therapy, such as the ability to assess gender identity or to discuss racial or sexual orientation similarities and differences with clients.

To assess and enhance these multicultural abilities in their supervisees, supervisors must possess these abilities themselves. This point cannot be overstated. Supervisors must possess more than rudimentary multicultural skills. As discussed in the next section, the less multiculturally adept the supervisor, the more likely there is conflict in the supervisory relationship, with negative consequences for the therapeutic services offered to clients.

INTERACTION OF MULTICULTURAL IDENTITIES

A key factor in therapists' individual potential to become multiculturally competent is their own identity. In the Heuristic Model of Nonoppressive

Interpersonal Development (Ancis & Ladany, 2001), multicultural identities in the supervisory dyad are said to influence both supervision and psychotherapy outcomes. Because the model is based on research and theory from a U.S. perspective, the model should be applied cautiously, at best, outside the United States. An important assumption in the model, supported by contemporary theory and research, is that identity-based factors (e.g., racial or gender identity) are more explanatory of intrapsychic or interpersonal psychological processes than simple knowledge of demographic factors such as race or gender (Cass, 1979; Chan, 1989; Cross, 1971, 1995; Downing & Roush, 1985; Fassinger, 1991; Hardiman, 1982; Helms, 1990, 1995; Helms & Cook, 1999; McNamara & Rickard, 1989; Ossana, Helms, & Leonard, 1992; Phinney, 1989; Rust, 1993; Sodowsky, Kwan, & Pannu, 1995; Sue & Sue, 1999; Troiden, 1989). A second assumption is that for any demographic factor (i.e., gender, race, ethnicity, sexual orientation, disability, or socioeconomic status), people belong to either a socially oppressed or a socially privileged group. In the United States, socially oppressed groups include women, people of color, gay men/lesbians/bisexuals/ transgendered individuals, people with disabilities, working-class individuals, and non-Christians. Socially privileged groups include men, Whites, European Americans, physically-abled people, middle- and upper-class individuals, and Christians. In this framework, a given individual can belong to both socially oppressed and socially privileged groups when more than one demographic factor is considered as, for example, a gay, disabled White, Jewish, middle-class male who has AIDS.

Furthermore, Ancis and Ladany (2001) propose that people progress through phases called Means of Interpersonal Functioning (MIF) that include thoughts and feelings about themselves in relation to their identification with different groups, as well as behavioral manifestations of these thoughts and feelings. A woman, at various points in her life, for example, will have a different understanding and emotional reaction to what it means to be a woman. According to the model, people progress through similar phases of MIF with respect to each demographic factor, and these phases have common and unique features depending on the group in question. For example, in less developed stages of MIF, both men and women are complacent about societal change, but each group is unique—women tend to feel less empowered, whereas men tend to perceive greater entitlement. Moreover, each individual is more or less advanced in terms of MIF with respect to various demographic factors. As shown in the following illustration, a White woman may be highly aware of sexism but lack awareness of her White privilege.

The four stages of MIF are based on Helms's (1995) model of racial identity development but expanded to include multiple demographic factors, as follows: (a) *adaptation*, characterized by complacency and apathy regarding the socially oppressive environment and a superficial understanding of differences among people (e.g., "color-blind" perspectives such as "there are no racial differences because we all belong to the human race" or "homosexuality is a sin"); (b) *incongruence*, characterized by confusion and some awareness of oppression from new knowledge gained in the social environment but a lack of commitment to advocacy (e.g., a woman learns of salary discrepancies based on gender but remains silent about her sense of injustice); (c) *exploration*, identified by strong emotions, such as anger toward the oppressive environment, as well as curiosity about and insight into cultural issues (e.g., an African American man actively explores African culture, including clothing and food); and (d) *integration*, which involves an integrative awareness and interpersonal proficiency in associating with various socially oppressed and privileged groups.

The four MIF stages are further conceptualized as fluid; people are said to move back and forth across the stages depending on the environmental context. For example, a White person in the incongruence phase, in terms of race, may become less sensitive to racial issues if not exposed to persons of color or issues salient to persons of color for a prolonged period of time.

Interpersonal relations in supervision can be described based on each individual's stage with respect to a relevant demographic factor. Expanding from Helms's (1995) and Cook's (1994) models, as well as the empirical literature in supervision (e.g., Ladany, Brittan-Powell, & Pannu, 1997; Rarick, 2000). Ancis and Ladany (2001) identified four types of relationship interactions: (a) *progressive*, which occurs when the supervisor is at a more advanced stage of MIF than the supervisee; (b) *parallel-advanced*, when supervisor and supervisee are at comparable, advanced MIF stages; (c) *parallel-delayed*, when supervisor and supervisee are at comparable, delayed MIF stages; and (d) *regressive*, when the supervisor is at a less advanced stage of MIF than the supervisee. Regressive relationships, typically occurring when the supervisor lacks multicultural training (Constantine, 1997), are uniquely problematic for supervisees.

Interpersonal relations from the MIF perspective are multidimensional and hence, very complex when we consider the many cultural groups to which an individual belongs. The interaction is rendered even more complex when the therapy relationship is added to the mix. For example, when the therapy relationship is regressive due to the supervisee's lacking awareness of women's issues relative to a female client, a likely outcome is the client's decision to terminate treatment prematurely. In such cases, the supervisor may need to attend directly to the supervisee's level of identity development as a woman. However, if the female supervisor is at the adaptation or incongruence stage in her own identity development, supervisory discussions about feminist awareness are unlikely to take place. On the other hand, the supervisory relationship may be regressive, but the client's care will not be compromised if the supervisee ignores the supervisor's lack of guidance and attends to her client's concerns from a feminist perspective.

The task for the supervisor, then, is to identify the type of interaction occurring in the therapy relationship to facilitate the most positive supervision experience possible. In supervision, processes and outcomes can be predicted based on interpersonal relationship interactions. We might expect, for example, that progressive and parallel-advanced relationships characterize the most productive supervision processes and outcomes, whereas parallel-delayed and regressive interactions produce the least effective ones. Specifically, more advanced relationships enjoy a strong supervisory alliance and observable gains in the supervisee's multicultural competence, whereas the latter might have a weak alliance and no growth in cultural competence.

SUPERVISORS' MULTICULTURAL SKILLS

Having discussed the necessary therapy competencies and identity development stages for supervisors, we now turn to the multicultural competencies that supervisors need to facilitate positive changes in their supervisees. Based on previous conceptualizations (Ivey, Fouad, Arredondo, & D'Andrea, 1999; Porter, 1995; Sue et al., 1992), Ancis and Ladany (2001) identified six domains of supervision competencies. These domains include (a) *supervisor-focused personal development*, that is, the development of the supervisor's self-awareness in relation to cultural issues (i.e., an active exploration and challenge of biases, values, and worldview in relation to supervision); (b) *supervisee-focused personal development*, or the supervisor's facilitation of self-awareness in the supervisee (i.e., exploration of biases that may impede effective and competent practice); (c) *conceptualization*, that is, facilitating the supervisee's understanding of individual and contextual factors in clients' lives, (d) *skills/interventions*, or helping the supervisee learn new methods of assessment and interventions, such as culturally sensitive verbal and nonverbal interventions; (e) *process*, or attending to multicultural processes in the supervisory relationship (e.g., discussion of similarities and differences between the supervisor and supervisee across demographic factors); and (f) *outcome/evaluation*, that is, the supervisor's ability to assess the supervisee's multicultural competencies and recommend appropriate remediation for a supervisee who is lacking in this regard. As with identity development, the greater the multicultural skill of the supervisor, the greater the likelihood that the supervisee's multicultural competency will be enhanced.

Certainly, it can be argued that all supervision experiences have a multicultural component and that the elements just discussed are present in all supervisory dyads and groups. There are, however, specific situations when it is necessary to address multicultural issues extensively, and this topic can become a major focus in the work of supervision. We turn next to these kinds of events.

As with other events described in this book, Markers in multicultural awareness events range from the obvious to the covert. Easily identifiable Markers are supervisees' comments about clients that reflect a multicultural stumbling block or difficulty. As one example, a supervisee might demonstrate multicultural insensitivity when discussing why a female client seems unhappy in her marriage by saying, "Andrea is unfulfilled because she's childless." Other explicit Markers occur when a supervisee expresses concern about a poor connection with a client due to a lack of experience with the client's cultural group (e.g., limited contact with people who are transgendered or with people from Pakistan). Other readily evident Markers include statements suggesting a universality mentality (e.g., believing that "no clients can benefit from advice" or "all clients need to be confronted") or reflecting an etic rather than emic perspective (i.e., seeing people only through the cultural lens of mainstream U.S. culture). A supervisee may, for example, conceptualize a client as needing to move away from parents when the client's ethnic culture is collectivist, emphasizing family interdependence.

Some multicultural event Markers are subtler and reveal themselves only through discussion. Consider the following actual case as an example: A supervisee, physically abled, was seeing a client who had the same disability as the supervisee's supervisor. Presumably, this situation could result in a rich discussion about cultural issues specific to the client's (and supervisor's) disability. The supervisee, however, was uncomfortable with the topic and did not reveal the client's disability to the supervisor for six sessions, even though it was intricately related to the client's psychological concerns. It was only by listening to a tape of the therapy that the supervisor learned that the client had a disability. Bringing this observation to the supervisee's attention, the supervisor helped the supervisee see how the client's presenting concerns could be conceptualized in light of the disability.

In other less obvious circumstances, a supervisor may notice that a supervisee omits mention of the client's race when it's clearly related to the therapy process. Supervisors, like therapists (Thompson & Jenal, 1994), need to initiate difficult discussions of cultural similarities and differences. Supervisees' biases are more likely to be revealed and worked through when the atmosphere encourages these types of important discussions.

Finally, Markers can occur when multicultural issues arise between supervisee and supervisor, both in a subtle and not-so-subtle fashion. For example, a supervisee may make a slip of the tongue statement that reveals a bias or lack of knowledge. Or, in the context of discussing racial differences, the supervisee may say something such as, "I have no problem with race." Dismissing the topic suggests a problematic reaction that needs to be faced, as shown in the following two case illustrations.

Task Environment and Resolution

After the Marker signals a need to raise the supervisee's multicultural awareness, the task environment proceeds with some or all of the following interactional sequences: an exploration of feelings, an assessment of multicultural knowledge, a focus on multicultural awareness, a focus on skill (conceptual), a normalizing of the supervisee's experience, and a focus on the supervisory alliance. Although these sequences are typical, they may not all be present or take place in this order. Each event will unfold differently, and the various interaction sequences may repeat in a recursive fashion.

In almost all multicultural awareness events, there is a marked level of affect on the part of the supervisee. Initially, supervisors are called to explore these feelings to uncover the multicultural issues. A supervisee may experience anger when recognizing oppressive acts made against a client or may feel guilty when recognizing personal privilege in relation to disabled clients. At first, the supervisee may attempt to maintain a distance from these feelings because of an almost automatic tension that accompanies discussions of differences. Recognizing the supervisee's discomfort, the supervisor will need to normalize the experience, which will in turn facilitate exploration of this sensitive topic.

Classic to all multicultural education is the assessment of knowledge, followed by attention to enhancing self-awareness, all of which should enhance competencies. At some point in the task environment, then, the supervisor needs to ascertain how much the supervisee knows about the specific multicultural issue at hand. The supervisor may ask the supervisee pointed but open-ended questions (e.g., "What have been your experiences working with Latino clients?"). Understanding the supervisee's level of knowledge and awareness in a given area, the supervisor may work toward furthering the supervisee's development by helping him or her examine personal and socialized biases toward a client's cultural group. Of critical importance is the supervisor's role in helping the supervisee translate new awareness into actual skills when working with a client. To do so, the supervisor might, for example, initiate a role-play to model a discussion of racial differences with a client.

Perhaps the most critical task in a multicultural awareness event is ensuring that the supervisory working alliance remains strong. The emotional bond, or trust, between the supervisee and supervisor must be solid enough to tolerate mixed feelings supervisees may experience in these kinds of discussions. Of course, aside from the emotional bond, there needs to be both an acknowledgment and an agreement that supervision involves working through multicultural challenges for both supervisee and supervisor to grow personally and professionally. Without such an agreement, the resolution of a multicultural awareness event will likely be limited.

Even with a solid alliance in place, working through all the suggested interaction sequences in a single supervision session is unlikely. More likely, partial resolutions will occur, such as a demonstration of increased knowledge of a multicultural issue, enhanced self-awareness, or a more complex conceptualization of the client. Ideally, a plan for the supervisee to engage in directed reading or experiential activities should follow these partial resolutions. More complete resolutions, such as integrating multicultural skills with treatment planning for a specific client, may require multiple supervision sessions or even multiple supervisors over a period of time.

Our next case illustrations are multicultural awareness events with varying degrees of resolution. In both examples, race is the primary multicultural factor because it is one of the most sensitive factors in any social relationship. Supervision events dealing with gender and sexual orientation are covered in chapter 7.

A PARTIALLY RESOLVED RACIAL AWARENESS EVENT (CROSS-CULTURAL THERAPY)

Tammy is a 28-year-old White woman and an advanced practicum student working in a university counseling center. One of her clients, Charles, an African American graduate student in his early 20s, is suffering from both depression and anxiety, feeling isolated on a predominately White college campus. Tammy and Charles worked together for two sessions when Tammy brought this case to her supervisor.

The supervisor, also a White woman, perceives herself at the MIF integration stage, that is, she defines herself as having sufficient knowledge, self-awareness, and skills to work with people from both socially oppressed and socially privileged groups. When it comes to her racial identity, however, she is most likely at the exploration stage, just beginning to examine what it means to be White in relation to people from other racial groups. Despite this, she considers herself relatively skilled in terms of multicultural supervision, although the journey to this point was arduous, and she recalls many mistakes along the way.

Marker

Tammy: . . . and he's unhappy to be at this school because he finds himself alone a lot. He also has difficulties making friends. I think part of the problem is he wears this African clothing, and he probably intimidates people. He also seems so angry all the time. I think if he just chilled out for a little while, things would be better for him.

Supervisor: Sounds like he can come across as intimidating.
reflects Tammy's experience

Tammy: Yeah.

Supervisor: And you see his anger and presentation as a put off to other people? *clarifies that this is Tammy's perception*

Tammy: Yes, definitely!

The supervisor makes a mental note about Tammy's desire for her client to "chill out," a pretty affect-laden statement that may be a Marker for a multicultural awareness event. To be certain, though, the supervisor decides to assess Tammy's racial identity, wondering whether Tammy is at the adaptation stage, which would be the case if she is unable to appreciate racial differences expressed in unexpected ways. Based on what the supervisor heard about Charles after the intake session, she hypothesizes that his racial identity may be at the exploration stage (i.e., more advanced than Tammy's). If so, the therapy relationship is a "regressive" one, a clear risk for a poor therapy outcome, if not a premature termination.

Realizing that Tammy is feeling put off and possibly threatened by her client, the supervisor continues to explore Tammy's experience of Charles as a way to assess Tammy's discomfort and determine whether the problem in the therapy alliance is due to racial tension.

Supervisor: So, what's it like to be in a therapy session with him? *deliberately vague*

Tammy: I don't know . . . um, he's different than other clients that I'm used to seeing. *avoids expressing negative feelings*

Supervisor: How so? *probes*

Tammy: Well the most obvious is that he's African American. I'm from a small town in the Midwest, so I've only known a few African American people in my life, and none very well. *hesitates*

Supervisor: So you're a bit uncomfortable with him for this reason? *reflects*

Tammy: (*quietly*) I guess so, yeah.

Now understanding that Tammy's reactions to Charles are related, at least in part, to her limited personal contact with African Americans, the supervisor moves into the task environment. She begins by assessing Tammy's comfort level with her client to determine the extent of skill difficulties due to Tammy's limited interracial experience. To do so, the supervisor continues questioning but shifts gears to get a clearer understanding of Tammy's knowledge about working with African American clients.

Assessing Multicultural Knowledge

Supervisor: Tammy, can you say more what you know about working with an African American client.

Tammy: It's not a problem.
defensive

Supervisor: Hmm. I'm not sure I was implying that I thought it was a problem for you.
backtracks, noting Tammy's resistance

Tammy: Having him as a client is just different, I guess. But I like to think of myself as color blind.
self-protective
[*extended discussion about the meaning of being "color-blind" in Tammy's worldview*]

Because Tammy's response ("color blind") and the elaboration of this construct suggest that she may be at the adaptation stage of racial identity, this signifies a critical point in the supervision event. To avoid a rupture in the working alliance, the supervisor must proceed with caution. At this point, recognizing that focusing directly on Tammy's lack of multicultural skills would be threatening, the supervisor decides to demonstrate her understanding through reflection and empathy.

Focus on the Supervisory Alliance

Supervisor: So you kind of see him as a person and don't really see his race?
assures Tammy that she understands

Tammy: Yeah, in a way, I guess. But it's hard not to think of his race because he kind of puts it right out there!
feeling understood, takes a risk

Supervisor: Kind of like he lets you know who he is from a racial standpoint?
continues to reflect

Tammy: Yeah. It just doesn't seem necessary, and like I said before, it may be what keeps him from making friends more easily.
rationalizes her discomfort

Focusing on her client, Tammy is feeling heat in this conversation about her personal views on race. Because Tammy is more comfortable with cognition than emotion-based discussions, the supervisor decides to make the point through a conceptualization of the client. This plan is undertaken in lieu of continuing an unproductive, tension-filled discussion of Tammy's feelings toward African Americans.

Focus on Skill (Conceptual)

Supervisor: Could you say some more about what may make it difficult for Charles to make friends?
redirects, focusing deliberately on the client rather than on Tammy

Tammy: Well, if I focus just on the way he dresses, it's like he has on a shield of armor. That makes him less approachable. It's funny! While he comes across as angry, it's a quiet sort of angry. Angry and yet reserved. He seems so reserved that I get the sense that people, even if they did want to talk with him, would be scared he wouldn't respond well.
feels more comfortable

Supervisor: How might he respond?
seeks to draw Tammy out

Tammy: They'd probably think he would not respond at all, or start talking about the problems of the Black man. You know what I mean?
worries about the supervisor's reaction

Supervisor: He may be off-putting to White people?
demonstrates understanding

Tammy: Yeah.

Supervisor: Is that how he comes off to you in your sessions with him?
probes Tammy's projection

Tammy: (*quickly*) No, not really. With me, he's pretty nice and relatively easy to talk to. I just sense this big load of anger. But I was meaning more in other realms of his life.
denies her apparent discomfort

Supervisor: Okay, so it seems that in your work with him, he comes across as sociable, but your concern is that others may not give him the chance to show his sociability?
reflects and summarizes to communicate understanding

Tammy: Exactly.

Tammy still denies the difficulties she has with her client because of racial tension, instead focusing on how Charles puts off the other people in his life. The supervisor persists, however, in communicating her understanding of Tammy's perspective through reflection and summary. This approach pays off. Despite her lack of self-awareness, the supervisee indicates willingness to explore her interactions with the client. For this reason, the supervisor redirects the discussion to focus on the therapy relationship.

Focus on the Therapy Relationship

Supervisor: Earlier, you also mentioned that he can appear kind of intimidating.
begins with Tammy's perceptions

Tammy: Yeah, on top of the way he dresses, he's a big guy.

Supervisor: Physically big?

Tammy: Yes.

Supervisor: (*gently*) So, maybe you do feel a little intimidated when you are in the room with him?
challenges Tammy's projection

Tammy: Oh yeah.

Supervisor: What else?
probes tentatively, to avoid raising Tammy's defenses

Tammy: It also feels a little scary.
more genuine

Supervisor: How so?

Tammy: I don't know, it just does. Being in this tiny room, just me and this big guy.
implies feeling threatened

Supervisor: So then, how do you suppose your scary feelings influence your work with him?
leads gently

Tammy: I don't know. At times, there's a lot of silence in our sessions. He doesn't say much, and I guess I don't know what to say.
admits feeling insecure

Supervisor: Why do you suppose he doesn't say much?
more cognitive

Tammy: I just don't know.

Supervisor: It sounds, maybe, like you just really don't know him?
offers a different perspective

Tammy: That's true, I guess.

With gentleness and patience, allowing Tammy to stay in the cognitive realm where she is most at ease, the supervisor helped Tammy recognize she is having difficulty understanding her client. At this point, there are a few roads the supervisor can take. One is to become didactic and explain what may be happening in terms of a specific regressive racial identity interaction. The problem with this approach is that Tammy is so anxious that she may be unable to work with this interpretation. Rather, she may hear only part of the message, get defensive, and block out the meaning entirely. Instead, the supervisor decides to help enhance Tammy's awareness of racial issues in hopes that this awareness will increase Tammy's receptivity to other, more directive suggestions. Knowing that Tammy's gender identity is advanced and that she can conceptualize gender dynamics adeptly, the supervisor uses this area of strength as an analogy before addressing Tammy's limited self-knowledge with respect to race.

Focus on Multicultural Awareness

Supervisor: Perhaps there's another way to approach this. Suppose for a moment, you were to observe a client and counselor working together. The counselor is a man, and the client is a woman who identifies herself as a feminist, and during this session, you observe that not much is being discussed. Given the limited information I just gave you, what are some thoughts you might have about what's going on with these two?
uses a metaphor to help Tammy get some distance

Tammy: Well, first off, I guess I would wonder if he is able to relate to a woman.
enjoys the diversion

Supervisor: Hmm.

Tammy: I see where you are going with this, but I think my situation is different.

Supervisor: How so?
open, wondering if Tammy feels patronized

Tammy: My client is the guy in our relationship, so he doesn't have to get to know me.

Supervisor: Okay, but what about the two of you in terms of race?
more direct, realizing that Tammy did not understand the analogy

Tammy: What do you mean?

Supervisor: Do you suppose that part of the "stuckness" you are experiencing with Charles is a struggle between two people of different races?
more pointed, feeling frustrated

Tammy: I guess anything's possible, but I'm not completely getting it.
senses the supervisor's frustration

Supervisor: Would it be okay if I challenged you with something?
asks permission, to avoid raising Tammy's defensiveness

With this last strategic question, the supervisor puts Tammy in a bind. If Tammy answers in the affirmative, she agrees to be challenged. If she says no, however, her resistance will be brought into awareness, and the supervisor can then help her work with her reluctance to be challenged in this area.

Tammy: Ah, sure.

Supervisor: You mentioned earlier that you have not associated often with African American people and that you tend to take a "color-blind" view when it comes to race.

Tammy: Hmm.

Supervisor: Well, perhaps there is another way to look at race. I know you're very knowledgeable when it comes to gender issues. In fact, you really seem to have a complex grasp of gender dynamics in interpersonal relationships.
supportive

Tammy: Thanks.

Supervisor: But I'm picking up a disconnect between how you understand gender and how you understand race. In the case where the client is a woman, and the therapist is a man, you understand that the therapist may not understand the client if he were to approach the relationship as "gender blind" or essentially that gender doesn't matter.
uses support to cushion the confrontation

Tammy: But gender obviously does matter.
tries to stay with it

Supervisor: Exactly, and very likely, so does race . . .

Tammy: (*pause*) I kind of see the parallel you are drawing, but what am I still missing?
more receptive

Supervisor: Well, one area has to do with White privilege. Have you heard this term before?

Tammy: Yes. In Dr. Fels's class.

Supervisor: As a White person you—and I—experience certain privileges in our culture.
more didactic

Tammy: But, as a woman, many of those privileges are taken away.
wants to show her knowledge

Supervisor: That's true, but for an African American man, it's likely that different privileges are absent, some of which you would never know about unless you walked in his shoes.

Tammy: Now I get what you were saying before . . . that's an interesting way of looking at it.

Supervisor: Good. Say more about what you are thinking.
reinforces and encourages

Tammy: I suppose I ultimately don't know how he must feel or why he does what he does, including how he dresses and so forth.
understands the parallel

Tammy has just scratched the surface of her understanding of racial issues in therapy and has, to this point, shown a limited degree of cross-racial awareness; that is, Tammy only recognizes that she does not understand Charles, her client, as fully as she'd thought. The supervisor worked hard to get Tammy to a point where she began to see that she has some racial issues to identify and work through, but Tammy's defensiveness and low level of racial identity development slow this process. Recognizing that the session will end only with a partial resolution, the supervisor hopes that with some more directive work, Tammy may try to learn more from Charles about his experiences as an African American man. To be sure that Tammy doesn't go away from the session feeling bad about herself or about the tough interaction they have had, the supervisor begins by normalizing Tammy's confusion. Then, when Tammy seems worried about how she's being viewed, the supervisor brings the supervisory alliance into the foreground.

Normalizing the Supervisee's Experience

Supervisor: You're on the right track. My sense is that there are lots of exciting and some even disturbing things you can learn about in relation to the African American culture and how African Americans are treated in this country. As with other things about becoming a therapist, the first step is to recognize that there is something more to learn. And what I know about you, Tammy, is that you are willing to put yourself out there and learn new things.
offers support

Tammy: I know that I need to learn and I *want* to learn. Sometimes, it's hard to see your blind spots.
relieved

Supervisor: Of course. For me, too!
reassures

Tammy: I'm worried that you think I'm . . .
(*falls silent*)
takes a risk, worrying about evaluation

Focus on the Supervisory Alliance

Supervisor: Tammy, it's just that we now know one area we need to work on together. I think you're strong enough to face and accept your need for growth here.
recognizing Tammy's worry, emphasizes their collaboration

Tammy: (*quietly*) Okay, thanks.
feels reassured

Supervisor: How has this session been for you today, though? (*softly*) Tough?
offers Tammy the chance to vent

Tammy: Yeah, a little. But I needed a push and you pushed me. (*smiles*)
more secure

Supervisor: (*smiling*) Yeah, well, we all need a push sometimes in this business! Thanks for hanging in there.
points out the trust between them

Resolution

Tammy: Okay, but what should I do now?
feels a need for direction

Supervisor: How about some "homework?"

Tammy: Great!
[*discussion of what Tammy can do to raise her awareness of White privilege in relation to people of color*]

Because Tammy showed a desire to work in this area, the supervisor decides to begin with something cognitive, working with Tammy's strengths. She may suggest that Tammy read Helms's (1992) *A Race Is a Nice Thing to Have: A Guide to Being a White Person or Understanding the White Persons in Your Life*, for example. Once supervisees like Tammy are more accepting of their lack of self-awareness and knowledge, they can benefit from experiential and didactic activities.

This event ends with a partial resolution. Because Tammy showed some ability to tolerate the difficult feelings that began to emerge and was willing to show her concerns about being evaluated in this area, the supervisor feels confident that she can help Tammy manage and deal with the feelings and insights likely to emerge in the journey to come.

A more complete resolution of a racial awareness event would only be possible with supervisees who began at a more advanced stage, fully understanding their White privilege and being open to considering their personal racism. With such supervisees, a successful resolution of a racial awareness event might involve not only an observable increase in self-awareness, but also an ability to integrate this awareness into a conceptualization of past and future interactions with clients.

In the next event, a Marker occurring in a group supervision session signals the need for raising a supervisee's racial self-awareness. This event illustrates a successful resolution in a cross-cultural supervisory relationship.

A SUCCESSFULLY RESOLVED RACIAL AWARENESS EVENT (CROSS-CULTURAL SUPERVISION)

In this case, the supervisor is a 35-year-old White man with considerable experience as both a therapist and a supervisor. The supervisee is Sally, a 25-year-old Chinese American woman in her first practicum experience at a university counseling center.

The Marker takes place during a group supervision session. Sally is one supervisee with three others (Jennifer, Michelle, and Danielle, all of whom are White women). The conversation picks up during the group's discussion of how to attend to multicultural issues when conceptualizing diverse clients. When the supervisees seem unsure about how to begin, the supervisor suggests that they focus on themselves as a group of people from diverse backgrounds.

Marker

Jennifer: It seems hard to do when so few of our clients are from diverse backgrounds.

Michelle: Yeah, I only have one client in my whole caseload that is a person of color.
(*Danielle and Sally nod their heads*)

Supervisor: Well let's bring it to the here and now, so that we can have something to focus on that we all share. How do multicultural issues play out in this group supervision?
(*prolonged silence*)

Jennifer: I'm not sure what you mean.
wants to please but confused

Supervisor: How do all of you suppose that multicultural issues play out in this group?
directs comments to the group but is deliberately vague to let them lead

Jennifer: I'm not sure that they do.

Supervisor: Well, let's take a step back and look at the composition of this group. I am a White man, we have three White women, and one Asian woman.
(*some tense smiles*)
recognizes the need to be more direct

Jennifer: I guess I never thought of Sally as Asian. Rather, she is just like all of us.
feels the need to protect Sally

Supervisor: So you kind of see her as White?

At this point, the supervisor is embarrassed, realizing that his response was, like Jennifer's remark, a statement about Sally in the third person. The supervisor considers pointing out this slip, knowing that taking responsibility for his insensitive behavior would be a good model for his supervisees. Afraid, however, that pointing out how Sally was objectified would be distressing for her, the supervisor decides not to self-disclose but rather to speak with Sally directly.

Jennifer: Yeah, I guess.

Supervisor: (*gently*) Sally, what's that like for you to hear that the group sees you as White?

Sally: It's okay with me. I guess I don't really see myself as that different from the rest.
wanting not to be singled out

Supervisor: Hmm.

Sally: (*pause*) Although, I guess I obviously am!
realizes that she needs to be genuine

Michelle: But we don't think of Sally as so different. We all get along great, and we don't feel a need to put our differences out there. You know, just because I'm Irish American, doesn't mean I have to make sure I mention it as part of every conversation.
coming to Sally's defense, to lessen the potential for conflict

Supervisor: I see. It seems that we have a very cohesive group, and part of that cohesiveness involves bonding in ways that we are similar, rather than ways that make each of us unique.
reassures and includes himself in the group to lower the supervisees' anxiety

Sally: Kind of.

Supervisor: Okay, well we are about out of time today, but what I want to encourage each of you to do over the next week is look at ways that your differences can create bonds among you. Also, look at how these differences may create conflict. And in the end, how do your similarities and differences lead all of you to better understand your clients from a multicultural perspective? Okay?
realizes that there is not enough time to work through this racial challenge but wants to highlight the importance of what has begun
[All nod, with varying amounts of enthusiasm]

After identifying a Marker for all the group members, the supervisor decides to begin working individually with Sally on her apparent acceptance of her peers' multicultural insensitivity toward her. The first sequence in their individual supervision session is a focus on awareness. The supervisor suspects that Sally sacrificed her feelings to avoid conflict with her peers and to not stand out as different. Thus, the supervisor starts by reminding Sally what had taken place during the group session.

Focus on Multicultural Awareness

Supervisor: I wonder if we could start with what happened in group supervision the other day? Would that be okay with you?
asks permission

Sally: Yeah, I've been thinking of it as well.
shows a willingness to consider race

Supervisor: What have you come up with?
gives her room to express herself

Sally: I think I'm still in shock about what was said. I mean, also a part of me isn't sure that anything was wrong with what was said.
reflects on the dissonance she experienced in the group

Supervisor: Hmmmm. Say more about that conflict.
wants to facilitate Sally's movement from adaptation to incongruence

Sally: I guess, in many ways, all my life I have tried not to put any of my differences out there. Growing up, it was important that I try to fit in with everyone else—most or all were White. It didn't matter to me that I was Chinese. In fact, my parents made sure that we always spoke English at home, and both my brother and I have American names.
sensing the supervisor's openness, wants to self-explore

Supervisor: So it seems like it was important for you to kind of fit in, and perhaps not be noticed?
reflects

Sally: Yeah, definitely.

Because Sally brought up her parents' motivation to become acculturated, the supervisor decides to help Sally go deeper into her self-understanding.

Exploration of Feelings

Supervisor: So what happened the other day when your racial difference was being discussed?
offers Sally permission to express negative feelings and perceptions

Sally: I felt really uncomfortable. I didn't want to be the center of attention, especially because of my race.
open, but continues to downplay the effect of the discussion on her

Supervisor: Could you say some more about feeling uncomfortable?

Sally: I felt kind of put on the spot. Like I had something to be ashamed of.
feeling supported, takes a risk

Supervisor: Uh huh . . . All right . . . Can you keep talking about your feelings of shame?

Sally: I began to wonder what my parents would think, and I could even hear my father's voice saying, "Make sure you fit in!" and "Be sure not to cause waves!"

Supervisor: You really are showing some good insight.
reassures

Sally: (*laughs*) It doesn't all feel that great, though!
more genuine

Supervisor: (*smiles*) Yeah, that makes sense. Were there other feelings you had?
implies that mixed feelings are the norm in such circumstances

Sally: This happened a little later. I found myself kind of angry. I don't know why, and it's not something I typically feel.
intellectualizes her anger

Supervisor: Talk about your anger some more.
encourages a stronger expression of feelings

Sally: I think I was a little angry at my parents for wanting me to hide a part of me. I was also angry at my friends, who in a way, are dismissing a big part of me. *takes a risk*

Supervisor: Yes. Do you think maybe they didn't want to see who you are, or they're afraid to see you as different from them? *backing off, offers an interpretation*

Sally: Exactly! And that really bothered me. In fact, I spoke with a couple of them after our group session, and we talked a lot about it. They apologized for what they said, but I think I'm also angry with myself for not noticing all this before. *blames herself in an effort not to feel hurt or acknowledge her peers' insensitivity*

Supervisor: You feel like you're partly to blame for everyone else not noticing it? *reflects*

Sally: Yeah.

Sally is working diligently at understanding her problematic reactions to her peers' comments, but she has difficulty accessing her felt experience of anger and feels awkward about having criticized her parents. Knowing that Sally will want to save face, the supervisor worries that Sally may get mired in self-blame. To that end, he decides to normalize Sally's experience, thinking that, at some future point, they will need to talk about anger.

Normalizing Experience

Supervisor: Hmm. Well, you certainly have a right to feel angry. I guess I'd also like to add that what you are going through is very normal. Your heightened awareness as well as your feelings of anger, discomfort, and even shame.

Sally: Really? *feels understood*

Supervisor: You have really experienced here what Janet Helms calls an "encounter event." It happens when we have been denying a part of ourselves and then all of a sudden are psychologically shaken a little and we begin to see things a little differently. *offers a cognitive construction to help the supervisee see her experience as less unique*

Sally: (*nods*)

Supervisor: I've had a number of these experiences myself. One of my earliest was when I began to recognize all the privileges I have because I'm White in our society. It wasn't easy for me to see it, but as my eyes began to open wider, I also remember feeling really angry and guilty, and some shame as well. *self-discloses to put Sally at ease*

Sally: Wow! That's really helpful. So I'm not losing my mind? (*laughs*) *relieved and more comfortable*

Supervisor: No, not at all. You're doing some really good work, although it's really hard work because it is so full of emotions.

Sally: That's for sure. Just what I need, more work in graduate school! (*both laugh*)
uses humor to avoid more embarrassment

As shown in this excerpt, the supervisor self-disclosed about his own multicultural journey, and this intervention helped Sally see the universality of the struggle. In this next sequence, the supervisor concludes the event by offering his perspective on Sally's learning in this supervision session. Specifically, he points out her increased awareness and suggests possible next steps for her continued growth. Although they could continue to focus on Sally's experience as a first-generation Asian American woman, the supervisor suspects that her discomfort may relate to her having expressed anger more directly than usual.

Resolution

Sally: So where do I go from here?
willing to learn but uncomfortable with the personal encounter with her supervisor

Supervisor: Well, part of the work is done by you as you recognize how your interactions with others are, in part, influenced by your being a person of color. Another place to begin to look at, which we can think about in here, is how your awareness, as it grows, may start to influence your work with clients. We also can look at how your blind spots around race and other multicultural issues, such as your gender, may influence your therapy with clients. How does all that sound?
offers a direction for the future, recognizing Sally's desire to stay in the student role where she's more comfortable

Sally: Pretty overwhelming!

Supervisor: Well, we'll try our best to not make it too overwhelming. We'll just take it one step at a time . . .
emphasizes collaboration

In this case, the supervisee was open to her encounter experience with people of a different race. She may have seen it more clearly coming from someone in authority. In this event, Sally contended with an internal conflict—wanting to deny the racial insensitivity she experienced but also wanting to please her supervisor, a White male, who is older than she and an authority figure. Sally's readiness for this experience may have also been facilitated by the multicultural focus in her didactic coursework and knowing that self-exploration is an important part of her training.

As Sally gains self-awareness as an Asian-American woman, she may begin to see that, with some clients, her race is denied or even a source of conflict in the therapeutic relationship. If this occurs, Sally will need to find a way to manage her feelings about her clients' dismissal of a central aspect of her identity, recognizing all the while that she has done the very same thing to herself.

SPECIAL CONSIDERATIONS

Next, we describe additional supervision conditions that can either facilitate or hinder the extent to which a multicultural awareness event is successful.

Supervisor Heal Thyself

As mentioned throughout this chapter, supervisors must undertake their own journey toward multicultural development. A sure sign that a supervisor has *not* developed adequately in this regard is a remark such as, "I have completed all the multicultural growth I need."

So what can supervisors do to become more multiculturally adept? As with any self-training, they can begin by reading relevant literature (e.g., Ponterotto, Casas, Suzuki, & Alexander, 2001) and attending continuing education seminars that address various multicultural issues. A literature review and continuing education can help with the knowledge aspect of multicultural competence. As for the self-awareness aspect, supervisors need to put themselves in situations in which they can examine their own biases toward different cultural groups, including their own. Supervision of their therapy as well as of their supervision are two places in which self-examination can occur. Other situations include peer supervision and clinical situations that serve diverse clients from multiple cultural groups.

Of course, this self-training plan seems intense, given all other supervisory responsibilities. Interestingly, supervision of therapy for postlicensed clinicians, as well as supervision of supervision, is unusual in the United States but common in other countries. In the United Kingdom, for example, the professional expectation is that people will seek supervision of their therapy and supervision of their supervision throughout their career. Professional growth and development are lifelong commitments, and clinicians who engage in these activities are often the most proficient in their practice. Research suggests that experienced therapists, who are considered "master" (Jennings & Skovholt, 1999) or "passionately committed" (Dlugos & Friedlander, 2001) by their peers, do engage in lifelong supervision and consultation activities.

When Supervisory Relationships Are Regressive

As mentioned earlier, regressive supervisory relationships (i.e., when supervisors are less multiculturally adept than their supervisees) are highly problematic. Some research suggests that more than 10% of supervisees see their supervisors as multiculturally insensitive and view their behavior as unethical (Ladany et al., 1999).

Regressive relationships are also present when a supervisee's multicultural development is stifled. As an example, a supervisor may overlook an important Marker when a supervisee makes racially insensitive comments. Alternately, a supervisor may listen to, and perhaps even empathize with, the supervisee's insensitive statements, without challenge. These processes are likely to occur when supervisors are either in the incongruence or adaptation phase of their own cultural identity. More disconcerting is if the supervisor's lack of multicultural awareness in supervision mirrors the supervisee's lack of multicultural awareness in therapy (i.e., a multicultural parallel process). Such processes are recipes for harmful client experiences.

Supervisors who are resistant to developing their multicultural competencies pose a unique challenge for training sites and academic programs that rely on them for graduate training. Ideally, multicultural training should be offered to supervisors and faculty on an ongoing basis. It behooves directors of training to cease using supervisors who resist self-examination and continuing professional development. Though sadly, instituting such a policy is easier said than done.

A Word or Two About Social Class

An important aspect of multiculturalism is social class, which intersects with race, ethnicity, gender, and other variables to influence the psychological experience of an individual (Fouad & Brown, 2000; Liu, 2002; Liu, Ali, Solek, Hopps, Dunston, & Pickett, 2004; Nelson, Englar-Carlson, Tierney, & Hau, 2004). Social class is difficult to define. It may refer simply to one's current level of income in comparison to the norm; it may also refer to one's level of education and cultural sophistication. Liu et al. (2004) argue that regardless of the technical definition of one's social standing, from a psychological standpoint, the critical definition of social class resides in an individual's subjective experience of class.

One can currently be a member of middle, upper-middle, upper, or educated classes and still maintain the identity of one's origins—as a member of a lower, lower-middle, or working classes. Some people may experience powerful psychological reactions to others based on the interaction of subjective experience of social class with the perceived social class of others (Liu et al., 2004; Nelson et al., 2004). Because subjective experience of social class is invisible, it is easy to overlook in discussions of difference. Moreover, as people compare themselves to others, they may carry a sense of shame about their own experience as less cultured and less "in the know" (Nelson et al., 2004). Such shameful experiences can render discussions of social class somewhat sensitive. Yet, countertransference reactions to clients, as well as transference reactions to supervisors, can be based in a supervisee's experiences of internalized social class. One example would be a supervisee from a working- or lower-middle class background providing therapy to a client from a highly privileged background. The supervisee might react to the client out of shame, envy, or resentment or may harbor doubts about self-efficacy. Hence, social class is another critical multicultural variable to consider in supervision.

What About Gender, Sexual Orientation, Religion, and so Forth

In both case examples, we focused on race as the arena in which the most difficult and challenging multicultural situations tend to arise. Sexual orientation and gender issues are addressed in chapters 6 and 7, respectively. Although space limitations preclude extensive discussions of ethnicity, age, disability, and religion, we suggest that similar dynamics can occur with these factors, as with our discussions of race throughout this chapter.

Religion is a multicultural factor, however, that warrants attention because of its inherent difference from other multicultural variables. The primary distinction is that religion is not ascribed to an individual in the same way as gender, race, or ethnicity. Moreover, religion has historically been used to oppress various groups—consider, for example, slavery, the Holocaust, and religious institutions condemning gay men, lesbians, or bisexual individuals.

When supervisees possess religious (or other) beliefs oppressive toward others, supervisors should require them to consult professional and ethical guidelines that, by and large, do not condone oppressive practices. Applicants to graduate programs should be advised up front that the culture of graduate education and training does not tolerate oppressive attitudes or behaviors toward clients or colleagues. Like other basic skills, multicultural skills must be monitored to ensure minimal levels of competence, and resistance to self-knowledge and growth in this area should be handled in the same way as a supervisee's resistance to self-examination in other clinical arenas.

CONCLUSION

Multicultural events are among the most difficult events to work through in supervision, and commonly, supervisors are getting up to speed with their supervisees. Addressing multicultural issues is an affect-laden enterprise that has implications not only for client care, but also for supervisees' and supervisors' professional and personal development. In the end, we encourage supervisors to embrace these challenges because, as difficult as they are, they are equally enriching.

4

NEGOTIATING ROLE CONFLICTS: IF IT WERE EASY, IT WOULDN'T BE CALLED SUPERVISION

A smile is the chosen vehicle for all ambiguities.
—Herman Melville, 1852

Conducting psychotherapy is work, and supervising it is work. Work-related stress and its many hazards figure prominently in the industrial and organizational psychology literature (Beehr & Newman, 1978; Newman & Beehr, 1979; Osipow & Spokane, 1984). One notable source of stress is the competing behavioral expectations for different work roles. Juggling multiple role demands can confuse and overwhelm an individual struggling to define a professional identity.

Since the 1970s, several authors have acknowledged the potential for damaging role conflicts in supervision. Early literature on conflict in supervision describes not only supervisees' personal issues and anxiety as a source of conflict (Mueller & Kell, 1972) but also theoretical differences (Moskowitz & Rupert, 1983; Wolberg, 1988), dual role definitions—supervisor-as-teacher and supervisor-as-evaluator (Hassenfeld & Sarris, 1978; Robiner, 1982).

Abundant evidence suggests that a good relationship—characterized by warmth, rapport, and mutual respect—is a key component of high-quality supervision (Friedlander & Ward, 1984; Nash, 1975). Although trainees learn quickly that different supervisors have distinctive supervisory styles or approaches (Friedlander & Ward, 1984), it may be less obvious that supervisors play different social roles in this relationship and expect their supervisees to follow suit. Role ambiguity can arise with a lack of clarity about the supervisor's expectations, the methods for fulfilling those expectations, and the evaluative consequences for failing to do so (Biddle, 1979; Van Sell, Brief, & Schuler, 1981).

Interpersonal or relational supervision, however, with its shifting focus on the therapeutic and supervisory relationships, likely differs from any supervision a beginning trainee may have experienced in other occupational settings. Without adequate preparation, or "role induction" (Bahrick, Russell, & Salmi, 1991; Ellis, Chapin, Dennin, & Anderson-Hanley, 1996), a supervisee may not appreciate the importance or complexity of this supervisory approach. At times, the process is collegial and consultative; at other times, particularly when a client is at risk, the supervisor may play a managerial role. Supervisors are also teachers—offering feedback, developing skills, and discussing theory. Although the aims differ, when the supervisee's personal issues are addressed, the supervisory session can resemble a psychotherapy session, with the supervisee in a client role in relation to the supervisor.

Experiencing oneself as a competent, authoritative therapist who develops and carries through a treatment plan can conflict with the experience of being subordinate or "one-down" in supervision (Holloway, 1984). This duality was illustrated in a case study of parallel processes in psychotherapy and supervision (Friedlander, Siegel, & Brenock, 1989). Content analyses of the supervision sessions showed that the supervisor was authoritative yet nurturing and supportive; the verbal interactions were largely supervisor "one-up"/supervisee "one-down." As a therapist, the supervisee's behavior in the therapy relationship mirrored the supervisor's behavior. Interacting with the client, the supervisee was one-up, authoritative, nurturing, and supportive.

Though in this case, the supervisee managed the dual roles well, maintaining a positive relationship with the supervisor even when the therapeutic relationship foundered, as conflict can arise when an individual sees the role demands as contradictory or unrelated to job performance (Caplan & Jones, 1975; Cooper & Marshall, 1976). In the extreme, supervision can seem like a double bind to the supervisee who feels criticized for a client's deterioration yet is expected to expose areas of weakness to the supervisor (Olk & Friedlander, 1992; Ward, Friedlander, Schoen, & Klein, 1985). When asked to disclose personal information, the supervisee may feel defensive or threatened, believing that the supervisor sees personal or professional inadequacy.

Role conflict can also affect the therapeutic relationship. As a therapist, the supervisee is expected to develop treatment strategies and apply them effectively with clients but may fear jeopardizing a client's welfare if the supervisor's directive goes against the supervisee's better judgment. If the supervisee follows his or her own sense of what is needed with the client, he or she risks putting himself or herself in a tenuous position with the supervisor.

Research in this area indicates that role ambiguity, as well as role conflict, affect (and are affected by) the supervisee's level of anxiety, satisfaction with clinical work (Olk & Friedlander, 1992), and the supervisory relationship itself (Ladany & Friedlander, 1995). Role ambiguity, defined as "a lack of clarity regarding the expectations for one's role, the methods for fulfilling those expectations, and the consequences for effective or ineffective performance," occurs when, for example, the supervisee is unsure how to prepare for supervision, about the kinds of material to present, how autonomous to be, or how best to use the supervisory process (Olk & Friedlander, 1992, p. 390). A national study suggested that role ambiguity can occur for trainees at any level of experience when a lack of agreement exists with the supervisor about the goals and tasks of supervision (Ladany & Friedlander, 1995). When this agreement is not in place and there is a poor emotional bond (mistrust, dislike, or disrespect), role conflict can ensue. In a recent qualitative study, trainees who felt harmed by their supervisors' behavior had significant role difficulties (Nelson & Friedlander, 2001). On the Role Conflict and Role Ambiguity Inventory (Olk & Friedlander, 1992), participants scored well above the normative means, and in interviews, they described intense feelings of anxiety, anger, and self-doubt, as a result of the problems with their supervisors.

Whereas role ambiguity is salient for beginning trainees (Olk & Friedlander, 1992), role conflict tends to afflict experienced therapists who have a clear idea about what should and should not happen in the supervisory process (Friedlander, Keller, Peca-Baker, & Olk, 1986; Olk & Friedlander, 1992). Although serious role conflicts are not frequent (Olk & Friedlander, 1992), many individuals will experience at least one problem of this kind if they work with numerous supervisors throughout their training.

Because supervisors' styles and preferred roles in supervision vary considerably (Friedlander & Ward, 1984), it is easy to see how problems develop when a supervisee encounters a supervisor who behaves much differently from what was experienced in prior relationships. As therapists gain experience and move from setting to setting, they may be exposed to very different supervisory approaches. Supervisors who work with beginners tend to have an evaluative, task-oriented style (Friedlander & Ward, 1984), focusing primarily on the client and skill development. With more experienced therapists, most supervisors use a collegial, interpersonal style, especially in outpatient settings with less seriously disturbed clients (Friedlander & Ward, 1984). Research suggests that conflicts often occur when supervisees expect *only* a directive, task-oriented *or* an exploratory, interpersonal style (Moskowitz & Rupert, 1983). In Exhibit 4.1, items from the Role Conflict and Role Ambiguity Inventory (Olk & Friedlander, 1992) illustrate

EXHIBIT 4.1
Role Conflict and Role Ambiguity Inventory

Items Indicating Role Conflict

1. I have felt that my supervisor was incompetent or less competent than I. I often felt as though I was supervising him/her.
2. I have wanted to challenge the appropriateness of my supervisor's recommendations for using a technique with one of my clients, but I have thought it better to keep my opinions to myself.
3. I have believed that my supervisor's behavior in one or more situations was unethical or illegal, and I was undecided about whether to confront him/her.
4. My orientation to therapy was different from that of my supervisor. She or he wanted me to work with clients using her or his framework, and I felt that I should be allowed to use my own approach.
5. I have wanted to intervene with one of my clients in a particular way, and my supervisor has wanted me to approach the client in a very different way. I am expected both to judge what is appropriate for myself and also to do what I am told.
6. My supervisor told me to do something I perceived to be illegal or unethical, and I was expected to comply.
7. I got mixed signals from my supervisor, and I was unsure of which signals to attend to.
8. When using a new technique, I was unclear about the specific steps involved. As a result, I wasn't sure how my supervisor would evaluate my performance.
9. I disagreed with my supervisor about how to introduce a specific issue to a client, but I also wanted to do what the supervisor recommended.
10. Part of me wanted to rely on my own instincts with clients, but I always knew that my supervisor would have the last word.
11. I was not comfortable using a technique recommended by my supervisor; however, I felt that I should do what my supervisor recommended.
12. I disagreed with my supervisor about implementing a specific technique, but I also wanted to do what the supervisor thought best.
13. My supervisor wanted me to use an assessment technique that I considered inappropriate for a particular client.

Items Indicating Role Ambiguity

1. I was not certain about what material to present to my supervisor.
2. I wasn't sure how best to use supervision as I became more experienced, although I was aware that I was expected to behave more independently.
3. My supervisor expected me to come prepared for supervision, but I had no idea what or how to prepare.
4. I wasn't sure how autonomous I should be in my work with clients.
5. My supervisor's criteria for evaluating my work were not specific.
6. I was not sure that I had done what the supervisor expected me to do in a session with a client.
7. The criteria for evaluating my performance in supervision were not clear.
8. The feedback I got from my supervisor did not help me to know what was expected of me in my day-to-day work with clients.
9. Everything was new, and I wasn't sure what would be expected of me.
10. I was not sure if I should discuss my professional weaknesses in supervision because I was not sure how I would be evaluated.
11. My supervisor gave me no feedback, and I felt lost.

continued

12. My supervisor told me what to do with a client but didn't give me very specific ideas about how to do it.
13. There were no clear guidelines for my behavior in supervision.
14. The supervisor gave no constructive or negative feedback, and as a result, I did not know how to address my weaknesses.
15. I didn't know how I was doing as a therapist, and as a result, I didn't know how my supervisor would evaluate me.
16. I was unsure of what to expect from my supervisor.

Note. For scoring the RCRA Inventory, see Olk and Friedlander (1992).

situations in which ambiguities or conflicts can arise between the educational, therapeutic, collegial, and managerial functions of supervision.

Without discussing how supervision will take place and how performance will be evaluated, the supervisee is vulnerable to both role ambiguity and role conflict. Although many authors emphasize the need for discussion in conflict situations, the degree to which the supervisory relationship should be focal in such discussions is controversial (Moskowitz & Rupert, 1983). Some authors suggest only a limited discussion of supervisees' feelings (Wolberg, 1988), but interpersonal theorists advocate a frank discussion in which the supervisor acknowledges a part in the impasse (Frawley-O'Dea & Sarnat, 2001). The rationale for this approach is that exploration of conflicts in the supervisory relationship fosters the supervisee's personal growth and learning (Moskowitz & Rupert, 1983), paralleling the experience of clients in therapy.

It is not common for supervisees to initiate discussions of this kind (Moskowitz & Rupert, 1983), due to their one-down status in the relationship. Unresolved conflicts may result in supervisee passivity or false compliance (Rosenblatt & Mayer, 1975). In extreme cases, supervisees falsify their notes or behave in other ways to conceal the difficulties they have with clients (Ladany, Hill, Corbett, & Nutt, 1996; Nash, 1975). Since supervisors expect supervisees to demonstrate competence, as well as expose weaknesses and vulnerabilities, the stage is set for strategic self-presentation (Ward et al., 1985).

More than any other critical event described in this book, role conflict events directly affect (and are affected by) the quality of the supervisory relationship. Because such conflicts can cause irreparable ruptures in the learning alliance (Ladany & Friedlander, 1995; Nelson & Friedlander, 2001), supervisors need to recognize these problems when they first arise. Infrequent, temporary ruptures in the supervisory alliance, if repaired successfully, can provide important learning experiences (Gray et al., 2001), but prolonged role difficulties can be quite destructive (Nelson & Friedlander, 2001).

In this chapter, we present and illustrate a process model for recognizing and working through role conflicts in supervision. The chapter concludes by discussing special considerations surrounding this critical event.

PROCESS MODEL

Our process model of working through role-conflict events in supervision derives from Safran, Crocker, McMain, and Murray's (1990) task analysis for repairing ruptures in the therapy alliance. The model begins with the Marker, arguably the most critical aspect of this event. For role relationship problems, the first supervisory task is to identify the Marker as either role *ambiguity* or role *conflict*. In many instances, role ambiguity can be corrected efficiently by addressing and clarifying expectations, whereas role conflict requires more sustained attention.

Marker

The clearest Marker for role ambiguity is when the supervisee inquires about how supervision works or about expected roles and responsibilities in supervision. The supervisee might ask if a given topic is appropriate for discussion or raise a concern about the evaluation process. Other Markers may be less distinct, however. The supervisee who fails to bring a tape (as requested) to supervision may either not understand what is expected (role ambiguity) or may resist the supervisor's influence (role conflict). Because role conflict, more so than role ambiguity, tends to signal mistrust (Ladany & Friedlander, 1995), a feeling of tension in the relationship signals that the supervisee may be experiencing more conflict than ambiguity.

Other Markers of role conflict include the supervisee's (a) direct or indirect (sarcasm, defensiveness) expression of anger or other negative feelings about the supervisor or supervisory process; (b) expressed disagreement about the goals or tasks of supervision or about the supervisor's evaluation; (c) overcompliance (rapid agreement with the supervisor without exploration or elaboration, i.e., "lip service"); (d) noncompliance (nonresponsiveness or begrudging acceptance of the supervisor's input); (e) avoidance (arriving late, canceling, or failing to attend supervision, coming unprepared, ignoring the supervisor's comments, or skipping from topic to topic); and (f) self-esteem-enhancing behaviors, such as justification or self-aggrandizing (cf. Safran et al., 1990).

Task Environment and Resolution

The Task Environment in role-ambiguity events is a straightforward clarification and negotiation of expectations for supervision. In more challenging role-conflict events, the Task Environment proceeds with at least two stages: *exploration of feelings* and *focus on the supervisory alliance*. In the exploratory stage, the supervisor tries to ascertain what the supervisee is experiencing in the interaction as it unfolds. Some supervisees may be angry and defensive; others may be confused, hurt, or embarrassed. With this understanding, the supervisor can attempt to clarify the competing role expectations and rebuild trust and a sense of ease in the relationship. To do so, the supervisor needs to encourage the supervisee's expression of negative feelings and acknowledge the supervisor's own contribution to the conflict.

A successful repair of the alliance, or Resolution, occurs when supervisees express an understanding of the impasse in a way that indicates they no longer experience the feelings aroused by the conflict. This shift might be an emotional one, signaled verbally or nonverbally, or an expression of insight (e.g., "Now I see why I reacted as I did to what you said"). In many cases, the Resolution involves renegotiating the goals and tasks of supervision.

In the following two sections, unsuccessfully and successfully resolved role-conflict events in supervision with the same supervisee illustrate the many-layered complexities of this critical incident. The event begins when the supervisee tells the supervisor about a troubled therapeutic relationship. Ruptures in the therapeutic alliance often signal to the supervisor that a different supervisory approach is needed to ensure the client's welfare. Yet in these two excerpts, the supervisor responds in different ways, with role conflict ensuing in both instances. In the first illustration, the supervisor switches from a consultative to a therapeutic role; in the second illustration, the switch is to a managerial role.

AN UNSUCCESSFULLY RESOLVED ROLE-CONFLICT EVENT

In this event, Alex, a 30-year-old advanced practicum student in a family service agency, discusses his work with a difficult couple, who have abruptly quit treatment. In response to the supervisor's query about Alex's emotional reaction to the couple's decision, Alex defensively justifies their right to terminate. The role conflict, which causes a rupture in an otherwise solid supervisory alliance, begins when Alex's supervisor switches to a therapeutic role, failing to address the basis for Alex's defensiveness, instead forging ahead with a personal agenda (i.e., probing Alex's feelings).

Marker

Alex: . . . and at the end of the session, they told me they won't be coming back again. They're done. There was no leadup to it, just, "BAM! Goodbye," you know. Maybe three minutes before the end of the session.
describes a therapeutic rupture

Supervisor: Wow! That's a surprise! Did you have any inkling this was coming?
questions his understanding of the therapy event

Alex: No, not at all. I handled it okay, though.

Supervisor: Yeah? What did you do?

Alex: Well, I asked Alicia to explain, since she was the one who told me. And she said it was just too hard for her to arrange things to get here—needing a babysitter, a taxi, and all that, and so I . . . and Lamont didn't think he should take any more time off from work. So I said I understood and that they could come back any time if they wanted to, just to give me a call. I remembered to remind them, though, that I'd be leaving the clinic in a month.

Supervisor: How's this feeling for you?
explores his experience

Alex: Okay. I think clients have the right to make these kinds of decisions for themselves. I'm not so sure it's all these external reasons, though, but I just think they feel they've gone as far as they can. I know that when I start working for managed care, couples might only get a few sessions or even *no* sessions, so this kind of thing happens and . . .
defensive self-justification

Supervisor: But how did it *feel* to have them quit like that?
redirects

Alex: All right, I guess. It was a choice point, and I decided not to force the issue.
intellectualizes

Supervisor: Was there something going on for you that was uncomfortable?
redirects, more strongly

Alex: I don't know what you mean.
confused or defensive

Supervisor: Well, I've been asking about your emotional reaction to their dropping out, but you keep telling me what you *think*, not what you *feel* about it.
confronts his intellectualizing

Alex: (silence)

Supervisor: You look kind of tense, or at least that's what I'm seeing.
feedback, wanting to encourage Alex to express negative feelings

Alex: I don't think this is about *me*! Maybe we don't agree about Alicia and Lamont leaving. It's not just how I feel . . . I don't know, it's also how you . . . (softer) I mean, I think we should be talking about *them*, not *me*.
avoidant, defensive; discloses his expectation for a client-focused supervisory process

Supervisor: Yes, I think so, too, but you're obviously having a lot of feelings or reactions about it. Negative ones, I suspect. Can we talk about them?
continues to focus on Alex, asking permission to encourage collaboration

Alex: This isn't *my* therapy!
reveals the basis for his discomfort

Supervisor: No, but your reactions are important. I'm wondering if this has something to do with the potential for violence in this couple. Maybe this is why it's hard for you to work with them.
offers an interpretation of his behavior

Alex: I don't think they're hard to work with—they simply decided to quit.
defensive

Supervisor: Yes, but as we've talked about it, you've continued to avoid looking at your emotional reactions to their leaving.
confronts his avoidance

Alex: (*louder*) Are you saying I'm defensive?
angry

Supervisor: Well, yes, I guess I am.

Although the supervisor may be correct in assuming that countertransference is behind Alex's defensiveness, repeated probing of his feelings about the case is ineffective—indeed, judging from his reaction, potentially harmful. At this point, it is abundantly clear that the supervisory alliance is in trouble, and the supervisor switches to focus on the supervisory relationship. Despite the supervisor's attempt to be empathic, Alex's feelings are so strong that he is even less willing and able to examine the rupture between them, let alone consider his handling of the therapy case.

Focus on the Supervisory Alliance

Supervisor: Your view of what should happen in supervision is not what's happening right now, then, I take it?
frustrated, attempts to clarify the incongruence

Alex: No, not really. I mean . . . I want to focus on what . . . on what I'm doing in therapy, my skills, my case conceptualizations, that's where I need the help. Not my feelings so much about what you and I are talking about all the time.
explains his understanding of the supervisory process and the basis for his discomfort

Supervisor: It seems too much about you, about us, and not enough about the clients? About what you feel you want to learn in supervision?
reflects

Alex: Exactly!
feels understood

Supervisor: It seems that focusing on your feelings is making you feel like a client. Do you feel that I'm seeing you as the problem . . . having the problem . . . or . . . ?
clarifies perception of his discomfort with the therapeutic aspect of supervision

Alex: I think we should be dealing with my work with my clients. I don't see . . . want to be . . . feel like I'm in therapy myself here. If we disagree about Alicia and Lamont, that's one thing, but . . .
reiterates his expectations for supervision as client-focused

Supervisor: Let's back up for a minute, Alex. It's important for you and I to get square with each other before Alicia and Lamont come in. They're not here right

now—*we* are, and we have our wires crossed. We can't help them until we get them uncrossed.
refocuses on the supervisory relationship and the need to repair their alliance

Alex: (*silence*)
frustrated

Supervisor: I think our different expectations about supervision may be getting in the way. Do you agree?
labels the role conflict

Alex: Mm.

Supervisor: You said you see supervision as primarily . . . or only . . . for you to get input, feedback on your technical and diagnostic skills. Also you said you don't want to feel like a client in therapy here.
reflects his expressed expectations about supervision

Alex: Right.
tentative

Supervisor: I think the problem we're having is one of not seeing supervision the same way . . . in a couple of different ways, actually. In your mind, it should all be focused on the clients and your work with them, right? That's the first way. And then, second, you don't want me to come in and overturn your decisions.
restates the role conflict

Alex: Well, yeah.

Supervisor: And, in my mind, supervision involves looking at the therapist closely, that you, me, whoever is the therapist is a big part of the equation in any therapy. Who you are, what you do, how you feel, your own emotional baggage. No two therapists would approach a case the same way. And—parenthetically—I think the therapist's issues get stirred up much more working with couples and families than individuals, but that's a whole other discussion! Anyway, I see looking inside at you, the therapist, is crucial, and supervision is the place to do it. It's not about being a good therapist. You *are* a good therapist, and you can become a *better* therapist. So in other words, it's not something that's *wrong* or a *problem* or whatever about you, Alex, that makes me ask you these things. We all have our blind spots, myself included. I do this kind of work with all my supervisees, and the more you, as a therapist can take a good, hard look at yourself, the better therapist you'll be. You're at the point now in your training that this would be more beneficial in some ways than our focusing on every intervention you make, I think.
didactic, describing expectations for supervision, wanting to reassure and bolster Alex's self-esteem

Alex: Oh! Well, I didn't . . . I mean . . .
confused

Supervisor: Sometimes it may feel like therapy in here, but the main difference is that the purpose of my asking you to look inside at how you feel is for you to work better with your clients, not simply for your own personal growth. I'm not your therapist, and

I would only focus on your personal issues as they affect your work with clients. If I feel a supervisee needs to work on an issue with a therapist, I generally say so. *clarifying the boundaries of supervisee-focused supervision*

Alex: Okay.

The event ends here, unresolved, with the supervisee still confused and frustrated. Seemingly compliant, he shuts down, unwilling to disclose further. A close look at the process shows that although the supervisor recognized Alex's discomfort and annoyance, the managerial style was one-sided and thus, ineffective. Frustrated with attempts to clarify the role conflict and reassure Alex, the supervisor addressed him in a didactic, authoritative manner. Although explaining the problem that arose between them at length, the supervisor did so only from a personal perspective, without acknowledging a role in the impasse or encouraging Alex's disclosures about his experience. By approaching it in this way, the supervisor implied that this view was the only correct one. Understandably, Alex continued to feel criticized, not only for how he handled his clients' termination but also for being defensive in supervision. In the end, rather than disclose his feelings about either the therapy or the supervision, he paid lip service to the supervisor, just wanting the session to end.

A SUCCESSFULLY RESOLVED ROLE-CONFLICT EVENT

The next excerpt, beginning like the previous one, illustrates a successfully resolved role conflict. In this event, Alex's expectation of a collegial supervisory relationship falters when the supervisor criticizes his behavior, revealing the supervisor's managerial perspective on the relationship. As follows, when Alex becomes defensive, the supervisor quickly recognizes the Marker and shifts the focus from the therapy relationship to the supervisory relationship. As the event unfolds, Alex acknowledges his supervisor's authority, and the supervisor acknowledges Alex's need for greater collaboration. In other words, each moves toward the other—their expectations are less polarized, and a good working relationship is restored.

We pick up the Marker when, as in the previous excerpt, the supervisor begins to explore Alex's feelings about Alicia and Lamont's decision to terminate treatment.

Marker

Supervisor: How's this feeling for you?
explores his experience

Alex: Okay. I think clients have the right to make these kinds of decisions for themselves. I'm not so sure it's all these external reasons, though, but I just think

they feel they've gone as far as they can. I know that when I start working for managed care, couples might only get a few sessions or even *no* sessions, so this kind of thing happens and . . .
defensive self-justification

At this point, seeing Alex's comments as an intellectual response to a tricky clinical impasse, the supervisor might decide that the problem results from Alex's inexperience with premature termination. If so, the supervisor might proceed in a teaching mode by, for example, describing various ways to handle the termination, viewing the videotape of the session, working with Alex to formulate an understanding of this therapeutic rupture in light of the couple's history, and so forth (see chap. 2 on skill deficits). Or, as in the previous illustration, the supervisor might focus on Alex's feelings. Instead, as follows, the supervisor decides to point out Alex's error and offer a directive about how to proceed with his clients. The supervisor begins by revealing concern about the couple's potential for violence, which Alex interprets as criticism. As the supervisor becomes more directive, Alex becomes quieter, suggesting discomfort and defensiveness. His expressed confusion, coupled with passivity, signals the supervisor that the supervisory alliance needs attention before they proceed with a discussion of Alex's clients.

Supervisor: But weren't we concerned that there may be some violence going on between them that they were inching closer to telling you about?
raises concerns about Alex's handling of the therapy event

Alex: What do you mean?
somewhat defensive

Supervisor: I'm concerned that these external reasons are a cover up and that the real reason they've left is the violence. Maybe not, maybe so. But we need to figure out a way to be sure that's not the case, offer Alicia a chance to come in on her own. I'm not comfortable leaving this the way it stands.
explains concern about his handling of the therapy event and provides a directive for action

Alex: (*silence*) I don't understand what you mean. (*quietly*)
confused, possibly defensive

Supervisor: I'd guess . . . we need to figure out how to handle it from here. It was a mistake to say "goodbye" and leave it at that, when you had so much prior evidence that there could be some abuse going on in this couple. She could be in real danger, or the baby could, and we won't know it. I understand fully your wish to respect their decision, but . . .
clarifies and defends perceptions of the case

Alex: But . . . are you saying . . . ? (*silence*)
initiates a challenge and backs off

Supervisor: What?

Alex: (*silence*)
threatened, defensive

At this moment, the Marker is complete, with the supervisor abundantly aware of the role conflict that Alex feels. The Task Environment begins with a shift—the supervisory relationship becomes the figure, and the therapy process, the ground—with a recursive movement between an exploration of here-and-now feelings and an explicit focus on the alliance. In essence, the supervisor's intent, at this point, is to help Alex express his discomfort with what is occurring between them and to explore his reactions to feedback. He, understandably, is reluctant, and the supervisor encourages his disclosure by demonstrating an openness to his negative feelings about their interaction. When Alex indicates feeling criticized, the event moves to the next stage.

Exploration of Feelings *and* Focus on the Supervisory Alliance

Supervisor: I sense some tension between us right now . . . ?
shifts focus to supervisory relationship

Alex: Mmhmm. I guess it's . . . (*quietly*)
reluctant, anxious

Supervisor: Something about what I said is bothering you. Was it . . . ?
gives Alex permission to express negative reactions

Alex: I don't see it as a "mistake" really, but as a "decision," or rather, a choice point.
defensive, intellectual shift

Supervisor: I see. You see my saying it was a "mistake" as different from considering it a choice point or a decision because that word, "mistake," implies . . .
attempts to clarify

Alex: (*interrupting*) Well, it implies . . . uh . . . a criticism, and . . .
reveals the source of his discomfort

Supervisor: Yes?
encourages his disclosure; hesitant to assert negative feelings

Alex: and it . . .

Supervisor: I guess it seemed off base to you?
prompts in order to demonstrate an openness to Alex's negative feelings

Alex: Mm hm.

Alex may feel highly sensitive to negative feedback due to his own personal history or because of prior harmful supervision experiences. Alternately, he may question the supervisor's authority to criticize his work. Or he may accept his supervisor's authority but be upset that their interaction is less collegial than what he expected. The following dialogue clarifies the latter explanation for the impasse and shows the discrepancy between Alex's expectation for collaboration and the supervisor's authoritative feedback. Recognizing the role conflict for Alex (between being a competent therapist who makes decisions and a supervisee who needs directives), the supervisor acknowledges that the previous response was ineffective, and indeed, perceived by Alex as "disrespectful." At this point in the event, it becomes clear that for Alex, the conflict arose in this supervisory interaction (i.e., it does not signal a pervasive difficulty in the relationship).

Supervisor: Yes, I can see that. Thank you for being frank about your reaction. It must've seemed heavy-handed, top-down authority, to you—my putting it that way.
acknowledges Alex's discomfort; reflects personal perspective on their interaction

Alex: (*more strongly*) Well, I know you're my supervisor, and you *are* . . . you *do* know more than I do about doing therapy, but in this situation, I don't think what I did was a "mistake." I know we disagree about it, and maybe I could've done some things differently, but . . .
acknowledges authority and expresses his need to be responded to differently

Supervisor: My jumping the gun to say we'd need to hold onto this couple, that it's dangerous, that it's abuse, that you made a mistake . . . in my doing that it seemed to you that I was discounting you as the therapist in charge of this case, knowing what's happening with them?
reflects personal experience

Alex: Yes.

Supervisor: (*pause*) Well, I clearly didn't give you feedback in a way that was helpful to you.
acknowledges a part in the problem

Alex: (*pause*) Well, no.
relieved

Supervisor: I'm sensing that you want our supervision to be more collaborative?
seeks to clarify expectations

Alex: Well, it *has* been pretty collaborative . . . up . . . up until this point. I was just surprised, that's all, when you said the word, "mistake."
indicates that this is a rupture in a solid supervisory alliance

Supervisor: So this seemed like a departure from the way we have been working until now? Or the way that I've been giving you feedback? Sounds like it felt disrespectful of you.
seeks to clarify Alex's perspective on the rupture

Alex: Right.

For a Resolution to the role conflict, the alliance must be repaired. To do so, the supervisor acknowledges that the feedback, although not intended to be disrespectful, had that effect for Alex. Because, in his view, the supervisor's behavior was a departure from their good working relationship, the supervisor reflects on the covert basis for the shift in behavior toward him. The acknowledgment of a mistake and the personal basis for it, along with empathy for his discomfort, frees Alex to express the conflict he experienced more clearly—competent therapists don't "screw up."

Supervisor: (*pause*) Well, this makes me think that I need to take a look at what's going on for *me* here, since what I said was so far off base for you. (*pause*)
explores personal responsibility for the rupture in the alliance

And I know that my *intent* certainly wasn't to be disrespectful of you or your work. You've handled the case very well to this point. I've had no cause for concern.
reassures him of his competence

Alex: (*quietly*) Thanks.

Supervisor: I understand now. I see that I was hasty in that . . . in jumping to that. I'm sorry. (*pause*)
apologizes

I think the potential for violence in this couple is a bit frightening for me, honestly. It pushes some of my own buttons. I may have jumped too quickly to my own conclusion about what should happen next with them because of that.
discloses the covert basis for involvement in the problem

Yes, definitely, my *own* issues got stirred up here, and I think I went about it the wrong way with you.
models acknowledgment of weaknesses

Alex: That's okay. I understand it now.
still uncomfortable

Supervisor: But at the time . . .
recognizes his discomfort

Alex: At the time, it seemed . . .

Supervisor: Yes, it must've seemed too strong, too quick.
shows empathy

Alex: Yes. And I just don't want to be seen as a jerk, you know, calling them back and saying, "Hey. Come back," you know, "I screwed up."
acknowledges that the directive threatened Alex's self-esteem

Supervisor: Of course! Now I see why you reacted as you did to my comment. But before we go on to talk about how to handle this couple, let's just see if *we're* on the same wavelength now, or . . .
shows understanding and refocuses on the supervisory alliance

Alex: Well, I feel better. I do. I think you're right. We weren't on the same wavelength about supervision. And . . . (*silence*)
hints at other negative feelings

When people interacting with each other use the identical metaphor, this mirroring suggests that they are indeed on the "same wavelength"—in this case, moving toward a repair of the alliance. As the event resolves, Alex's growing comfort is revealed by his next disclosure.

Resolution

Supervisor: Something else?
gives permission

Alex: I'm feeling better about what happened with you and me, but maybe I'm feeling worse about what happened with Lamont and Alicia.
acknowledges self-doubt

Supervisor: First, before we go back to them, can we stick with us a moment longer . . . can you tell me how you're seeing our supervision together?
asks permission to work it through to the end

Alex: Well, as I said before, it's been pretty good for me overall.

Supervisor: But maybe I need to be a bit more sensitive and more collaborative with you. Sometimes, though, I may contradict you or your decisions.
acknowledges the need to change in relation to him in some (not all) respects

Alex: I know. That's all right. I hadn't thought about *why* you were saying what you were saying, how you thought they [clients] are not safe together. I only reacted to being told I was wrong. I didn't want to hear that! I got defensive!
indicates a shift toward being able to see the supervisor as a person, not only in a supervisory role; admits his fear of negative evaluation

Supervisor: Of course! No one likes to hear they're wrong. And again, I'm sorry. I think this case stirs up a lot for both of us.
reassures him and moves to the therapy relationship

Alex: (*pause*) I realize now that I wasn't 100% comfortable with their decision to quit therapy, and maybe when you said it was a mistake, it forced me to face how uncomfortable I really was with how I handled it at the time.
acknowledges self-doubt and possible projection
   I reacted against you because you labeled what I didn't want to see! (*laughs*)
insight

Supervisor: (*laughs*) Yes, of course! What's even more fascinating about all this is the parallel between you being faced with their decision to quit and my being faced with your decision to let them! Neither of us is happy with how we acted in the moment.
draws attention to the parallel process

Alex: Wow! (*pause*) I didn't want to just categorically say, "No, you can't quit," but I didn't know how to go about keeping them here.
shows understanding

Supervisor: Well, we found out from what happened between us that being authoritarian or heavy-handed is *not* the way to go. Maybe we'd best start by reviewing the tape at the point where Alicia told you they were quitting. Let's see if we can figure out a more collaborative or problem-solving approach with them that might be effective.
suggests that understanding their interaction can inform the therapy

Alex: Great!

Before transitioning to the therapy relationship, the supervisor clarified the supervisory roles, thereby modeling behavior change. In the Resolution phase of the event, Alex acknowledged his defensiveness and explored the basis for it—the supervisor's criticism echoed his own self-criticism and doubt. Hearing his insight, the supervisor came to recognize the parallel process—Alex's difficulty handling his clients' resistance and the supervisor's difficulty with Alex's resistance. (Rather than using the term *resistance*, which Alex would find pejorative, the therapist described the parallel process behaviorally, both from his perspective as therapist and from the supervisory perspective.) The episode ended with a return to the therapy relationship, this time with the understanding that collaborative problem solving may more effectively melt resistance.

As shown in this excerpt, some role conflicts are caused not by widely divergent expectations about the supervisory process but rather by ego-threatening clinical material. In this case, Alex's sense of competence is shaken by his clients' abrupt termination from therapy. Rather than put his self-doubt on the table for discussion, he rationalized the couple's termination somewhat defensively.

In contrast to the previous, unsuccessful handling of the same situation, this supervisor acknowledged a role in the impasse and attended to Alex's feelings about it. Reflecting on a personal internal state, the supervisor disclosed the basis for the abrupt role shift—the discomfort of Alex's handling of the case in light of personal responses to the clinical material. In the Resolution, both recognized a parallel between Alex's mishandling of his clients' behavior and the supervisor's mishandling of Alex's behavior. Insight into this parallel amused them, and their lighthearted laughter signaled that the supervisory alliance was restored. With the role-conflict event ended, they can now turn their attention back to the therapy relationship.

SPECIAL CONSIDERATIONS

As illustrated in both excerpts, role conflict arose with the abrupt shift in the supervisor's behavior, away from the collegial role Alex had come to expect. In the first case, the supervisor's shift in focus to Alex's personal feelings about his clients and the supervisory process was perceived as inappropriate and threatening. In the second case, the supervisor's shift from colleague to case manager raised Alex's defenses, interpreting it as personal criticism that mirrored his own self-criticism and doubt.

Because the different social roles in supervision carry distinctive expectations for behavior, it is important to know what supervisees expect. In a study of supervisees' expectations (Friedlander & Snyder, 1983), beginners, as well as advanced trainees, expected their supervisors to behave like "evaluative experts" more so than "attractive supporters" (p. 343). Although experience level was not related to expectations, confidence level was. Supervisees with a stronger sense of self-efficacy as therapists had greater expectations for their supervisors to be trustworthy, supportive experts and for supervision to further their own and their clients' development.

These results suggest that role conflict can arise when the supervisor fails to be *both* evaluative and expert *and* trustworthy and supportive. If supervisees view their supervisors as less experienced or competent than themselves, they may be highly sensitive to the evaluative aspects of supervision, believing that a collaborative relationship is more appropriate. Alternately, if supervisors always assume a friendly, consultant role, rarely offering feedback, supervisees may be uncomfortable because they expected more didactic learning or a greater focus on personal issues. Indeed, role conflict often arises when the supervisor only assumes a single role in supervision. The supervisor who, for example, repeatedly probes for the supervisee's personal disclosures, offering little feedback or suggestions for skill development, may be seen as intrusive, possibly even unethical.

In group supervision, the potential for role conflict is heightened due to the multiple relationships supervisees have with their peers. Interpersonal problems, allegiances, and rivalrous competition within the group will undoubtedly affect the mood and process of supervision. Supervisees tend to have acute awareness of each other's skills and deficiencies, which are naturally distributed unevenly within any group. In cases of extreme heterogeneity, giving and receiving feedback can be a source of tension, particularly if supervisees expect their peers only to be confirming and collegial. Problems may occur when the supervisor focuses on individuals' personal issues in a round-robin, "hot-seat" kind of process. Unless there is a strong sense of safety and norms of risk taking and confidentiality, supervisors would be wise to function primarily in their educative and collegial roles in the group, saving the therapeutic and evaluative functions of supervision for one-on-one relationships.

Thus far, we have only discussed various roles played within the supervisory relationship. Role conflict can pose even more problems, however, when there are dual relationships. Supervisors in academic settings commonly have multiple relationships with their supervisees, who may be students in their classes, research assistants, or advisees. Keeping these different roles separate is difficult because the evaluative component may be more salient in one relationship than in others. Mindful of the potential for conflict, supervisors can explain the differing role expectations to their supervisees and avoid problems by, for example, not discussing coursework or research during a supervision hour and not referring to personal issues revealed during supervision in other contexts.

In clinical settings, however, the multiple relationships are less distinct. With one supervisee, a single individual might serve as internship training director, individual supervisor, and group cotherapist. As part of a clinical staff, supervisor and supervisee also function as colleagues and may develop a friendship outside of work. Keeping these roles distinct and the supervisory relationship intact can be a significant challenge.

CONCLUSION

In other occupations, supervision tends to be straightforward and administrative, with the managerial and evaluative aspects clear to all parties. In our field, however, supervisors need to balance managing client welfare with promoting their supervisees' professional development, and these dual responsibilities can sometimes collide. By its very nature, clinical work places complex and extraordinary demands on therapists and supervisors. Although supervisors and supervisees cannot help but be affected by the intimate material discussed in therapy relationships, their openness and willingness to explore personal reactions to that material can affect the direction and ease of the supervisory process. With support and understanding of the various aspects and role demands of this endeavor, supervisees can benefit greatly from a fluid shift in focus from their clients to themselves.

5

WORKING THROUGH COUNTERTRANSFERENCE: WHEN SUPER-VISION IS NEEDED

With the intimate nature of the work, supervisees must face the inevitability of ambivalence, their reactions of hate as well as love, the presence of destructive as well as constructive forces, and the realization that we are all vehicles for one another's inner worlds.

(Arkowitz, 2001, p. 54)

Handling a critical incident involving countertransference is as tricky, as the concept is nebulous. Successful countertransference resolutions can not only move the client's therapy forward in a positive direction but can deepen the supervisee's self-understanding as a therapist, professional, and person. Unsuccessful resolution of countertransference can damage both the supervisory and therapy relationship.

Recognized as an empirically supported, effective element of the therapy process (Gelso & Hayes, 2001), managing countertransference is crucial in supervision. Raising the topic in the context of nonpsychoanalytic therapy often causes confusion because the term *countertransference* derives from analytic notions about unconscious processes, though neo-Freudian writers (e.g., Little, 1951) broadened the definition to include conscious and unconscious processes. Whereas *transference* refers to a client's reaction to the therapist based on projections deriving from past experiences with influential others, countertransference refers to feelings a client elicits in the therapist— feelings that either reflect the therapist's own problematic transference issues or reactions to the client's attitudes, characteristics, or behaviors.

When speaking of managing countertransference in supervision, we typically refer to the supervisee's reactions to his or her client(s). However, we can also refer to the supervisor's reactions to the supervisee. In the following sections, we discuss classic and contemporary views on countertransference in psychotherapy and review theoretical and empirical literature on working with countertransference in supervision. Two process models illustrate how a supervisor can help a supervisee work through feelings of countertransference toward a client. Finally, as special considerations for this event, we discuss transference and countertransference that originate in the supervisory relationship.

COUNTERTRANSFERENCE DECODED

Skillful countertransference management in supervision requires understanding the complexities of the phenomenon. Two definitions currently prevalent in the professional literature, include the common classical definition, which views countertransference as an impediment to therapy—an intrusion of the therapist's own issues into the therapeutic process (Hedges, 1992; Ogden, 1982). The other, more contemporary definition views countertransference as the therapist's emotional reactions to the client's interpersonal demands in the therapeutic relationship (Frawley-O'Dea & Sarnat, 2001; Grinberg, 1979a, 1979b; Hedges, 1992; Ogden, 1982).

Traditionally (i.e., in the Freudian sense) countertransference is an impediment (Hedges, 1992). In classical psychoanalytic training, supervision accompanies personal analysis to help a candidate come to terms with unconscious, drive-based fantasies that can threaten the capacity to maintain neutrality in session with an analysand. The goal of supervision is to help analysts rid their work of intruding unconscious material.

Interpersonal theorists view the therapist's countertransference reactions not as a product of unconscious fantasies, but of the therapist's unique psychosocial history. From the interpersonal viewpoint, familial factors, particularly relationships with early caretakers, create expectancies for relationships that influence social behavior in adulthood. Typically, supervision involves identifying how the therapist responds in an unconscious, habitual fashion to interpersonal situations in therapy that mimic a familiar historical relationship. Whether seeing therapists' reactions to clients as reflections of unacceptable unconscious fantasies or viewing them as repetitions of therapists' early experiences with others, many supervisors emphasize countertransference as an impediment to effective treatment.

Alternatively, countertransference can provide the therapist with a window to the client's inner world. Related to the concept of *projective identification*, this form of countertransference, with roots in the early object–relations theory of Melanie Klein (1975), is called *projective counteridentification* (Grinberg, 1979a, 1979b). From an object relations perspective, we all experience emotional reactions and self-perceptions that we deny because acknowledging them would constitute a threat to our stable sense of self. One way to avoid awareness of these unwanted perceptions and experiences is to project them onto others or see others as possessing the same traits, feelings, experiences, and motives that we would rather deny. In projective identification, however, a more primitive process takes place. We not only view others as possessing our projected, unwanted feelings, but also behave in a way that actually induces others to experience those feelings and perhaps act on them. Doing so allows us to disavow the unwanted feelings or expressions.

For example, an angry client may do something (e.g., repeatedly forget to bring payment for therapy sessions) that at first, induces frustration in the therapist. Eventually, however, as the client continues provoking, the therapist may come to dislike the client and consciously wish to discontinue treatment. As the "passive recipient" of the client's projections and introjections (Grinberg, 1979a, 1979b), the therapist begins to feel self-disgust for experiencing such hostility toward the client. ("Good therapists don't hate their clients, do they?") Because these feelings are distinctly unfamiliar, they likely result from the process of projective counteridentification. To short-circuit this downward spiral, the therapist must recognize the client's self-loathing and how it drives the actions that cause rejection by others. With this understanding, the therapist may be able to convert feelings into empathy and reverse the noxious counteridentification that threatens work with the client.

From their medical model perspective, analysts have said a fair amount about when countertransference is likely to occur and how it manifests. The edited book *Countertransference* by Epstein and Feiner (1979), for example, is devoted to explaining countertransferences that arise when working with severely regressed clients or clients with borderline personality disorder or disorders of the self. Other authors focus on kinds of client problems, such as incest—ripe for countertransference reactions (McElroy & McElroy, 1991). (See chap. 8 for a discussion of vicarious traumatization.)

Contemporary research on countertransference (e.g., Hayes, McCracken, et al., 1998; Rosenberger & Hayes, 2002) provides valuable information about its typical origins (family problems, unfulfilled needs, performance anxiety), triggers, manifestations, and consequences. Interestingly, the experienced, expert therapists interviewed by Hayes et al. indicated that countertransference frequently occurs in their practice. Considering that countertransference, by definition, is often an unconscious process, its prevalence was likely underestimated (Hayes et al., 1998). If, as suggested (Rosenberger & Hayes, 2002), countertransference can be used to a therapist's advantage, then supervisors need information about its behavioral signals, how it may affect therapeutic and supervisory interactions, and steps to work through its entanglements.

WORKING WITH COUNTERTRANSFERENCE IN SUPERVISION: TEACH OR TREAT?

Although Freud and other early analysts are generally credited with discovering countertransference, the idea was in the air, so to speak, long before. In 1853, Baron Ernst Von Feuchstersleben wrote, "Since in the so-called psychical mode of cure, one personality has to act upon another . . . the treatment in most instances demands a second education of the physician" (cited in Ekstein & Wallerstein, 1958, p. 242). In the early days of psychoanalysis, "problems about learning" due to countertransference were handled within the context of supervision, but by the mid-20th century, U.S. analysts insisted on a split between personal or training analysis and supervision (Ekstein & Wallerstein, 1958, p. 137). Taking the most conservative position on this issue, Arlow (1963) argued that a supervisor should comment on the supervisee's countertransference reactions to patients only in extreme circumstances. Personal growth and development were the domain of the training analyst, not the supervisor.

In the "teach or treat" controversy (McKinney, 2000, p. 567), one side maintains that supervision's sole purpose is to enhance technical skills, whereas the other side argues that working through countertransference is essential to protect clients from a supervisee's neurotic acting out. In 1976, most analysts surveyed tended to ignore a supervisee's countertransference or only approach it cautiously (Goin & Kline, 1976). Not to violate the supervisee's privacy, the supervisor would simply encourage the supervisee's further self-analysis. The prevailing wisdom was that the supervisor's obligation ended after pointing out the supervisee's failure to interpret significant clinical material (Barnat, 1980).

In contemporary psychoanalysis, however, examination of countertransference is the sine qua non of relational supervision (Frawley-O'Dea & Sarnat, 2001; McKinney, 2000). Based in social constructionism, relational supervision's guiding principle is that supervisor and supervisee work collaboratively within each other's subjective realities, cocreating meaning from felt experience. As in relational psychoanalysis, transference and countertransference phenomena in supervision are seen as inevitable and mutually reinforcing. To be fully present in the supervisory relationship, the supervisor and supervisee must move back and forth from regressive experiences to open, observing spaces. There is no assumption that the supervisor has the Truth (i.e., greater knowledge of the patient, the therapeutic work, or the supervisee than the supervisee has). Indeed, the supervisor's authority has less to do with a socially sanctioned role but intersubjective wisdom demonstrated in relating with the supervisee (Frawley-O'Dea & Sarnat, 2001).

In the context of discussing countertransference love and hate, analysts identified other feelings that a supervisee may experience, such as jealousy (Searles, 1979) and shame (Hahn, 2001), as well as the attitudes that supervisors may witness when their supervisees experience countertransference. Considering supervisees who act out sexually with their clients, Celenza (1995) explained that typically the supervisee views countertransference "love" for the client as empathy when, in fact, this feeling is substituted for hate or used as a defense against profound feelings of vulnerability. Celenza's observation is supported by research showing that when countertransference is present, supervisee and supervisor often disagree on the strength of the supervisee's connection with the client (Ligiero & Gelso, 2002).

The clinical literature gives more guidelines for working with countertransference in supervision than any of the other critical incidents discussed in this book. These guidelines tend to be fairly general, however, and focus more on the Markers of countertransference, such as supervisee hostility or withdrawal, than on the mechanics of resolution. In terms of Markers, some authors note the supervisor's experience of the supervisee, whereas others focus on the supervisees' conversations about the client. For example, unaware of emotional distancing from a client, a supervisee may either idealize the supervisor or respond indifferently to input (Hahn, 2001). In reporting on a case, the supervisee may make extraneous and critical comments about the client, or the client's stories may reveal unconscious perceptions of the supervisee's countertransference (Barnat, 1980).

One kind of countertransference, *theme interference* (Caplan, 1970, cited in Bernard & Goodyear, 1998), occurs when a supervisee loses objectivity about a client because of overgeneralized personal experiences with similar individuals. Consider a female supervisee who responds to a highly masculine male client with extreme trepidation based on her many negative personal experiences with men like him. Supervisory strategies to overcome theme interference involve unlinking the supervisee's experience of the client from her stereotype or challenging the stereotype itself (Bernard & Goodyear, 1998). (See chaps. 3 and 7 on gender and cultural misunderstandings for process models on working with theme interference.)

Writers on the side of "teach, don't treat" recommend clarification and confrontation, pointing out the supervisee's "learning blocks" (e.g., Fleming & Benedek, 1983, p. 78) to catalyze self-analysis of the countertransference. With a supervisee who is eager to learn, empathic, responsive to feedback, and can also self-observe, the supervisor can patiently encourage introspection and allow the supervisee to decide individually whether personal therapy is needed. With a more defensive supervisee who refuses to acknowledge his or her countertransference, the supervisor is obliged to recommend personal therapy (Fleming & Benedek, 1983).

The most oft-discussed supervisory phenomenon related to countertransference is, of course, parallel process. Traditionally, parallel processes were said to arise from supervisees' unconscious identifications with clients

(Searles, 1955). Although the concept can be defined in various ways, we refer to parallel processes as similarities between a specific therapeutic interaction and the supervisory interaction, originating in either interaction and mirrored in the other. Because being supervised and being seen in therapy both involve help-seeking, similarities in the process are natural and expected (Ekstein & Wallerstein, 1958). Thus, some authors look at parallel process only as a serendipitous event in supervision. Like other authors (Ekstein & Wallerstein, 1958; Loganbill, Hardy, & Delworth, 1982; McNeill & Worthen, 1989), however, we value working explicitly with parallel processes to further the supervisee's personal and professional growth.

Searles (1955), the first analyst to discuss parallel process, called it a *reflection process*. Although most contemporary writers recognize that parallel processes can originate in either the supervisory or therapeutic relationship (Bernard & Goodyear, 1998), early authors saw it strictly as "upward bound" (Frawley-O'Dea & Sarnat, 2001, p. 17). This is because supervisors considered to be more knowledgeable and self-aware than supervisees can point out that a supervisee may unconsciously reenact some aspect of the client's functioning through projective counteridentification (Grinberg, 1979a, 1979b). In contrast, parallel process in psychoanalytic relational supervision is not something the supervisor observes in the supervisee so much as something in which the supervisor is actively involved in creating, enacting, and processing (Frawley-O'Dea & Sarnat, 2001).

Research on critical incidents in supervision (Heppner & Roehlke, 1984; Rabinowitz, Heppner, & Roehlke, 1986) shows that supervisees, particularly the more advanced ones, value a focus on transference and countertransference in supervision. In one case study (Martin, Goodyear, & Newton, 1987), the recognition and resolution of countertransference characterized the best sessions, as rated by both supervisee and supervisor, and in another case study (Friedlander, Siegel, & Brenock, 1989), verbal communication processes in the supervisory relationship mirrored verbal communications in the therapy relationship. The supervisee was one-down and cooperative in supervision, but she was dominant and nurturing in therapy, just as the supervisor behaved toward her in supervision.

The most clinically rich study on parallel process (Doehrman, 1976) involved in-depth interviews of supervisees and supervisors. The qualitative results showed convincingly how a supervisee's parallel emotional reactions to the supervisor and the client could derail the supervisory process. When, however, the transference-countertransference shadows came to light, supervisees behaved more genuinely and spontaneously in their therapeutic relationships with clients.

In our process model of working through countertransference, described following, the events we present are ones in which countertransference is the primary phenomenon addressed. In general, the supervisor's strategies involve exploring the supervisee's feelings to determine the nature of the countertransference and identify its causes, conceptualizing the therapy process in light of the supervisee's new understanding and planning action to facilitate the supervisee's withdrawal from the client's drama.

A countertransference event contains two important interaction sequences, *focus on countertransference* and *attend to parallel processes*. These two sequences are not unique to critical incidents involving countertransference, however. As illustrated in other chapters, a focus on countertransference and an interpretation of parallel processes occurs during other kinds of events—role conflict, misunderstanding, or events focusing on supervisees' problematic feelings and behaviors.

PROCESS MODEL OF A COUNTERTRANSFERENCE EVENT

Markers

Like other events, the most difficult aspect of countertransference events is identifying what specifically needs addressing (i.e., the Marker). For this reason, treating an incident in supervision as a countertransference event ideally should only be done when a well-established, positive relationship with mutual trust and respect exists and where the supervisee's personal boundaries are clear to both parties. Of course, these ideal conditions occur most often when the supervisee is experienced, skilled, and has no active or minimally significant personality problems or emotional difficulties.

Unfortunately, this best-case scenario is not always possible. Sometimes countertransference interferes with therapy at the outset, before the supervisory relationship is established. Whereas therapists should avoid making premature interpretations of their clients' unconscious material, supervisors cannot always avoid focusing on countertransferential material when a client's welfare is at stake. Sometimes, the supervisee lacks awareness about when it is appropriate to mention personal issues in supervision, fearing that revealing personal problems will be damaging. And sometimes, what at first seems to be countertransference in the therapy relationship is really transference or countertransference in the supervisory relationship.

Thus, it is crucial, before undertaking the steps outlined in the following process model to identify that countertransference—and not something else—is indeed the problem. As discussed earlier, countertransference can arise from the supervisee's psychosocial conflicts or be a counteridentification to the client's conflicts. Naturally, the first variety is easier to detect and work with. Although not a litmus test, traditional or classic countertransference Markers may be distinguished from projective counteridentification Markers by the extent to which the supervisee's feelings toward the client are familiar or unfamiliar. Having a familiar feeling, even if uncomfortable, reflects classic countertransference. The supervisee may not be able to make sense of feelings toward the client, but these feelings are ones the supervisee owns—they are personal, recognizable, and familiar. Feeling distinctly uncomfortable with a client, however, and sensing that this discomfort is unfamiliar or unrecognizable—extreme, inappropriate, or uncharacteristic—may signal projective counteridentification.

Supervisees, who know themselves well and are aware of how their responses to a given client reflect feelings about someone else in their life, might clearly ask their supervisor to help sort out these feelings (e.g., "He reminds me so much of my father, I just can't shake it!"). Less aware supervisees might recognize that responses to a given client are troubling, but they still do not understand the reasons. The supervisee vaguely knows that some kind of countertransference is occurring (e.g., "I'm just disliking him so much—he's just the kind of person I try to avoid!"). Still less aware, a supervisee might complain about a vague, uneasy, or uncomfortable feeling toward a client with no idea that this feeling might reflect personal issues or relationships (e.g., "I have to admit, I wasn't looking forward to my session with her this week").

These hypothetical statements are not, of course, sufficient Markers in and of themselves, because the relational context, discourse, and knowledge of the supervisee are needed to distinguish countertransference events from other kinds of events. The last statement, for example, "I have to admit, I wasn't looking forward to my session with her this week," could signal a skill difficulty (see chap. 2) rather than countertransference, if the supervisee's reluctance is primarily due to a lack of understanding about how to help the client.

The countertransference Markers discussed so far are verbal statements. Countertransference can also be evidenced by a supervisee's behavior, either in supervision or in therapy itself. Excessive passivity or activity, for example, or seductiveness, forgetting important details, arriving late, and so forth, could signal the presence of countertransference. Countertransference that underlies these kinds of behaviors is less conscious and therefore, more challenging to recognize. Perhaps the clearest indicator of countertransference is a supervisee's notably uncharacteristic behavior. Any of the preceding examples that occur regularly with several different clients, might signify a skill difficulty or some problem other than countertransference, which by definition, is particular to a single therapy relationship.

Because of these complexities, the Marker may be lengthy. But once the supervisor judges that countertransference is evident, the task is clear—identify and understand it and ascertain that it does not unduly interfere with the therapy. Ideally, a successfully resolved countertransference event should enhance the supervisee's professional development and work with the client.

Interaction Sequences

The first step in the process environment is exploring what may occur in the therapy relationship beyond the supervisee's awareness; undertaken not only to put the countertransference in a context but to expose what happens to set it off. The next step explores the nature of the supervisee's countertransference by looking closer at the supervisee's present feelings toward the client, contrasted with previous feelings toward the same client or with similar clients. Ideally, this step should "click" for the supervisee (i.e., result in some new self-understanding).

In this step, supervisor and supervisee begin by identifying specific client behaviors that gave rise to the countertransference. The extent of interpretation depends on the supervisee's self-awareness as well as the comfort level in discussing personal issues with the supervisor. If the trust is strong and the supervisee understands the boundary between supervision and therapy, this step might include an extended discussion of personal difficulties or troubling relationships.

The final two steps in the model are interpretation of the parallel process and the Resolution. This event involves planning for future therapy sessions despite what has been discovered. The parallel process step is an optional one, only necessary when some recognizable similarity in the therapeutic and supervisory processes exists. When there is a sound basis for interpreting a parallel process, it is desirable to do so because it teaches the supervisee, in a personal way, about the power of unconscious processes. The Resolution—planning for action—is necessary on two levels. First, on a practical level, it ensures that the supervisee has the tools to overcome the block caused by countertransference. Second, on a less-conscious level, it helps the supervisee regain confidence in approaching difficult situations with a client.

SUCCESSFUL RESOLUTION OF A CLASSIC COUNTERTRANSFERENCE EVENT

In the following illustration, Janice, a 28-year-old experienced postdegreed supervisee and her female African American supervisor have worked together for many months and have a good, mutual understanding of the client under discussion. The bond between them is strong: Janice has previously disclosed quite a bit about her life and personal issues, and they know that Janice values the opportunity for personal growth in supervision.

In this event, Janice discusses her work with a client, Marcus, a 40-year-old, single White man with a narcissistic personality disorder, who has made demonstrable progress in therapy to this point. The Marker begins when Janice describes a rupture in the therapeutic relationship and her negative feelings toward her client.

Marker

Janice: I hate to admit it, but I've been real rocky with Marcus for a few sessions. I want to . . . have been trying to understand it, but I think I'm going through a period where I don't really want to work with him. You know, I feel myself getting bored with him because he's very, very dramatic. He does things, oh, like, for a lot of attention. I always feel drained when I walk out of there, more so than before, and one session he started crying because he was happy, which was good, but he was crying. He had his head down and peeked up above both hands like this [*demonstrates*] to see if I was looking at him, you know. I thought, "Come on, you know, like . . ."
expresses embarrassment and confusion about her negative reactions to her client

Supervisor: So it seemed insincere to you?
clarifies

Janice: Yeah. It didn't seem genuine, and the other people watching the session said it didn't seem genuine. You know, I don't know, it's really hard to work with him at this point because like . . . (*pauses*)
mistrusts her own perceptions

Supervisor: He isn't likable.
gives Janice permission to express negative feelings

Janice: No, he whines, and I don't care as much. I don't care about helping him as much as I did (I'm a little embarrassed to say this) because he doesn't, he wasn't, it seems like he's trying to get something other than help, you know.
expresses shame

The supervisor knows that Marcus' transferential feelings toward Janice are strong; thus his behavior is not unusual or surprising. Rather, what was notable and caught the supervisor's eye was Janice's expression of exhaustion, boredom, dislike, and impatience; feelings she has never expressed before. Because Janice owned these negative feelings, doubted her own perceptions (" . . . and the other people watching the session said [his behavior] didn't seem genuine"), and expressed a need to understand these reactions, countertransference seemed likely. What is not clear, however, was the extent to which Janice's reactions stemmed from her own issues (i.e., the classic kind of countertransference). She seemed aware that her feelings toward Marcus were troublesome, but she wondered whether it was his behavior or something in herself, which gave rise to these feelings. This uncertainty prompts the first step in the event, an exploration of what is occurring in the therapy that might touch off Janice's strong feelings.

Exploration of the Therapy Relationship

Supervisor: You feel manipulated, it seems. Tell me a bit more about the last few sessions with him.
reflects Janice's feelings and explores, to figure out what the client might be experiencing
[*extended discussion of the previous sessions*]

* * *

Janice: Yeah. There is a big, a lot of time I don't feel in control of . . . if, because he isn't, it isn't like we're working on his problems. But there's something else going on, like he's trying to get so much of my attention all the time, not to help him, but just because he wants my attention.
describes her uneasiness

Supervisor: What is it that you think he's asking you to do, though, that you think you can't or shouldn't do?

Janice: It's like, "Jump on my merry-go-round, be in my real life. Don't be the therapist. Be totally wound up with me." Yeah, it kind of sounds like, "I want you to be my therapist, but I wish you could get on this merry-go-round and be as happy as I am, and be my friend and everything and feel everything that I feel." He came to that realization, but the session was bad because it was sort of like I was bursting his bubble, you know. Because he was on a high, high, high, and I was trying to bring him back to reality. And I couldn't do it, and he was getting really angry during the session. And I said, you know, "What's going on here?" because we were getting nowhere. And he said, "I feel like you're not understanding me, you're not listening to me, you don't understand what I'm saying."
explores her understanding of the impasse

And he said, "Don't you realize how far I've come?" and he went into one of the spiels about how he used to let everything affect him dramatically, and now he's got a rein on that but that *I'm* telling him that everything is going to get worse again. This wasn't what I was saying, but that's how I think he was kind of hearing it.
expresses some negative feelings about the client and an awareness of transference

At this point, the supervisor realized that Janice was reliving the emotion of her last session with Marcus. To create meaning, which would give Janice a handle on what she is experiencing, the supervisor offers a synthesis of what she has heard thus far.

Supervisor: There's a lot there! You seem to feel at a loss about how to both be with him and also move things forward. And he's seeing it very "black and white."

Janice: Yeah.

Supervisor: But something nagged at you, it seems. You felt it was a bad session? Too personal or . . . ? Are you just concerned because it was conflictual, or . . .
seeks to identify specifically what led Janice to feel badly

Janice: It felt like we were fighting, like it was a tug of war, every little sentence. Okay, everything I said he took wrong. I mean I was happy for him. He's made gains and I know he will . . . I'm thinking that he has, he has gone backward. So I should, I probably should have just bared with him the whole session, not introducing any reality. Just staying with him, with him being happy, you know, and later bringing in reality. I think that I tried to prevent him from, like, falling on his face.
offers her understanding of the rupture alliance and her part in it

Supervisor: Yeah, you tried to cushion the fall.
reflects Janice's good intention

Janice: Right. I shouldn't have done that, and it was like the whole session was pull and tug. We just weren't . . . we just weren't on the same plane. I don't know.

Janice, an experienced therapist, shows her ability to listen to the "melody," the latent content, in her work with Marcus. By the end of this step in the event, she had expressed less annoyance with Marcus and less self-blame. With the supervisor's help, she gained some distance and began assigning meaning to the impasse in the therapy process.

Focus on Countertransference

Supervisor: I think the thing is . . . it's almost like you're seeing it in black and white, too, almost—either to be with him—high in the sky—or to do what you *did,* try to cushion the inevitable fall. Let's see if we can understand what put you in this frame of mind, okay? Let's see if . . .
identifies Janice's cognitive distortion and asks her permission to explore it more deeply

Janice: (Yeah)

Supervisor: Let's see if we together can figure out what's happening to you right now with him. The bit you said about the merry-go-round makes me wonder. He seems very childlike, you know.
emphasizes collaboration and offers her own perception of the client

Janice: Yeah. Yeah. I think, "childlike," yeah, that was something that later, after the session, I realized that bothered me. Because I've seen him like that before, but it was real different. Like two sessions ago, he was like Maria [*another client*], very adolescent-like, and I felt like I was talking to her, not to Marcus. And I realized it bothered me, because he's 40 and acting like a child! It never bothered me before because when he's an adult and he's sincere, we can talk about how painful it is that he had all these tragedies as a child. I can deal with that, but when he acts like a baby, I sit there, and I want to shake him and say, "Don't act like a kid."
labels the source of her discomfort

Supervisor: Any idea why that bothers you so much?
asks Janice to consider a more personal explanation

Janice: No really, because . . . except it gets, it just gets really draining sometimes to sit there and all the time be empathic with him. I'm not sure if that's it or because he's so needy.

Supervisor: When you say you want to shake him, it sounds like . . . oh, like he's frustrating you.
reflects

Janice: Yeah, like . . .

Supervisor: But, what *is* frustrating you? What's frustrating you with him?
probes

Janice: Because it's frustrating for me to think that he's sitting there being so needy for some attention and wanting me to feel sorry for him. But then he flips into critical mode. (*embarrassed*) He actually told me, "Be sure to prepare for our next session!" It was his parting shot when he left!

Supervisor: It's hard to feel empathy for someone who's blasting you!

Janice: Yes! Right, and I can *do* that, but when he's not genuine about it, I *can't* do it, and it's frustrating. It's frustrating, one, to think I can't be empathic with him anymore when I *have* been, and two, it's frustrating to try to fake it. I don't want to have to do that, you know. If he's sitting there and zapping me for every little ounce I have left, I can't do it.

Supervisor: So, when he's acting like a child, you feel like a bad therapist, and that's frustrating you, like your hands are tied. There's nothing you can do. *describes the sequence that led to her negative self-representation*

Janice: Sometimes it is, but sometimes it's just frustrating, you know, I think, "why doesn't he just, you know, get on with it? Stop acting like a child, grow up, get on with it, you know." I don't know why I feel that, you know, I don't know. If he's sincere and acting like a child, it doesn't bother me, but . . . *allows herself to verbalize some hostility toward the client but then becomes confused*

Supervisor: Maybe it's the insincere . . . or is it the *manipulative* child that bothers you? *proposes a specific client behavior that may be problematic for Janice*

Janice: Yeah, manipulative, exactly! And he knows I wasn't listening to him and that the session wasn't on target like it used to be. You know, I know he's pretty perceptive. He can tell if I'm interested, and . . . *identifies the source of her shame*

Supervisor: So what he was saying was true?

Janice: Yeah.

Supervisor: It was upsetting you because he hit the nail on the head.

Janice: Yeah. (*laughs*)

Realizing that Janice is feeling victimized by her client—she doesn't know what is happening and why it feels out of control—the supervisor helps Janice use her self-knowledge to look deeper within herself for answers.

Supervisor: So maybe the disturbing part of it was the inappropriateness of him acting like an authority and telling you, "You're doing a terrible job and shape up." And he expects his due, and you feel he is not real appreciative of . . . *offers an interpretation of Janice's discomfort with the client*

Janice: You know, it's . . . it does bother me when he pulls me a lot, and you know, I started thinking I was trying to figure out why it bothered me so much. "Why can't I help this person? Why is he aggravating me so much?" And this has been going on for a few weeks now, and there's been a time that I could hardly deal with myself, and I felt like, "I can't, I can't, I can't, I don't have anything left

for you. So if you need me, be genuine and I'll help you, but don't sit here and babble in front of me about things you're really not serious about." You know what I mean? I started thinking maybe that was it and 50 zillion hypotheses about why I can't do this.
self-explores

Supervisor: I think that makes a lot of sense. Can we look at that some more?
reassures her and asks permission to explore it further

Janice: Uh-huh.

Supervisor: You were feeling overwhelmed and barely able to hang in there yourself, and here you've got this demanding, manipulative child that's taking unfair advantage, who's also turning you around, treating you sometimes like a parent, sometimes like a friend.
summarizes Janice's latent feelings in response to the client's transference

Janice: That just made a lot of sense, because I never thought about it like that, but that sounds just like my mother, because that's what she does. She has all these roles, you know, and I go home, and she's very manipulative and she does all these things. (*quieter*) I told you she's a drug addict—?
insight about a parallel relationship in her own life

Supervisor: Yes, you did.

Janice: Well, I can't *make* her get help. I've tried! But to me, she'll come up and she'll be real authoritative and she'll say, "da, da, da," like a parent. And I'm not a kid. Then she'll be like a kid, not the parent. Then she'll try to be my friend, and she'll want to go out with me. She'll want to go out dancing with me and my friends. And I think that's not appropriate, and it's like . . . I don't . . . I don't like her. And that's probably why I'm not liking Marcus very much lately. Right before my vacation, when I went home, I had a good session with him, but after my vacation . . . oh! Maybe that's why . . .
insight about the timing of her countertransference

Supervisor: So maybe some of those things, some of those same things maybe got stirred up with your mother. And with Marcus, you're feeling like, "Grow up and take responsibility for your problems. And be genuine. If you say you really want my help, I'll be there for you, but if you act whiny and childlike . . ."
suggests further parallels

Janice: With her it's like, it's not even, it's, "Grow up. Grow up. Grow up." All the time. "Why are you so immature? Why can't you be the mother?" kind of thing. "Why can't you get help?" It's not so much that she's whiny, but one minute she'll be genuine, and then she'll turn around and snap your head off. And like . . . it's like when he (*client*) tells me, "Prepare for our session tomorrow," and where did that come from . . .
explores her feelings in both relationships

Supervisor: Yeah. I can understand how you're feeling: "How dare you, how dare you say this to me?"
reflects

Janice: So, I guess in a lot of ways they're the same, and I don't . . . I don't want to help her anymore. I don't talk about it because I can't help her, you know. She has to do it on her own, go for help or whatever. It's different. I *can* help him. I *can't* help her. She has to help herself. I can't do it, and she just . . . she stresses me out too much so I can't, but I can help him. They're different, though. They're alike, and they're different.
makes a distinction between the two relationships

Supervisor: Um hmm

Janice: But I think you're right. They probably pull the same things out of me.

This is the most powerful aspect of the event. Based on their exploration of the therapy process, the supervisor took her understanding of the client's transference toward Janice and Janice's latent feelings toward her, the supervisor, and offered a metaphor—a demanding, manipulative child. This metaphor "clicked" for Janice when it brought her mother to mind. Note the back-and-forth exploration of her feelings in the previous speaking turn.

Janice knows that her complex feelings toward her mother need expressing because they interfere with her work as a therapist. Because the boundaries of supervision are clear, she discloses this information to get a handle on her reactions to Marcus, not to elicit a therapeutic response from the supervisor. The supervisor, knowing that Janice does not want or expect to linger on her problems with her mother, delicately moves the discussion back to the issues at hand. Because Janice's insight about her mother seems helpful to her, in the next sequence, the supervisor focuses on the parallel process, hoping that Janice might recall that her best work with Marcus has been insight oriented.

Attend to Parallel Process

Supervisor: When we first started talking, we were talking about how you were in a dilemma because you felt like the only two options you had were either to get on his merry-go-round or stay off it and tell him to knock it off.
recalls the original therapeutic dilemma

Janice: Um-hmm

Supervisor: Right. Let's think for a minute about you and me here. Here, for example, I could have said to you, "Well, Janice, just snap out of it." That wouldn't have been very helpful to you, would it? You would've felt that I wasn't being empathic, right?
focuses on the supervisory process

Janice: Um-hmm

Supervisor: Or I could have said, you know, "Okay. Go with your feelings. Run with it. Do more with it." That probably wouldn't have helped you either.

Janice: No.

Supervisor: But what we *did* do was, "Let's see. Let's see if we can understand why you're having such difficulty with this guy." And that's what I'm trying to help you to see, to understand.
identifies her own supervisory strategy as collaborative and interpretive

Janice: How I don't have to be black and white, you mean?

Supervisor: Yes, I guess what I'm saying is that what we've been doing together is what you need to be doing with Marcus. Let's see if we can understand how you're feeling now. Let's see if we can understand what it means that you feel I have to be with you on your merry-go-round, that I have to be with you in everything you do, or else.
uses the parallel process to suggest how to get back on track in the therapy relationship

Janice: I guess that would get me back in the mode of therapy.

Supervisor: Yes! Somehow that got derailed along the way.
suggests a basis for the therapeutic alliance rupture

Janice: Yeah, it would help because if I didn't have to be empathic all the time, I could just do something different. I wouldn't be so drained, you know, if he could do more of the putting it together instead of me just sitting there reflecting. I think the thing that . . . the thing that helped was when you said, "He does this . . . he makes you feel this, and this . . . you don't like it when he's this, and this way," and those things are things I felt for somebody else, you know, for my mother.
summarizes her insight about the countertransference and its negative effect on the therapy

In this case, the parallel process worked both ways. First, Janice presented her dilemma with Marcus in "black-and-white" terms, just as Marcus saw his dilemma with Janice. Next, Janice understood that the helpful aspects of the supervisory process—empathy, collaboration, and interpretation—could lead to insight for her client as they did for her. The next and final step in the event involves making this second link more explicit.

Resolution

Supervisor: And this, what I'm doing with you, is what you can do with him. The same thing. "Is this what's going on? This is what is going on right now between you and me. What do you think about that? How do you see it? What does it remind you of?" And maybe he can see that it has to do with his abusive parents. Maybe he can figure out that he's trying to be the child and make you the mother because he never had a mother who acted like a mother and never had a father, and he could never be a child. This is why he wants to be on the merry-go-round, and "I want you to be up there with me. Why can't you play with me? I was never allowed to play my whole life! Why can't you do that?" And then . . . he can . . . then the 40-year-old can then snap back and say, "Oh, you're my therapist! Of course you can't do that!"
offers a possible sequence of exploration, interpretation, and insight

Janice: Right. It feels funny because it feels like I used to do that with him, and it feels like I haven't done any of that for a long time. I don't know why. Maybe it's just because my brain went on vacation or something . . .
recalls her own skill

Supervisor: Well, there may be a lot of reasons. First of all, he changed quite a bit. Things are going better in his life, and he isn't in a depressed state. He's going through a new phase in his emotional growth. It's not surprising that you came up with the metaphor of a merry-go-round (or maybe *he* did, it doesn't matter) because when you're in there together, your unconscious minds come together. I mean, a merry-go-round is what a child is on. You didn't say "an airplane"; you said "a merry-go-round." That's a 6-, 7-year-old, and he's reexperiencing that life stage. And we know he's got issues about merger with his mother that he's projecting onto you, and you've got a stress that is very similar in your life to a stress that he's reexperiencing in the therapy.
offers a perspective on the impasse in the therapy process based on a conceptualization of the client's progress and Janice's countertransference

   I think what you're going through is very common for long-term dynamic therapy with someone who's as disturbed as he is.
reassures

Janice: Do you mean the part of running into something in your life that's similar to theirs, or the part of falling off track?

Supervisor: Both, but the part, yeah, the part that falls off track and loses empathy, gets frustrated, and doesn't know how to get to the next phase, having things get pulled out that are going on in him and also in you. It's what all experienced therapists go through. And this issue is for you to understand it, you know. Just as it is the issue for him to understand the stage he's at. He's on a high. He's on a merry-go-round.
suggests that Janice can handle her countertransference through insight

   You say, "That's wonderful. Let's figure out what triggered it. Let's figure out what puts you in this frame of mind. Let's see if we can understand it. What does it mean in the context of your life?" These are the questions you need to ask him.
suggests possible interventions

Janice: You know, that transactional analysis with the parent, the child, and the adult. Sometimes when I'm sitting in there, I think about that, and I think that I'm trying to be the adult here, and he's just bouncing around from all three of them. He's not telling me when he's changing, and that's when I get confused.

Supervisor: Exactly. But it's very difficult to maintain your position when you've got somebody who's jumping around all over the place.
empathizes

Janice: And sometimes, I know, I can get into being the parent, too, or even the child when I get defensive. But not as much as he does! Oh, God, is that confusing! (*laughs*)
owns another aspect of the countertransference

Supervisor: Yeah! Hopefully, though, understanding all this will help you feel more in control in your sessions with him.

Janice: Yes. The session before I went on vacation . . . I can't remember what we were talking about . . . but I felt like I really wanted to help him, like the caring part was coming back, and I was really involved in it. It was more like that, and plus I knew I was going on vacation and was going to have two weeks away from him. I thought that was just wonderful, having a break. And then when I got back, you know, I started . . . sometimes I forget that he's a client, that he projects a lot of things onto me that aren't me, and I shouldn't react to them. It's hard to keep that in mind. I think what I need to do is just sort of push aside all the nongenuine stuff and keep in mind there's a reason he's doing that. Then I can look for genuine material. And when he's not being genuine, I can just blow it off.
further insight into the cause of the rupture and how she can avoid it in the future

Supervisor: That'll work, you think?

Janice: Yeah, it'll help to sit there thinking about him as somebody who needs me to help him understand what's going on. I think I can deal with him, and I understand a lot more things that would never have clicked for me before, like about my mother. (*silence*)

Supervisor: Well, we've covered the waterfront here today, haven't we?
brings them back to the here-and-now

Janice: Yes! We *have*!

Supervisor: I'm impressed with your willingness to look at what's going on for you so openly.
reassures, in case Janice is embarrassed later on

Janice: Yeah, well, I had to.

Supervisor: I imagine some other things might kick in later on for you about all this, when you think over what we've talked about.
Janice: (*smiles*) I hope so!

With the new knowledge that her client pulls from her responses similar to those she experiences with her mother, Janice felt more in control of her work with him. Working it through as she did in this episode, Janice gained important knowledge about how to work with challenging clients and about therapy in general. The supervisor alluded to the likelihood that Janice would have some more thoughts about her relationship with her mother, but further discussion along these lines in supervision was neither appropriate nor necessary.

SUCCESSFUL RESOLUTION OF A PROJECTIVE COUNTERIDENTIFICATION EVENT

In the next scenario, the supervisee, Marcia, a 34-year-old predoctoral intern in a community mental health agency, is experiencing a strong sense of inadequacy related to her client, Lauren, a 19-year-old White bartender "with an attitude." The Marker occurs when the supervisee expresses frustration over being unable to do something for her client. As in the previous illustration, exploration of the therapy relationship is the first step in the process. As the event unfolds, it becomes clear that a parallel process is operating, but the supervisor decides not to make it explicit. An important aspect of this event is the need to help Marcia determine whether her reactions come from within, representing her own unresolved emotional issues or if her reactions are an introject (a "taking in") of the client's disavowed experience. In this illustration, when it becomes clear that countertransference, based on projective counteridentification, is occurring, the supervisor educates Marcia about the meaning and uses of that awareness.

The Marker, in this instance, is succinct and begins with Marcia expressing frustration over feeling inadequate with her client. As the supervisor begins to learn how Marcia is reacting to Lauren's presentation, she notices a discrepancy between how Marcia is experiencing this particular client *versus* how she experiences other clients. Inquiring about this observed discrepancy is crucial to confirm or disconfirm the presence of projective counteridentification.

Marker

Marcia: I think I'm over my head with Lauren. I just get the feeling that she wants something I just can't provide, like I'm not hip enough, you know? I don't know how to get close to her, and in fact, I feel like I don't want to work with her. I don't know what's going on here!
doubts herself, confused

Supervisor: Well, let's see if we can tease it out. Can you tell me more about what's been going on?
slows Marcia down, joining with her and seeking clarification
[*extended discussion about what's been taking place in the therapy*]

* * *

Supervisor: Tell me how she looks.
asks for a visualization to help Marcia access her feelings

Marcia: She's just so cool, you know, kind of sarcastic and funny. And she wears those pants and boots that all the kids are wearing now and the hair all up and crazy. She just doesn't seem all that interested in me. I feel like she thinks she got the wrong counselor.

Supervisor: What does she do that results in your feeling this way?
focuses Marcia back to the client's behavior

Marcia: She just acts bored in session or looks at the ceiling or rolls her eyes. She says, "I don't know" when I try to reflect her experience. She seems so blasé, like I'm not doing anything to help her. Am I overreacting here?
feels a mixture of frustration and shame

In this early part of the event, the supervisor observes that Marcia is unusually anxious about her work with Lauren, and Marcia has expressed strong feelings that suggest the presence of countertransference. Hence, the supervisor inquires specifically what Lauren is doing that results in Marcia feeling inadequate. This questioning is important, whether or not Marcia decides to call those moments to Lauren's attention or simply note them to craft an interpretive intervention. Before that can happen, however, it is important to identify how the countertransference was induced. Thus, the supervisor encourages Marcia to explore what was happening in the therapeutic relationship that led to her feeling inadequate.

Exploration of Therapy Process

Supervisor: Ouch. Seems like she's got you feeling like you can't live up to some expectations that you don't quite understand.
reflects and provides a cognitive construction of what might be occurring

Marcia: Yup. I feel like I don't and maybe *can't* get it. (*softly*) I also feel kind of rejected, like she doesn't think I'm capable enough to work with her.
deepens her experience

Supervisor: (*pause*) That's a tough one, just not feeling able to make something happen with her, and it seems also like feeling kind of pressured by her to make something happen and rejected because you can't.
normalizes and labels the client's interpersonal behavior
[*more discussion of how the client's behavior affected Marcia's feelings for her*]

* * *

Marcia: Yeah. I guess I just feel like whatever I decide to do, it won't be enough or adequate enough to meet with her approval. Isn't that ridiculous?
needs reassurance

Having worked with Marcia for a while, the supervisor knows that such strong feelings of inadequacy never came up for Marcia with other clients. In her responses to Marcia, the supervisor selects language that implies Lauren's potential influence on Marcia's experience of her. By doing so, she tests her growing feeling that Lauren's projections may cause Marcia confusion, shame, and feelings of incompetence. In the next sequence, the supervisor seeks to understand whether the feelings are simply in response to Lauren's behavior or due to Marcia's experiencing Lauren's disavowed feelings about herself.

Focus on Countertransference

Supervisor: You know, I haven't seen you feeling incompetent like this or feeling unable to measure up with any of your other clients. I just haven't heard you

express feeling pressured in this way before. Can you help me understand why this is happening now?
provides feedback and encourages collaboration to sort it out

Marcia: Well, I mean, sometimes I'm not sure where to go with clients, but no, I usually don't feel like they are pushing me away like this or like they don't believe I can help them—which is how I feel with her. I just . . . it's Lauren. She just gets under my skin somehow.
recognizes the unique quality of her countertransference

Supervisor: So, this is pretty unique to Lauren. You *do* feel some competency with your other clients, like even though you aren't sure where to go sometimes, you still know you have a connection with them, and you sense that they have some confidence in you.
validates and reassures

Marcia: Yeah. Lauren just seems to know how to make me question myself. As we're talking, I'm starting to feel some resentment toward her, and I don't like that. I don't feel like that at all with other clients. I mean, of course I don't feel like a total expert therapist, but I definitely know that I can usually think and respond on my feet. Not with Lauren, though. She seems to find that little unsure place in me and aim for it.
feels more confident, supported by her supervisor

At this point, Marcia described her countertransference and acknowledged her unfamiliar feelings unique to her experience with Lauren. Unlike other clients, Lauren can find a vulnerable spot in Marcia and poke at it. The supervisor, guided by her understanding of projective counteridentification and knowing something of Lauren's relational history, speculates that Lauren may be inducing some of her own feeling states in Marcia.

Supervisor: It feels lousy to be on the receiving end of that kind of hostility. Your feelings, though, give us important information about Lauren and how she feels about *herself*. Because your feelings with Lauren are pretty different from what you feel with other clients, it's possible that she is inducing some of that in you through projective identification.
empathizes and teaches

Marcia: So, I'm reacting to something that she experiences? And she induces that in me by . . . (*hesitates*)

Supervisor: . . . when she acts bored and sullen and when she pokes and prods you like she does. Does that make sense to you?
reminds Marcia of the behaviors that made her feel inadequate

Marcia: Yeah. Wow. How strange but real. It's weird because I know she must feel that way herself, incompetent like.
begins to put together her countertransference with her knowledge of the client

Once Marcia understands how she can look at her client through her personal experience of the client's projections, the supervisor transitions to a discussion of the particular client dynamics that may be finding expression in the therapy relationship.

Focus on Skill (Conceptual)

Supervisor: How do you know that?
probes to expand Marcia's understanding

Marcia: Well, her mother is a high school English teacher, and she just picked and picked at Lauren—about everything, schoolwork, clothes, friends, everything. She could never do anything right, and she wasn't very good in school, which is why I think she's such a rebel now. (*pauses*) Maybe I remind her of her mother because I'm kind of preppy looking.
understands the client's transference

Supervisor: Possibly, yeah. Most definitely. She could be resisting some aspect of her mother by not connecting with you. It also becomes understandable that Lauren herself is very familiar with feeling incompetent.

Marcia: Oh, yeah. I mean, I think that's why she left home at 17 and got her GED. She just couldn't stand her mother's expectations any more. She didn't believe she could live up to them anyway.
her understanding of her client reveals a shift toward empathy

Supervisor: So there could be two things going on. One, she may fear that you will judge her like her mother did, so she distances you. Another thing that may be happening is that she is tired of her own feelings of incompetence, so she's sharing them with you so that you can carry them for a while. Does that make sense?
interprets the client's projective identification and Marcia's projective counteridentification

Marcia: Like, she feels incompetent in light of the constant criticism she's used to. Yeah, but she can't allow herself to acknowledge that she feels incompetent, so she projects it into me. And, man, do I feel it!
expands her understanding

Supervisor: Yeah! She either consciously or unconsciously wants you to know how she feels.

Marcia: Well, I definitely do! (*laughs*)
feels more at ease

Supervisor: That's very useful information for us. Your capacity to feel that can be seen as a very deep kind of empathy. So whether or not she knows it, you are connecting deeply with her already.
normalizes and reassures
(*mutual laughter*)

Marcia: Hmm. I never knew empathy could be so painful!

Supervisor: A mixed blessing sometimes for sure!

The supervisor made a point of reframing Marcia's countertransference as a positive experience of empathy. In the preceding sequence, with the support of her supervisor, Marcia began distancing herself from her feelings of inadequacy and used them to understand her client's experience. Equipped with this awareness, Marcia can now consider how to intervene with Lauren in a productive way.

Resolution

Marcia: So, now what do I do now that I have a clue about what's going on between us?
still self-deprecates

Supervisor: Any ideas?
implies that Marcia is competent to figure it out

Marcia: Well, tell her that she seems to feel painfully inadequate?
hesitates

Supervisor: Or wonder aloud about it.

Marcia: Yeah, like, "Sometimes I wonder if all of those experiences with your mom just made you really question your abilities."

Supervisor: Sounds good to me.
supportive

Marcia: How would I explain to her how I know that? Do I tell her about my experience?

Supervisor: You don't have to tell her; you can simply interpret what's going on for her, or you could tell her. There are different opinions about whether or not it's productive to tell the client how you came up with your interpretation. How you manage that will ultimately be up to you and where you decide to land theoretically. A more traditional therapist would simply make the connection for her. A more progressive therapist might invite the client to discuss the therapeutic interaction with you, and you give your reactions. But that requires some skill and confidence—(*pauses*) maybe a little more than you feel right now.
offers a range of options, implying that Marcia is capable enough to figure it out

Marcia: Yeah. I think I'll start with just the interpretation.

Supervisor: Sounds like a plan.

In this event, Marcia expressed strong feelings of incompetence about helping her client. The supervisor acknowledged Marcia's feelings, then helped her examine their origins. Was feeling incompetent common for Marcia—something she does in a number of situations—or was it particular to her experience with this client? If Marcia's feelings of incompetence were familiar, the supervisor might have addressed the feelings directly or suggested personal therapy. In this circumstance, however, because Marcia's experience of incompetence with Lauren was extreme and unfamiliar to her, the supervisor intuited that Marcia may have received her client's projected feelings of inadequacy. To help Marcia understand how this happened, the supervisor taught Marcia about the client's projective identification, and without labeling it, Marcia's own counteridentification. Once Marcia began expressing an empathic understanding of Lauren, the supervisor helped Marcia use her own experience to understand Lauren more deeply and, with that understanding, make a plan to get the therapy back on track.

The supervisor might have pointed out the parallel process, showing Marcia that, in the supervisory relationship, interpretation, empathy, and guidance helped her get through the muddle and begin to feel more competent. In this case, the supervisor chose not to do so, because in her judgment, Marcia had enough to digest without this added piece. In future supervision sessions, however, the parallel process that took place in this session could be referenced and explained.

This simplified example illustrates how a supervisor might approach sorting out a classic countertransference from a projective counteridentification. Real life, however, is seldom this simple. In fact, a client's ability to induce specific feelings in a therapist depends in part on the therapist's proneness to experiencing those feelings in the first place, even in the absence of related emotional baggage. Competence issues are a good example of this nuance, because being inexperienced and in training lends itself naturally to feelings of inadequacy.

In countertransference events like these, the supervisor's job is to help the supervisee understand that projective counteridentification is normal and manageable. The supervisee can take heart by finding out, first, that bad feelings are not completely personal, and second, that these feelings offer a window onto the client's experience. If the supervisee uses that information wisely, showing the client the internal resources to manage the difficult feelings, the supervisee can effect deep insight and change in the client. Ultimately, the client may come to trust that unmanageable feelings directly can be shared, knowing that the therapist will contain them and help the client cope in a healthier fashion. When the process works, both supervisee and client learn to manage the seemingly unmanageable.

SPECIAL CONSIDERATIONS

Because transference is a natural phenomenon, occurring to some extent in all relationships, it is an expected part of supervisees' experiences of their supervisors. Likewise, it is normal for supervisors to have countertransferential responses to their supervisees. As eloquently put by relational psychoanalysts (Frawley-O'Dea & Sarnat, 2001; McKinney, 2000), the supervisory relationship models for the supervisee how to manage the subtexts of clinical discourse through the supervisor's wise handling of transference and countertransference phenomena.

Parallel processes often originate in the supervisory relationship, not in the therapy relationship (Doehrman, 1976). Whether the supervisor is in a clear position of power with the supervisee or the power relationship is subtler (as in postdegree supervisory situations), the supervisee will nonetheless see the supervisor as an authority figure. Naturally, the supervisor becomes a receptacle for the supervisee's projections about people in power, with all the accompanying associations. As discussed in other chapters, transference reactions to the supervisor can also reflect discomfort related to differences based on gender, culture, race, ability, age, sexual orientation, religion, or socioeconomic status. When the supervisor is unaware of this potential dynamic and conscious and unconscious reactions to the supervisee's transference, confusion can reign. More damaging are cases in which problems are attributed to the client when they more accurately reside in the supervisee or supervisor.

Making connections between attachment theory (e.g., Bowlby, 1979) and supervisory processes, Watkins (1995) identified three pathological attachment styles that can manifest themselves in supervision: compulsive self-reliance, anxious attachment, and compulsive caregiving. Compulsive self-reliance reflects an avoidant attachment style and may be evident when a supervisee refuses or resists help and has defiance, resentment, distancing, or disparagement for the supervisor. Curiously, just as compulsive independence masks feelings of dependence, compulsive self-reliance is likely to hide intense longings for help and approval. The anxiously attached supervisee, on the other hand, may cling to the supervisor, seek to be the favorite in the peer group, or test the supervisor's caring and availability in various direct and indirect ways. By contrast, the compulsive caregiver may manifest her or his problems in the supervisory relationship by, for example, expressing solicitous concern for the supervisor's personal and professional worries (Watkins, 1995). In the extreme, the compulsive caregiver may draw the supervisor into a role reversal, whereby the supervisor comes to rely on the supervisee's help in a pseudotherapeutic way.

These and other transference reactions to the supervisor may be most noticeable when the supervisee repeatedly comes late or avoids supervision sessions, forgets to bring clinical material, is too reticent or too active, expresses acute anxiety around the supervisor, or behaves in an ingratiating way toward the supervisor. Noticing these cues, the supervisor should find an appropriate time to inquire about the supervisee's experience of supervision in general and the supervisory relationship in particular. If transference is suspected, it should be addressed, but not in the same way a therapist might address a client's transference. Though in some instances the basis for the supervisee's transference may be so deeply rooted in personality conflicts or attachment styles that the supervisee is unsuited for the profession (Watkins, 1995), most transference phenomena in supervision can be dealt with in a straightforward, educational manner. After all, supervision is not about working through traumatic, formative experiences but rather, is about learning to think through interpersonal dilemmas and developing ways to resolve emotional entanglements (Ekstein & Wallerstein, 1958).

It is a different case altogether when the problem involves a supervisor's countertransference to the supervisee. Although countertransference in supervision may be experienced in much the same way as experienced in therapy, the consequences carry more risk. A supervisor who acts out countertransferentially with a supervisee can cause harm to a young professional who depends on the supervisor's evaluation to proceed in career development. Still more serious, countertransference in the supervisor, if not resolved, can put the supervisee's clients at risk.

The major conundrum is whether the supervisor's countertransference originates within the supervisory or the therapy relationship. Countertransference that originates with the supervisor may be due to long-standing personality conflicts or reactions to specific supervisee's (Bernard & Goodyear, 1998). Overidentification with the supervisee or wanting to be like a good parent, a supervisor may avoid challenging a supervisee, choose favorites in the supervision group, compete with other supervisors for the supervisees' regard, or view supervisees as an extension of her or himself (Lower, 1972). Countertransference reactions related to sexual attraction or to cultural differences from the supervisee are discussed in chapters 3 and 6.

Supervisors can also experience countertransference toward a client, even when the supervisee does not. In chapter 4, for example, we present a transcript in which the supervisor had a strong reaction to a potential child abuse situation. The supervisor's eventual insight into her reactions allowed her to "own" her part in the role conflict that developed with the supervisee, eventually moving the event toward successful resolution.

Supervisors may experience exaggerated or unrealistic affective, cognitive, or behavioral manifestations of countertransference to their supervisees (Ladany, Constantine, Miller, Erickson, & Muse-Burke, 2000). Interviews with experienced supervisors (Ladany et al., 2000) suggested various origins of these countertransference reactions: unresolved personal problems, environmental dynamics (e.g., divided loyalties within an agency), reactions to supervisees' interpersonal styles (e.g., defensive, guarded, passive, avoidant), or their behavior with clients in session. By and large, countertransference reactions troubled these supervisors. Their emotions included distress, fear, discomfort, frustration, anger, resentment, surprise, confusion, and self-doubt. Typically, they worried about their competence and judgment and had concerns about behaving with and evaluating their trainees appropriately. Most commonly, supervisors sought help from colleagues and recognized the parallel processes so that eventually they could discuss troubling issues with their supervisees.

All countertransference events on the supervisor's part are harmful, however. Most of Ladany et al.'s (2000) supervisors reported that the initial weakening of their supervisory relationship was rectified by their actions, resulting in a stronger bond with their supervisees. Indeed, when the supervisor recognizes countertransference as a reaction to the supervisee's transference, there is room for negotiation. Just as therapists can recognize projective counteridentification by a sense of unreality, supervisors can use their own feelings to detect projective counteridentification stemming from their supervisees' unconscious conflicts. The supervisor's reactions do not have to be extreme to be informative, and in fact, the more subtle ones may be the most instructive.

Take, for example, a supervisee who spends the session talking but without questioning or seeking input, allowing the supervisor no space to intervene. If the supervisor ends up feeling bored or tempted to "check out" of the interaction, this reaction might be a clue that the supervisee expects to be ignored or discounted by others. The supervisee fills the air with words, longing to make a connection but instead pushing others away. Recognizing an unfamiliar feeling of being discounted, the supervisor realizes that the supervisee behaves in similar off-putting ways with clients. In therapy, the supervisee waits until the client finishes speaking, then provides a reciprocal monologue. Supervisee and client function like two ships passing without connecting in a meaningful way. Understanding this dynamic, the supervisor can then relate a felt experience to a suspicion that the supervisee may be anxious about making genuine bonds with others. A responsive supervisee may explore this hypothesized dynamic and consider whether it could be operating in session with clients.

The supervisor's hypothesis may, of course, be inaccurate, but its disconfirmation prompts further attempts to understand personal reactions to the supervisee's behavior. The utility of such discussions lies not in the supervisor's accurate discernment but in the opportunity her or his reactions offer both parties to understand what "stirred" interpersonal space.

Before becoming supervisors, mental health professionals have had ample opportunity to be supervised themselves. They engage in various pursuits of self-knowledge and develop a greater awareness of interpersonal patterns. This experience, however, does not preclude the need for ongoing self-reflection. Supervisors in training usually receive supervision of their supervision, giving them the chance to examine and address countertransferential reactions with supervisees. Generally, however, after the predoctoral training experience, supervisors are on their own. As professionals, supervisors need to find opportunities to discuss their own countertransferential issues—whether they do so in peer supervision groups, psychotherapy, or through pursuing supervision of their supervision.

CONCLUSION

Because of its complexity, the concept of countertransference is difficult to understand, particularly in supervision, where it can occur on two levels simultaneously and originate in either. Managing critical incidents involving countertransference is tricky. A too heavy-handed approach to countertransference can result in the supervisee resisting all the supervisor's attempts to be helpful (Hunt, 2001). However, understanding and working through countertransference reactions can make the difference between adequate and outstanding supervision.

A major implication of this chapter is that effective supervisors must engage in activities that promote ongoing self-awareness. Placing a value on the interplay of personal and professional development cannot be understated. The time invested in understanding and working through countertransference and projective counteridentification can pay off in deepened supervisee awareness and development, as well as supervisor satisfaction for a job well done.

6

MANAGING SEXUAL ATTRACTION: TALKING ABOUT SEX IN SUPERVISION

Has it ever occurred to you that in your promiscuous pursuit of women you are merely trying to assuage your subconscious fears of sexual impotence?
Yes, sir, it has.
Then why do you do it?
To assuage my fears of sexual impotence.
—Joseph Heller, *Catch-22*, 1961

Therapists who sexually act out are a pernicious problem in our society, with approximately 5% of psychotherapists admitting to this unethical conduct (Bartell & Rubin, 1990). Not only does such behavior harm clients and their families, but it also erodes public trust in the mental health profession. Although sexual acting out is clearly unethical, having sexual feelings for a client is normal and relatively common, with more than 84% of therapists reporting that they found themselves sexually attracted to a client at some point in their practice (Pope, Keith-Spiegel, & Tabachnick, 1986; Rodolfa et al., 1994).

How to handle sexual feelings in therapy is probably the most uncomfortable topic in supervision. Not only is it simply unusual to discuss sex in the workplace, but supervisors also have an ethical and legal obligation to prevent their supervisees from acting out sexually with the clients in their care. This obligation can work at odds with the need to provide a safe learning environment for supervisees to explore their weaknesses and vulnerabilities, specifically around the normal range of sexual feelings bound to arise.

There are five ways sexual issues can arise in supervision. Supervisees can be sexually attracted to clients (Ladany, O'Brien, et al., 1997; Pope et al., 1986) and vice versa (Pope, Sonne, & Holroyd, 1993), supervisees can develop feelings for their supervisors (Melincoff, 2001) and vice versa, and supervisors can even become attracted to their supervisees' clients (Walker, 2003).

Although supervisors' attraction issues are discussed in the conclusion of this chapter, we focus primarily on critical sexual attraction events between clients and supervisees. Though the others certainly merit attention, client–therapist attraction is the most common, and arguably, the most problematic scenario.

Overall, the literature on therapists' attraction toward clients is scant (Gabbard, 1994, 1995; Pope et al., 1986), and the literature on managing sexual attraction in supervision is particularly sparse (Ladany, O'Brien, et al., 1997; Pope et al., 1986; Rodolfa et al., 1994). Generally, research has found that most postdegreed therapists become sexually attracted to at least one client during their professional lives (Bernsen, Tabachnick, & Pope, 1994; Pope et al., 1986; Rodolfa et al., 1994), yet only about half seek consultation or supervision to manage these feelings.

It is also common for therapists in training to have problematic attractions toward their clients. A qualitative study on this topic revealed some interesting patterns (Ladany, O'Brien, et al., 1997). Specifically, supervisees who felt attracted to their clients tended to respond to both physical (e.g., the individual's "template" of attractiveness) and personal characteristics of their clients (e.g., intelligent, vulnerable, needy, sophisticated). For most supervisees, their attraction developed in the initial phase of therapy, usually in the first three sessions, when the relationship develops most rapidly. In some instances, sexualized dreams alerted them to their feelings. Typically, they experienced negative emotions such as fear and guilt, which were more pronounced when they also noted their clients' attraction toward them. At times, supervisees saw their attraction to the client as facilitating their work, as they were more attentive and invested. At other times, it distanced them from what was actually occurring in the therapy process.

In Ladany, O'Brien, et al.'s (1997) sample, sexual attraction was just as likely to be brought to the supervisor's attention as not, and supervisors rarely facilitated the disclosure of a supervisee's sexual attraction toward a client. In one situation, when a supervisee described a client as the "most sensual" person the supervisee had ever worked with, the supervisor seemingly ignored the comment. In this case, the Marker for a sexual attraction event was clear, but as we will discuss, this is not always the case.

As much as theorists emphasize the need to assess expectations and set norms for supervision (e.g., Bernard & Goodyear, 1998; Neufeldt, 1999), research suggests that supervisors only rarely include sexual issues in their "getting to know you" role inductions (Ladany, O'Brien, et al., 1997). Setting the stage for this discussion is critical, however, if sexual issues are ever to be broached by a supervisee. Ladany, O'Brien, et al.'s participants indicated that when they felt safe enough to bring up the topic, they often received helpful responses such as validation, support, and normalization of their experience. These findings suggest the need for supervisors to explicitly make sexual attraction an acceptable topic for discussion. If the topic is not raised in the earliest phase of supervision, it can reasonably be introduced later on if the ground has been laid for making intimate disclosures in a safe atmosphere.

In the next section, we provide a process model for managing sexual attraction issues in supervision, followed by two case illustrations. In the first case, a supervisee is successful at managing her feelings toward a client. By contrast, in the second case, the supervisee adamantly opposes exploring the client's attraction to her, and in this circumstance, the event ends abruptly without a resolution.

PROCESS MODEL

Marker

Markers of sexual attraction on the part of supervisees can be obvious, as in cases where supervisees simply comment on what they feel and ask the supervisor for help or consultation. For example, a supervisee may report a romantic dream or fantasy involving a client. In these cases, it is clear to the supervisor that a sexual attraction event is unfolding. Other Markers of sexual attraction can be covert, however, when the supervisee is either unaware of sexual feelings or deliberately hides them from the supervisor (Ladany, Hill, Corbett, & Nutt, 1996). Observing a supervisee's session live or on videotape, the supervisor might notice that the supervisee dresses more fashionably or seductively on the days a certain client is scheduled. The supervisee may smile or laugh more frequently in session with this client or atypically begin sessions early or end them quite late. Covert Markers may also occur in supervision, when a supervisee repeatedly forgets to bring a tape, avoids showing the tape or discussing a particular client, or minimizes the therapeutic work with that client. Of course, these same behaviors could signal some other kind of event—a skill deficit, countertransference, role conflict, or other problematic behaviors. As in every critical incident, the Marker phase of the event continues until the supervisor is certain of the task at hand—in this case, to help the supervisee manage sexual attraction for a client.

Markers of sexual attraction on the part of clients is another matter altogether, particularly if the client's feelings for the supervisee are unnoticed or the supervisee's own behavior elicits the client's feelings. At times, a client might act out in a therapy session, for example, by asking for a kiss or touching the therapist inappropriately. Disturbed by these events, the supervisee is likely to address them in supervision. In other circumstances, however, only by observing the session does the supervisor recognize the client's attraction to the supervisee. As shown in the second illustration that follows, the supervisee may be unaware of the client's feelings and unwilling to see the process in the same way as the supervisor.

Task Environment and Resolution

The Task Environment in these kinds of events varies greatly depending on the stage and quality of the supervisory relationship, the client in question, the degree to which the supervisee is likely to act on sexual feelings, and the supervisee's comfort versus defensiveness in discussing sexuality. Typically, when there is no reason to believe the client or supervisee would act out, the supervision event proceeds with some or all of the following five phases: *exploration of feelings, assessing knowledge, normalizing the experience, focus on countertransference*, and *focus on the therapeutic process*.

Once the Marker has been identified (i.e., a recognition that sexual attraction issues need to be discussed), the supervisor begins seeking additional information about what is occurring in the therapy process by exploring the supervisee's feelings. It is, of course, understandable for the supervisee to feel discomfort or embarrassment—not only about sexual or romantic feelings that exist in the therapy relationship, but also about having to speak with the supervisor about them.

In the second phase, the supervisor should obtain a sense of the supervisee's ethical awareness. Specifically, is the supervisee knowledgeable about the prohibition of sexual relations with a client? Is the supervisee aware of the differences, both subtle and overt, between behaving unethically (dating a client and having sexual relations) and having the quite normal reaction of physical attraction? If the supervisor is satisfied that the supervisee's boundaries are solid, he or she can skip this step and proceed with offering the supervisee a normalization experience, essentially, helping him or her see that these experiences can be expected from time to time in therapeutic relationships. (Of course, such a discussion may not be as necessary for advanced supervisees as it is for novices.) If comfortable, the supervisor might choose to disclose about his or her own sexual attraction experiences as a therapist to facilitate the normalization process.

Once feelings are identified, knowledge is assessed, and normalization has been offered, the next stage involves helping supervisees explore their personal issues and possible countertransference reactions that may stem from the client's transference or projective identification. For example, a client may flirt with the supervisee, but the supervisee may be attracted to the client's vulnerability. In this phase, the discussion may involve talking about how the supervisee's interpersonal dynamics seem to influence therapy (e.g., how might the supervisee, consciously or unconsciously, be responding to the client's flirtatiousness?).

The Resolution phase of the successful event involves integrating all the previous work so the supervisee understands how to manage sexual feelings in therapy, and if this is part of the picture, without responding countertransferentially. Evidence that the event was successful however, may not be available until the next therapy session, when the supervisee becomes aware of and skillfully manages feelings as they arise with the client.

Partial or unsuccessful resolutions of a sexual attraction event, on the other hand, can occur at any moment during the Task Environment, when the process proves too difficult or threatening for the supervisee. Over-the-top anxiety or a lack of insight can derail the supervisee's ability to effectively describe, discuss, and manage sexual or romantic feelings. As other examples, the supervisee (a) may have trouble identifying feelings; (b) may not be well versed in ethics or may have personal boundary issues to work through; (c) may not be responsive to the supervisor's normalization experience (e.g., "I could never feel that way about a client because my religion forbids me from being attracted to people outside of marriage"); or (d) may have already acted out, for example, by seeing a client socially. In the latter situation, the supervisee's acknowledgement becomes a Marker for a problematic behavior event (see chap. 8).

Finally, resolutions may also be unsuccessful when multicultural and sexual attraction issues interact. Supervisees who never encountered sexual tension in cross-racial or cross-sexual orientation dyads, for example, may have a difficult time working through their personal reactions to clients who differ from them in these ways.

We now present two sexual attraction events that vary in the extent to which the issues are effectively addressed in the supervisory context. The first, successful event involves the supervisee's attraction toward a client, and the second, unsuccessful event involves the client's attraction toward the supervisee.

A SUCCESSFULLY RESOLVED SEXUAL ATTRACTION EVENT (SUPERVISEE TO CLIENT)

In this dyad, a female supervisor with 15 years of therapy experience and 10 years of supervision experience works with Leta, a 24-year-old woman in her second year of a doctoral psychology program. The setting is a community mental health clinic.

Though Leta is an advanced student, the supervisor assumes that sexual issues may never have been broached in her previous supervision experiences. Thus, during the initial discussion about the structure of supervision (e.g., confidentiality limits, weekly meeting times, the importance of being on time, and using all the time allotted), the supervisor includes sexual attraction issues in the context of explaining her various roles as supervisor (e.g., offer alternative perspectives, provide didactic information, question whether Leta's personal issues are interfering with the therapeutic relationship, make suggestions about technique, and so on) and Leta's various roles as supervisee (e.g., bring therapeutic challenges to supervision, be open to feedback, set goals for professional development, and so on). We pick up the process in the first session as the supervisor suggests possible topics of discussion for supervision.

Supervisor: So, there are lots we can talk about in the context of our sessions. Some things may be more challenging than others. For example, it may be relatively easy to bring up questions about how to intervene with a depressed client. You may ask at some point, "Now that I've developed a therapeutic relationship, what do I do?" On the other hand, supervision can also be a place to discuss your countertransference reactions toward clients. And these can come about in many shapes and sizes. For example, you may have a dream involving your client that alerts you to some countertransference. Feelings such as anger and frustration may be there. At times, it can also be expected that, as therapists, we find ourselves attracted to clients either in a friendship way or even be sexually attracted. These are things that may be experienced by you, and I hope that you and I develop the kind of relationship where we can be open to discussing all sorts of issues. How does that sound?

Leta: Wow. I guess I never really thought about some of the topics you mentioned.
shows interest

Supervisor: Such as . . .
leads

Leta: Well, like the dreams. I don't really remember any of my dreams, so I doubt that will ever come up. But I'm certainly open to talking about them if they do.
receptive

Supervisor: Sounds good. We'll just keep tabs on things as the semester progresses.

Leta: That works.

We now move forward to the seventh supervision session. Leta is working with Jim, a 30-year-old man in recovery for alcohol addiction. He attends Alcoholic Anonymous meetings and sought therapy to work on a host of issues related to his family of origin and interpersonal relationships. Leta and Jim have worked together for three sessions and, in fact, had a session earlier in the day.

As Leta begins the supervision session by updating her supervisor about all the clients in her caseload, the supervisor notices that Leta is dressed up a bit more than usual. Then, contrary to their norm (the supervisor usually begins by asking Leta what she'd like to focus on), Leta excitedly launches into a discussion of her clients.

Marker

Leta: So my second new client is Tom, who is having occasional panic attacks and wants to find a way to get rid of them. I'm feeling pretty confident about working with him since I've already worked with two other clients that have the same issues. And I'm also now seeing Jim, who's dealing with problems in his family of origin. He's really had a tough life, and with all he's gone through, he is still a very likable guy.

Supervisor: Would you like to talk more about Jim?
following Leta's lead

Leta: (*eagerly*) Sure. Let's see. Jim has just had a horrible family life. His father was an alcoholic and was physically abusive toward his mother. And, when he wasn't beating his mother, he was beating Jim. It's just so sad . . .

The supervisor notices Leta's empathy for Jim and wonders whether Leta is experiencing some countertransference or whether her exuberance belies something else that may be out of her awareness.

Supervisor: Can you say some more about your feelings of sadness?
encourages self-exploration

Leta: I guess I just feel bad for him that he had to go through all that. It's not surprising that he ended up becoming an alcoholic and has never been able to establish a healthy romantic relationship with someone. He's just such a sweet guy and deserves to be with someone nice after all he's been through.
begins with feelings but switches to the cognitive

Supervisor: What's it like having those feelings and being in the same room with him?
refocuses

Leta: Sometimes, when he's crying, I just have this desire to reach out and hold him. I, of course, would never do something like that, but it just seems that that's what he really needs in the moment. (*quietly*) Does that make me a bad therapist for feeling that way?
implies worry that her feelings are inappropriate

The supervisee does a nice job exploring her reactions to Jim but then catches herself and feels guilty for her honest reflections. Picking up on Leta's sense of guilt and her need for reassurance, the supervisor suspects that Leta's boundaries are solid and that she knows it would be unethical to pursue a relationship with her client. If, however, Leta's boundaries seemed questionable, the supervisor would be obliged to inquire further into Leta's understanding of appropriate limit setting with clients.

The Marker is now complete. Because there were several cues that Leta is attracted to Jim and that she may have lost her neutrality with him, the supervisor decides to address and manage Leta's sexual attraction. Moving to the Task Environment, the supervisor wants to be certain that Leta's boundaries are indeed intact. Asking Leta about them directly, however, risks raising

Leta's anxiety and shame to a disabling degree. For this reason, the supervisor deftly moves between two interactional sequences, an assessment of knowledge and an exploration of feelings, using fantasy to accomplish these ends.

Assessing Knowledge (Ethics) *and* Exploration of Feelings

Supervisor: Help me understand what you mean by feeling like a "bad therapist."
open-ended probes

Leta: (*softly*) I guess I feel guilty for having these feelings, and it's like I'm losing my objectivity.
embarrassed

Supervisor: It sounds like your feelings are real to you, and I don't see them as unusual under the circumstances. Also, your insight might help us know how to work with Jim more effectively.
reassuring and validating

Leta: Yeah, but why do I feel this way?
open, seeking help

Supervisor: Tell me more about what your experience is like working with Jim. If you were to meet him outside the therapy context, say at a party, what would your reactions be toward him?
avoids a direct answer but wants to assess Leta's ethical understanding indirectly

Leta: Oh, that's easy! He would just be someone I'd want to talk to more and get to know better.

Supervisor: Would he be someone that you would want to know more as a friend or perhaps in a romantic way?
gentle probe

Leta: I don't know if I would, but my friends probably would say I would!
frank

Supervisor: Interesting that your friends would say that.
wants Leta to expand on her previous comment without being directly questioned

Leta: Yeah, I don't know though. That just seems so wrong . . .

Supervisor: How are you feeling right now?
wants more clarity about Leta's comfort level before proceeding to the next stage

Leta: I guess I'm feeling a little embarrassed. I can't believe I'm telling my supervisor that I might be attracted to a client of mine! I guess I've *really* lost my objectivity!
self-aware

Supervisor: Actually, I'm quite impressed with your openness and your willingness to talk about your reactions. Sounds like you have a real question about whether your feelings are appropriate. What are you concerned about—about how I'm perceiving you?
reassures and reflects Leta's unspoken worry about evaluation

Leta: I guess that you might think I'm this boundaryless person who is "looking for love in all the wrong places!" (*both laugh*) But I think the bottom-line worry is that you would think I'm a terrible therapist for losing my objectivity and having these feelings.
uses humor (i.e., quotes a song) to relieve tension

Supervisor: I certainly don't think you're a terrible therapist.
reassures

Because Leta is concerned about being evaluated, the supervisor realizes she needs to normalize Leta's experience before they discuss where her feelings came from. Moreover, because sexual topics had been included in the previous role induction, the supervisor is more at ease to directly address Leta's sexual attraction toward her client. As shown, the supervisor discloses her own experience to further normalize Leta's feelings and lessen her embarrassment and concern about evaluation.

Normalizing the Experience

Supervisor: I want to say again that I'm impressed that you have the insight to recognize this possible attraction. It's not always easy to see or to acknowledge. Also, we (all therapists) should expect that occasionally we'll all be sexually attracted to a client every now and then. I know it has happened to me on a number of occasions. It's not always easy to see and then sometimes even harder to own.

Leta: Hmm. That's interesting. It's funny you mention it because Amelia and Sybil (*peers in supervision group*) have been joking with me about how cute he is and that it's too bad he's in therapy.
feeling more comfortable

Supervisor: How is that for you, then, when your peers joke about you with him?
explores

Leta: I guess, at some level, I kind of agree with them and wish that he wasn't in therapy.
acknowledges her attraction directly for the first time

Supervisor: Mhmm.

Leta: (*quickly*) Of course, now that we're in therapy together, he is obviously off limits. And at some level, that's fine, because he is the type of guy I typically get involved with, only later to learn what a mistake I made.
wants to reassure the supervisor that she will not act on her feelings

The supervisee accepted her supervisor's offer of normalization by acknowledging her feelings for the client more directly. Knowing it is important to use supervision to understand herself better in relation to clients, Leta opens up more, implying a willingness to consider her projections and actual responses to Jim. The supervisor takes this cue to begin exploring Leta's countertransference.

Focus on Countertransference

Supervisor: How so?
deliberately vague

Leta: I used to tend to get into relationships where I like to rescue the guy from his troubled life, only later to learn that it's all been a waste of time.

Supervisor: You kind of learned how futile it can be to try to help someone who doesn't want the help?
reflects to show understanding and gives Leta permission to explore further

Leta: Yeah!

Supervisor: You mentioned that you used to get into these kinds of relationships?
prompts

The supervisor is careful here, as she steps into the gray area between supervision and therapy. In her mind, she keeps track of the question, "How does what Leta is telling me affect her work with Jim or other clients?" If the conversation starts to slip too far afield, the supervisor will gently steer it back and consider suggesting a therapy referral for the supervisee. As shown following, Leta proceeds to explain what she has learned about herself in romantic relationships, and the supervisor is empathic without interrupting or offering interpretations or guidance.

Leta: Two years of therapy has helped me realize that many of the reasons why I get into these situations are from my own family and their crazy relationships. But I guess even after two years of therapy, old habits die hard . . .
implies that she does not feel a need for personal therapy or that she wants supervision to become like therapy

Supervisor: Well, the good thing is that we know the first step in managing countertransference is recognizing it.
offers a paradigm to help Leta make the link

Relieved that Leta has already worked on these issues extensively and understanding that Leta wanted her to know that she has got a good handle on her own problems, the supervisor deftly guides Leta back to the clinical material. In this next phase, there is a recursive movement between a focus on the therapeutic process with Jim and Leta's countertransference to him. This back and forth focus works well with an advanced supervisee, like Leta, who can handle multiprocessing.

Focus on the Therapeutic Process *and* Focus on Countertransference

Leta: So now that I've recognized it, what do I do?
seeks guidance

Supervisor: Well, the next step is to separate what is the part of the countertransference that is based on your issues versus the part of the

countertransference that is based on Jim's interpersonal presentation style. In addition, it's important for you to know that there may be a real aspect, or a nontransference aspect, to the attraction. We know that by Amelia and Sybil's reactions to Jim!
didactic

Leta: Yeah, he is cute! (*laughs*)
relieved

Supervisor: (*smiles*) So you mentioned that some of your stuff is that you have this desire to rescue people when they seem in need?
redirects

Leta: Yes, I'm a real wonder woman! But then it backfires. At heart, I know most people don't want rescuing in a relationship, but I can't help myself being drawn to guys that are kind of down and out (like Jim!) and want me to listen. I'm a sucker for it in my real life!
eager to explain her insight

In the next sequence, the supervisor uses open-ended questions to see if Leta can apply her insights to the therapeutic process at hand. It is not enough for supervisees to recognize their countertransference; they also need to use it to good advantage in their therapeutic work (see chap. 5).

Supervisor: Sounds like you already have figured out how these dynamics work— or don't work!—for you. How does that get played out when you are with him?
leads

Leta: (*pause*) Well, whenever he seems so despondent, I have this desire to help him feel better right away, like I want to stop his bleeding. Sometimes in session, instead of letting him cry, I talk to him and tell him things are going to be better. He usually responds by not crying anymore and thanking me for being so kind.
reflects

Supervisor: So you can see that your seemingly benevolent intervention ends up interrupting the therapy process.
helps Leta get more distance

Leta: Yeah, and I get reinforced for doing it!
insight

Supervisor: Good. So you see that one cue that your countertransference may be operating is an immediate desire to help.
clarifies

Leta: Yeah, that makes sense.

The supervisor and supervisee continue to explore internal cues that can alert Leta to her countertransference. Discussions like these are not only important preventative measures about sexual attraction triggers, but they also further the supervisee's ability to conceptualize her own contribution to the therapeutic process.

Supervisor: Now that we have talked about cues that you have some countertransference going on, what do you suppose he is doing that feeds into your attraction for him?
again, deliberately vague to see where Leta will take it

Leta: Hmm. Well, he does this shy-guy routine.

Supervisor: "Shy-guy routine"?

Leta: Yeah, when I ask him a tough question, he smiles at me and then looks at the floor and usually says he doesn't know and asks why the work is so hard. I then tend to let him off the hook, and we switch the topic. The way he does it is kind of cute, and the message I get loud and clear is that he doesn't want to talk about it. (*pauses*) But at the same time, the topics that I ask him about are exactly what he needs to talk about.
begins to put it together

Supervisor: Hmm. Hm.
encourages without interrupting the flow of Leta's associations

Leta: I guess his shy-guy behavior is another cue that something is happening, and instead of letting him off the hook, I could focus even more on the topic at hand.
demonstrates a greater ability to take an observing perspective

Supervisor: Exactly!

Leta: I could also probably point out his behavior and see what he does with it.
eager

Supervisor: Very good. You're getting the hang of it.

Now that there is clear indication that Leta's boundaries are secure, her ethics are sound, she knows herself, and she can recognize her countertransference, the event moves to the Resolution phase. The supervisor initiates a wrap-up that involves integration, consolidating what Leta has learned about herself, her client, and the therapeutic process.

Resolution

Supervisor: Now that we have gone through all of this, how do you feel about what you will do next with him?
probes for Leta's integration

Leta: I guess I feel I have some direction, but I'm still not sure what to do with these feelings, especially if they become more intense.
seeks reassurance

Supervisor: Say some more about your concerns.

Leta: I think I'm nervous about meeting with him again. What if all I can think of is our discussion about my possible feelings toward him?
unsure, seeks concrete suggestions

Supervisor: Leta, I know your boundaries are strong, and I have no fear that you'll act inappropriately. Here's a suggestion. When these feelings come up, think about the context—what is going on, what *he* may be avoiding looking at what sets off the shy-guy stuff. That'll help you get your perspective back, I think.
validates and offers guidance

Leta: Oh, yes, that's helpful!
relieved

Supervisor: But, it sounds like we may have some more work to do on this issue. But that's what supervision is all about. I appreciate you hanging in there with me, and I hope we can continue to talk frankly about your experiences. And also, as I've mentioned before, remember you have some say in this process, and we have multiple avenues to approach any issue, if things become too uncomfortable. How does that sound?
keeps the door open for Leta's further self-exploration

Leta: Okay. I'll let you know.

Supervisor: Sounds good.

In this session, the supervisor identified and explored Leta's attraction to her client, then worked to normalize it for her, and finally, managed the supervisee's feelings so they would interfere less with the therapy process. Clearly, the supervisee in this instance was mature enough to handle her embarrassment, disclose her true feelings, and engage in a discussion about sexual attraction without undue anxiety.

It should be noted, however, that Leta's attraction to her client was not "resolved." What was resolved was the managing sexual attraction event in the supervisory session. That is, Leta gained self-awareness to continue working with Jim productively and knows that her supervisor is approachable on this issue. Although the supervisor suggested what to do when the "shy-guy" shows up, Leta needs time to become adept at handling her interactions with Jim, while recognizing and accepting her attraction to him. Doing so over time, if successful, will help her identify and address her feelings and countertransference when they arise with future clients.

The process depicted here flowed relatively smoothly. There can be significant challenges, however, if a supervisor is uncomfortable talking about sexual attraction or tries interpreting a supervisee's behavior who is not ready to hear it. Similarly, supervisees can present challenges to the process when they lack self-awareness or are in denial of their attraction to a client, show discomfort or shame regarding sexual issues, or are limited in their ability to conceptualize the effect of their own personal issues on the therapeutic process. We turn to one of these more difficult cases now.

AN UNSUCCESSFULLY RESOLVED SEXUAL ATTRACTION EVENT (CLIENT TO SUPERVISEE)

The supervisor in this case is a 55-year-old gay faculty member with 25 years of experience as a therapist and 20 years of supervision experience. The supervisee, Jill, is a 35-year-old heterosexual woman completing her second practicum in a university training clinic for doctoral students. Although the possible need to discuss sexual attraction was raised early in the process of negotiating expectations for supervision, as we will see, the supervisee resists engaging in this sort of discussion.

In this illustration, personal issues and supervision dynamics lead to an unsuccessful sexual attraction event in which a female client, Rita, seems to be attracted to the supervisee. Unlike the supervisee in the previous case, Jill lacks the insight and openness to manage this work. Compounding the problem is Jill's homophobia, which is of personal as well as professional concern to the supervisor. We pick up the process near the beginning of the fourth supervision session, when both are engaged in reviewing the status of all Jill's clients.

Marker

Jill: And then there's my client, Rita. I just don't know why she keeps coming back to therapy. She initially came in because of a recent breakup of a relationship. But what really seemed to be happening was that she was just homesick. We never really talked about the breakup, and she hasn't brought it up since the intake. We've seen each other for five sessions, and the most recent ones are about nothing of substance. I think I'm just going to terminate with her or just ask her to "shit or get off the pot!"
wants to appear competently in charge; hides her insecurity and uncertainty about her client's agenda

Supervisor: Okay, perhaps we can talk a little more about Rita.
invites exploration

Jill: Alright, what do you want to know?
somewhat defensive

The supervisor is first alerted to the emotion in Jill's comment, "I just don't know why she keeps coming back to therapy." Jill's final comment ("shit or get off the pot") indicates her frustration with and disappointment in her work with this client. At this point, the Marker is not clear, because Jill's comments could signal either a skill deficit, countertransference, or as shown next, a sexual attraction event. To clarify the Marker, the supervisor probes by using Jill's metaphor.

Supervisor: You mentioned that she should "shit or get off the pot" . . .

Jill: Well, yeah. Every week, she comes in and doesn't really say anything. We talk about her parents, her classes, and her friends, but she really doesn't seem to want to work on anything in particular.
embarrassed, thinks that she should be able to direct the therapeutic work more effectively

With Jill reverting to a cognitive explanation, the supervisor still doesn't know what is happening in the therapy with Rita or in Jill's internal experience of her client. Thus, he refocuses Jill on her thoughts and feelings about what is taking place, deliberately being vague to avoid predetermining the direction of Jill's exploration.

Supervisor: What's that like for you?

Jill: (*strongly*) It's very frustrating! I just keep thinking, "There are a lot of other people that could use therapy, so I wish you would stop wasting my time!"

Supervisor: Seems like you would rather be pretty much anywhere other than in the room with Rita?
reflects Jill's annoyance, implicitly gives her permission to keep exploring

Jill: I probably wouldn't mind it so much if she wanted to work on something of substance.

Supervisor: So why do you think she comes to see you every week?
draws attention to the therapeutic relationship

Jill: I don't know . . . (*silence*)

At this point, the supervisor remains silent to facilitate Jill's self-reflection. Doing so allows Jill space to consider what is really going on for her in the relationship with her client. The Marker continues as Jill recalls a reaction to Rita that she had previously forgotten or dismissed as irrelevant.

Jill: It's funny. I became silent in our therapy session once, too, just like you are doing now, and all I could think about or focus on was Rita's ear and eyebrow piercings! I kept thinking about how painful that must have been to get done and how it might still hurt. It hurt me just looking at her!
able to reflect on her immediate experience with the supervisor

Supervisor: (*smiles*) You seem to be really struck by her piercings . . .
offers permission to explore this theme further

Jill: Yeah. I mean, I think it doesn't make her look pretty. One of her issues is finding a boyfriend and how "no guys seem to excite" her. I keep thinking, it's because they probably aren't excited by her! She's so painful to look at! (*laughs*) And it's also weird that she keeps asking me about my relationships and whether I am in a happy relationship.
notes that Jill missed an important therapy Marker and seems confused by it

Supervisor: How do you respond to her?

Jill: I let her know that my relationships are an area of my life that I keep private and that I don't discuss that part of my life with my clients. But it was also a bit

annoying because she seemed to keep wanting to know. At one point, I finally gave in and told her that I'm married to a man, emphasizing "man" because I didn't want her to get any funny ideas.
thinks the supervisor is questioning her boundaries

Supervisor: Funny ideas?
has an inkling of Jill's homophobia

Jill: Yeah, I have a sneaking suspicion that she wonders if she is a lesbian.

Supervisor: What makes you think that?

Jill: I don't know, it's just a weird vibe I get when I'm with her. Sometimes I think I catch her staring at me, and I feel really uncomfortable.
frank

Supervisor: Do you think she may be attracted to you?
direct

Jill: (*strongly*) I've been trying to avoid thinking like that!
puts up a wall

At this point, the Marker ends, and sexual attraction is clearly the issue at hand. Reacting to Jill's harshness and put off by her comments about Rita, the supervisor finds himself wanting to defend the client. Then, wondering whether Jill's own sexual orientation identity is not very advanced, the supervisor moves the event into the Task Environment by continuing to explore Jill's feelings.

Exploration of Feelings

Supervisor: What's it like to have to avoid thinking like that?
focuses on Jill's defenses

Jill: I really just don't want to go there!
resistant

Supervisor: (*slight smile*) Seems like you may be worried that she finds you sexually attractive?
uncomfortable, anticipating more resistance

Jill: Hmm. I really have not wanted to consider that.
reverts to the cognitive

Supervisor: Tell me how you are feeling right now.
focuses on immediacy

Jill: I just never in my wildest dreams thought I'd have to be talking about a girl client being attracted to me in supervision. No wonder she has all those issues with relationships!
wants to shift the focus back on the client

Supervisor: Okay, let's slow down a minute. What are you feeling right now?
frustrated, recognizes that he needs to reconnect with Jill

Jill: Kind of creepy, I guess.

Supervisor: Tell me what it's like to feel "creepy."

Jill: Just icky. I don't want to have to think about her being attracted to me.
more open

Supervisor: Say more about that.

Jill: Well, I just believe that a person's sexual orientation is a choice, and I wish she didn't choose to have to be that way—if she *is*, of course.
remains cognitive

Jill is having a difficult time staying in the here and now, and clearly, her homophobia is getting in the way of effective treatment with her client. Aware of his personal countertransference to her thinly veiled hostility, the supervisor decides to assess the extent of Jill's homophobia and try to diffuse the intense affect beginning to emerge between them.

Assessing Knowledge

Supervisor: Tell me more about sexual orientation being a choice.

Jill: I may have mentioned this before, but I'm a Christian, I believe in the Bible, and I've been told all my life that the Bible says that homosexuality is a type of sin.
sensing her supervisor's discomfort, justifies her attitudes

Supervisor: Hmm mm.

Jill: Of course, that doesn't mean I can't still be her therapist. The saying goes, "love the sinner, not the sin."

Supervisor: Okay.
has difficulty staying neutral

Jill: But then we learn in all these multicultural classes that maybe homosexuality is something you are born with. So I guess I just don't know for sure. But I don't believe what our one professor said when he said that Jesus may have been a homosexual because he seemed to hang out with a lot of men. That really bothered me!
wants to explain her position

Supervisor: Well, let's go back to something you said. You indicated that you were not completely convinced that homosexuality is a sin, given some things you have learned about people who are gay, lesbian, or bisexual.
clarifies the conflict

Jill: I *do* have a friend that's gay, and he thinks the Bible talks about a lot of things we don't consider appropriate today.
wants to show that she's not naive

Supervisor: (*interrupting*) Such as stoning adulterers and the treatment of women?
notes his own sarcasm as he speaks

Jill: Yeah, I guess.

Supervisor: So, there seems to be this conflict about whether or not homosexuality is a sin, and perhaps that one notion could really change a major part of your belief system?
implies that Jill needs to change

Jill: Yeah, absolutely! I'm not sure I can handle a major change in my belief system.
disregards his implicit suggestion

In this sequence, the supervisor also experiences a conflict. Trying to put his personal feelings aside, he wants to respect Jill's freedom to believe what she wants. Nonetheless, he is concerned about and feels responsible for the welfare of her client, who deserves an empathic, accepting therapist. Consequently, he switches gears, wanting to get a sense of how problematic Jill's belief system is for her work with clients. As we will see, at this point, even more of the supervisor's frustration surfaces.

Focus on Evaluation

Supervisor: So without a new perspective then, how are you going to be able to work effectively with clients?
confronts

Jill: (*sharply*) You don't think I can work effectively with clients?
increasingly defensive

Supervisor: I'm not convinced that people can so easily put away their biases when working with clients. If I told you that a major part of my belief system is to consider women as inferior to men, do you suppose I would be able to work effectively with women?
sensing his own frustration rise, he shifts away from lesbian, gay, bisexual, and transgendered (LGBT) issues

Jill: Well, that's different.

Supervisor: Hmm. How so?

Jill: I don't know, it just is! (*laughs anxiously*)

Supervisor: (*smiles tensely*) I guess I'm not convinced it's very different.

Jill: I don't know if I agree with you.

The supervisor is feeling personally vulnerable in this conversation. Realizing that Jill would be unlikely to persist as she has been if she were aware of his lifestyle, the supervisor considers whether to disclose his own sexual orientation. He decides not to, realizing that a disclosure would serve his own agenda more so than help Jill. Indeed, having this knowledge might also give Jill justification to dismiss his comments about tolerance ("Of course he thinks that way—he's gay himself!"). Self-aware, the supervisor knows that because Jill's attitude has triggered vestiges of his own internalized homophobia, he needs to guard against using his authoritative power to serve his own needs. To avoid revealing how offended he's feeling, the supervisor decides to take a didactic approach, hoping that a switch in focus will achieve the same end (i.e., to increase Jill's knowledge and sensitivity to LGBT—lesbian, gay, bisexual, or transgendered—clients). Unfortunately, however, as shown in this next sequence, the supervisor's abrupt shift causes a rupture in the supervisory alliance.

Focus on the Therapeutic Relationship

Supervisor: Fair enough. So then, what is it going to be like for you if Rita is sexually attracted to you and that's why she keeps coming back?

Jill: I don't know. I'm not ready to deal with that yet.
shuts down

Supervisor: How so?

Jill: Well, I just don't feel comfortable considering that option.
thinks the topic is inappropriate

Supervisor: Sounds like it's feeling kind of scary to look at that option.
tries to be empathic, having recognized his own judgmental attitude

Jill: I guess. I'm just not ready to look at that further in supervision.
adamant

With Jill increasingly defensive, the supervisor digs in his heels, and both parties want to flee the interaction at this point. It should be noted that the process took a downturn, not because the supervisor is gay, but because he was reactive to Jill's narrow-mindedness (a dynamic in supervision not limited to issues of sexual orientation).

Trying to salvage the situation, the supervisor finds himself in deeper trouble. Angry with Jill for what he considers obstinacy or lack of professionalism, the supervisor forgets his role as teacher and facilitator, as shown in the next sequence.

Focus on Evaluation

Supervisor: Hmm. It seems we've stumbled on another conflict. On the one hand, we need to make sure that you are providing adequate services to clients, yet on the other, you are telling me that you're not ready to examine your approach to this client more closely.
challenges

Jill: I guess so. At least not in *this* way.

Supervisor: Okay, well, one of the things that I need to do is make sure that clients are not being harmed, and supervisees who may be acting on oppressive belief systems fall under this realm. At this time, I am going to require that you do a few things, and you really are not going to have an option about whether or not you do them. First, you need to more closely examine the literature on working with gay, lesbian, and bisexual clients. Be sure to include the ethical issues as well. I'm going to ask for a report on this knowledge due to me in the next two weeks. Second, you'll need to visit the LGBT Student Alliance on campus, and talk with a representative about the important attitudes and beliefs that therapists need for working effectively with LGBT clients. And third, I want a five page self-reflection paper on your countertransference in relation to this issue and how your counter-transference may affect your work with LGBT clients.

The supervisor decided to address Jill's knowledge base with the intent to enhance her self-awareness of LGBT issues. Although he does not delude himself that she will become a self-aware clinician through these exercises, he hopes that her engaging in them will begin a journey. However, as he speaks, he realizes that the impasse may already be too great. Jill is increasingly defensive, feeling that her religion has been insulted. Thus, the supervisor decides to focus more directly on their relationship, hoping to repair the ruptured alliance.

Focus on the Supervisory Alliance

Supervisor: I know this is asking a lot, and I've moved much more into the role of educator. However, you are going to have to attend to this work in order for both of us to be doing our jobs appropriately. I know you are going to have a number of reactions to this assignment, and I hope that we can address some of these reactions in our work together.
senses Jill's resistance

Jill: (*tensely silent*)

Supervisor: What's happening for you right now?
realizes he needs to attend to Jill's feelings

Jill: I'm just curious if I'm the only person in the practicum that has to do this assignment?
still defensive, feels singled out

Supervisor: Sounds like you feel this assignment is unfair.
reflects

Jill: Well, yeah. With all my coursework and I have exams coming up, I'm not sure I'll be able to get to what you're asking for.
justifies her conscious intent not to comply

Supervisor: I hear that this assignment has taken you back a bit. (*pauses*) And maybe, in some ways, it feels punishing?
takes a risk

Jill: (*softly*) Yeah.
feels somewhat understood

Supervisor: And really, the required tasks I'm assigning you are a way to ensure that your work with clients is professional and competent, but also I want to attend to your growth as a therapist.
justifies his actions

Jill: Feels like your concerns about getting me to do this assignment overrides your concerns about my growth as a therapist.
confronts

Supervisor: Well, that may be the case, and I'm sorry that, at the moment, you don't see that they both are intertwined.
tries to stay neutral

Jill: (*louder*) I'm also not happy about how you ask me to be open in supervision, and yet when I am, I get nailed for it.
angry

Supervisor: I understand. That's a conflict that's inherent in supervision, and perhaps there are better ways for me to deal with it in the context of this issue. However, this is the best I have to offer at the moment. While you are doing your assignments, though, I will also think about my own role in our disagreement, okay?
intellectualizes, trying to avoid a hostile confrontation, then thinks he should own his part in the impasse

Jill: Okay. (*leaves abruptly*)

In this unresolved event, when the supervisor failed to address Jill's feelings in a nonjudgmental way, she became increasingly resistant and hid behind her religious beliefs to justify her defensiveness and homophobia. Given Jill's anger, it is unlikely that she will respond well to the supervisor's assignment, the intent of which was to prevent Rita, or future clients, from harm by Jill's judgmental bias. Unless the alliance is repaired, Jill is likely to become even more closed off and disclose less in supervision (cf. Ladany et al., 1996).

The next challenge for both members of this dyad depends on how Jill responds to her assignment. If Jill remains unreceptive to this learning challenge, the supervisor will need to decide how to evaluate and deal with her problematic attitude toward him and her client. From this event alone, however, it is unclear whether Jill's defensiveness signals a lack of receptivity to any challenge of her belief system, or some unknown countertransferential process (toward her client or her supervisor) is going on, or whether her resistance was a unique response to the supervisor's poor handling of the present situation.

What might have prevented this unfortunate lack of resolution? With Jill so entrenched in her prejudicial beliefs, the impasse could have been unavoidable. On the other hand, a switch from an authoritative to a collaborative supervisory approach might have been effective in this instance, particularly if the relationship had been strong until this point. Specifically, when the supervisor first intuited Jill's defensiveness, he could have focused first on her discomfort with the topic and then about working with a woman client who seems attracted to her. The supervisor could have pointed out that, even if he was wrong about Rita, sexual attraction by a female client is likely to occur at some point in Jill's career. Moreover, if the supervisor had helped Jill explore her feelings toward Rita, even if she expressed anger and disgust, perhaps the subsequent intervention would have been more palatable for her.

As a teacher, the supervisor could have explained that people at either end of the sexual orientation continuum often have feelings similar to Jill's when they lack experience and when they don't understand the experience of people at the other end of the spectrum. Reminding Jill of her role as therapist may also have been helpful. If Jill could be gently reminded that a professional attitude toward any client demands unconditional acceptance, regard, and caring concern, she might be motivated to work through her personal feelings of repugnance for LGBT clients.

If these sequences were to diminish Jill's defensiveness and she honestly began to examine her position, she might then be asked to consider how these issues could be made easier for her. Optimally, she would, on her own, suggest various educational and experiential activities (reading, speaking with a minister sensitive to LGBT issues, talking with peers, and so forth) to further her own learning agenda in this area. A successful Resolution would then involve a collaborative, productive discussion of how Jill could proceed therapeutically with Rita while attempting to overcome her own fears and prejudice.

SPECIAL CONSIDERATIONS

These two case illustrations represent opposite ends of the continuum for successful versus unsuccessful event resolutions. In the first event, the process achieved some closure when the supervisee felt better able to manage her sexual feelings toward the client. In the second event, the process stalled before the sexual attraction issues were fully addressed.

Though it would be easy to explain the different outcomes of these events in terms of heterosexual versus gay or lesbian attraction or in terms of differences in the two supervisees' multicultural competence and self-awareness, several other factors are involved in working through sexual attraction in supervision. These factors include the quality and stage of the supervisory relationship, the supervisee's level of insight, and the supervisor's knowledge about and comfort with discussing sexual attraction issues. Because such a discussion can create uncomfortable feelings in both parties, the supervisory relationship must be secure, with sufficient trust for supervisees to work through their discomfort. They must also be psychologically sophisticated enough to understand the connections between their own subtle or unconscious behaviors (e.g., flirtatiousness), feelings (e.g., arousal, nervousness), thoughts (e.g., "forbidden" fantasies), and defense mechanisms (e.g., denial, sublimation, projection, intellectualization, reaction formation). Finally, supervisors must be astute enough to recognize sexual attraction when the indicators are subtle and to have worked through their own personal issues enough to feel comfortable raising the topic with the supervisee.

Supervisees With Chronic Interpersonal Problems

Supervisees with characterological difficulties create problems across the board in their training, and adding sexual attraction issues to the mix creates a situation ripe for trouble. Supervisees with boundary problems, in particular, are more likely to facilitate—consciously or unconsciously—their clients' attraction to them, and they tend to be far less able to explore and work through these issues effectively in supervision. Hence, it becomes imperative for the supervisor to consistently and respectfully evaluate the supervisee's boundaries across a variety of clinical and collegial situations (Ladany & Muse-Burke, 2001).

In many cases, sexual attraction may not be the first or only issue that requires questioning the supervisee about behavior. In the short run, some supervisees may improve with personal therapy as a supplement to supervision. In the long run, supervisees with boundaries so loose that they pose a threat to clients may need to be removed from practice situations altogether (see chap. 8 on problematic behavior).

Sexual Harassment by Clients

Some clients try to initiate a romantic involvement or sexual contact with their therapists, often as a defense against the therapeutic work, and some clients talk in an overly sexualized manner in hopes of arousing themselves or their therapists. Novice or entry-level supervisees are particularly susceptible to these overtures, possibly because clients sense their insecurity and vulnerability.

In these circumstances, supervisors need to monitor the therapy closely to be sure that their supervisees are neither traumatized nor drawn into the client's acting out. In extreme cases, it may be necessary to reassign the case to protect the supervisee and allow the client to be helped by someone more capable of redirecting the therapeutic work.

Dressing for Unsuccess

One of the more tricky issues in supervision is the supervisee's dress code. The standard for professional dress can vary culturally, regionally, and from one clinical site to another. Moreover, naive, young supervisees, particularly those who have never worked in a professional capacity, may dress as they would for a social occasion without recognizing the implications or inappropriateness of their choices.

Because dressing seductively can trigger a client's sexual fantasies, or as mentioned previously, dressing up can signal a supervisee's conscious or unconscious attraction for a client, discussing an appropriate dress code is often necessary. To forestall the supervisee being humiliated, we recommend a preventative approach, that is, the topic of professional dress norms should be part of the "getting to know you" discussion in supervision or in the introduction to the clinical setting. In raising this topic, however, supervisors need to be sensitive to cultural differences in fashion to avoid unintentionally offensive implications.

In male supervisor/female supervisee dyads in which both parties are heterosexual, the relational power dynamics are pronounced, and the female supervisee is especially vulnerable (Nelson & Holloway, 1990; see also chap. 7). Talking about dress in cross-gendered heterosexual supervisory dyads or in same-gendered gay or lesbian dyads tends to be particularly uncomfortable. In these situations, it is wise to enlist the aid of a colleague, perhaps the director of the clinic, but preferably someone of the same sex as the supervisee, to discuss appropriate dress. Sensitively handling this situation ensures that the supervisory relationship is not unduly threatened by the supervisee's shame or fear of having unwittingly enticed the supervisor.

Sexual Attraction in Supervision

Until now, we have been discussing sexual attraction only within the therapeutic relationship. It is altogether possible, and indeed probable, that attraction can come to the fore in supervision. Because good supervisory relationships are close and personal and dynamics involved in attraction are complex and multifaceted, it is not uncommon for supervisees to develop romantic feelings for their supervisors (Bartell & Rubin, 1990; Melincoff, 2001; Pope, Schover, & Levenson, 1980; Rodolfa, Rowen, Steier, Nicassio, & Gordon, 1994; Yarris & Allgeier, 1988).

In a survey of predoctoral interns (Rodolfa et al., 1994), 25% reported being physically attracted to their supervisors. In another study with open-ended interviews (Melincoff, 2001), participants reported their attraction to supervisors in terms of physical (e.g., "good body for his age"), personal (e.g., genuine, caring, nice), intellectual, and professional characteristics. For some participants, the supervisors reminded them of past or present romantic partners, or their attraction was part and parcel of their idealization of the supervisor. The attraction caused positive and negative reactions—becoming energized as well as feeling guilt and shame, and the attraction both facilitated and inhibited the supervision process. The alliance was strengthened, on the one hand, but supervisees felt more guarded around their supervisors on the other. To manage their sexual attraction, many supervisees in the sample talked with peers or a therapist about their feelings, but most tried to ignore their sexual feelings by avoiding the topic, focusing on clients, or forbidding themselves to fantasize. In other instances, supervisees acknowledged the sexual attraction within themselves, recognizing it as normal or attributing it to stressors in their personal lives. Typically, supervisees did not disclose their feelings for fear of damaging the supervisory relationship or because the feelings weren't intense enough to affect their work. A number of participants indicated that they would have disclosed their attraction had their supervisors asked, even though the discussion would have been uncomfortable.

On the other hand, when a supervisor is attracted to a supervisee, which can occur in the normal course of conducting supervision, the issue of power comes into play, even though the feelings may be due to countertransference or the realistic aspects of the relationship. Such an attraction is likely to engender both positive and negative feelings in the supervisor, at points, inhibiting, and at points, facilitating the process and outcome of supervision. Even more problematic, however, is the supervisor's attraction to the one of the supervisee's clients (Walker, 2003). Although virtually no literature on the topic exists (Ladany & Melincoff, 1999), it seems reasonable that if the supervisor is aware of and able to manage his or her reaction, discussing it could serve as a normalizing model for the supervisee, particularly if both find the same client attractive.

Because of the power differential, it is vitally important to differentiate sexual attraction from sexual contact (Pope et al., 1986), the former being a normal response to human interaction and the latter being an unethical response on the part of professionals toward clients or trainees. Surveys suggest that approximately 5% of supervisors have sexual relationships with their supervisees (Bartell & Rubin, 1990). Bartell and Rubin differentiated between supervisor harassment, involvement, and discrimination. Sexual harassment occurs when supervisors make sexual advances toward the supervisee, ranging from physical assaults to repeated verbal innuendoes and threats (APA, 2002; Somers, 1982). Sexual contact constitutes harassment when the contact is unwanted and not consensual. Consensual sexual involvement is not harassment but is nonetheless unethical. All too often, sexual involvement begins as consensual, but later, it is perceived as coercive and harmful (Glaser & Thorpe, 1986). Sexual discrimination occurs when students who are not sexually involved with a supervisor are denied the same access to opportunities as those who do engage in such relationships. In both situations, the potential for personal and professional harm is great.

So what should supervisors do if they find themselves attracted to a supervisee? Prior to entering into any supervisory relationship, supervisors should be aware of how their own attraction to others develops—do they "fall" for others at first sight, or do these feelings emerge gradually? What characteristics of others, both healthy and unhealthy, facilitate their attraction? Is it vulnerability or dependence that enhances their attraction, or is it self-confidence in the face of ambiguity that makes someone attractive? Supervisors should be particularly careful if they tend to be attracted to others who are dependent and less powerful than themselves.

A priori introspection can go a long way toward helping supervisors manage their sexual attraction when it emerges. However, even with insight and immediate self-awareness, an attraction experience may come along that does not fit the supervisor's personal template. In these instances, it is imperative to consult with colleagues, one's own supervisor or therapist, and always document all supervisory interactions.

CONCLUSION

The supervisees in Melincoff's (2001) study noted that sexual attraction in supervision was not discussed adequately, if at all, in their training programs. In fact, many participants had experienced or were aware of student–faculty relationships minimized or overlooked by other faculty. These findings underscore the recommendations that sexual attraction be discussed as a natural part of clinical training and that supervisors consult their colleagues when such feelings arise. Dialogues about attraction in supervision pose a number of obstacles, however, due to the diffuse boundaries between the appropriate and necessary discussion of attraction and the inappropriateness of sexual harassment. Even under conditions where the discussion focuses on "maintaining appropriate boundaries," consultation is essential to ensure that the supervisor is protected and managing responses professionally.

For an educational discussion on this topic to take place, both supervisee and supervisor should have a good capacity for insight, and resistance to self-reflection should be at a minimum. If the supervisor can own the uncomfortable feelings—reasonable given the context—such modeling can normalize the discussion of the supervisee's experiences. Moreover, the supervisor should consider if and how parallel processes (countertransference and transference) may be the origin of these reactions. The sexual attraction, even having been discussed, may remain far from worked through. If, after consultation, the attraction on either side interferes too much with the process of supervision, a switch in supervisors should be considered. It should go without saying, of course, that changing supervisors does not justify acting on sexual feelings, even when the feelings are mutual (see the American Psychological Association Code of Ethics, 2002).

In sum, sexual attraction in therapy and in supervision can and does occur, and it warrants close attention. In this chapter, we have only tapped some of the myriad sexual attraction situations that can become a focus in supervision. As with other critical events, it is important for supervisors to recognize the Markers, then attend to these difficult issues unflinchingly. Due to the very nature of the problem, the supervisor's knowledge of its complexity, self-understanding and awareness, flexibility, and advanced preparation are essential to effectively monitor and manage sexual attraction when it arises with supervisees.

7

REPAIRING GENDER-RELATED MISUNDERSTANDINGS AND MISSED UNDERSTANDINGS: IT'S NOT JUST "HE SAID, SHE SAID"

Nolite te bastardes carborundorum.
—Margaret Atwood, *The Handmaid's Tale*, 1986

Professionals rarely disagree that gender is a "sticky wicket," in both their personal and professional lives. The war of the sexes rages on as cacophonously as ever in the history of humankind, and gender issues abound in the literature on psychotherapy and supervision alike. A supervisory relationship is influenced not only by the supervisor's and supervisee's sex, but also by the gendered expectations each brings to the interaction and the sex and gender configurations of the therapeutic relationships discussed.

Gender-related impasses (Twohey & Volker, 1993) can wreak havoc on a supervisory relationship and hamper both the supervisee's learning and the clients' progress. In qualitative studies of negative supervisory experiences, the supervisors' unwillingness to bring up gender differences was a factor contributing to some supervisees' feelings of being unsupported and discounted (Nelson & Friedlander, 2001; Walker, Ladany, & Pate-Carolan, 2003). Hence, supervisors are well advised to attend to the obvious and the subtle manifestations of gender and gender role expectations, both in supervisory relationships and in the therapeutic relationships under discussion.

In an extensive review of studies comparing demographically matched to nonmatched psychotherapy dyads, Beutler and Clarkin (1990) concluded that the matched pairs were relatively more successful. Explaining this finding, Beutler and Clarkin posited that what clients want is the familiarity and empathy that such matches seemingly offer. It is reasonable to assume that supervisees also expect a sense of ease if they have same-sex supervisors. Regardless of demographic characteristics, however, what people really want in a relationship is to share similar attitudes and beliefs with their clinicians (Beutler & Clarkin, 1990).

In a supervision study, the match or mismatch of gender attitude exerted some influence on supervisory style (Rarick, 2000). Supervisors with more progressive attitudes about gender than their supervisees tended to be more task oriented than supervisors whose supervisees had equally liberal attitudes, suggesting that a didactic approach may help supervisees who need gender-related education. Again, a demographic match seems less important than other factors, and supervisors need awareness of their supervisees' specific developmental and attitudinal needs to meet them at their level.

Many theorists and researchers writing about multicultural issues in psychotherapy and supervision regard cross-gendered relationships as cross cultural (Ancis & Ladany, 2001; Hansen & Gama, 1996; Munson, 1997, 2002; Reid, 2002; see also chap. 3). Whether the difference between supervisor and supervisee is due to ethnicity, race, sexual orientation, social class, age, gender, or some combination of these or other variables, it has the potential to occlude the supervisor's vision about the supervisee's experience and vice versa. In other words, ignoring gender differences is similar to ignoring any other cultural difference.

In this chapter we review the literature on gender in supervision, but reading is only a first step in learning to make gender a safe topic for discussion in supervision. The key to facilitating honest, meaningful dialogue about cultural factors is to engage in such conversations with others outside of supervision. Receiving one's own supervision, as well as attending training, workshops, and conferences that address gender differences in professional relationships, can help supervisors target their own biases, areas of discomfort, and defensiveness on this affect-laden topic.

One difficulty that plagues gender discussions is the inevitable temptation to stereotype. Indeed, some attitudes and behaviors *are* more characteristic of one gender group than another, but it is important not to assume that any particular set of characteristics applies to a given individual. No client or supervisee wants to be seen as representative of a class, but rather, understood for who that individual is, gender and all. The dilemma of "seeing but not seeing" gender in all its facets is a difficult one, best handled through dialogue—repeatedly, if need be.

In a supervisory relationship's early phase, gender should be discussed regarding cultural similarities and differences (e.g., race, age, sexual orientation, etc.) between supervisor and supervisee. Initial discussions about gender are not intended to put the matter to rest, however. Such conversations merely invite supervisees to discuss multicultural issues as needed or desired and open the door for ongoing dialogue about interpersonal discomfort related to these issues.

In this chapter, we consider ways to repair misunderstandings that stem from traditional gender role expectations for both women and men. In our definition, a *misunderstanding* can either be a point of impasse arising from differing expectations for behavior or a *missed understanding* about how gender dynamics operate in relationships. We focus on two areas: (a) empowering female supervisees and (b) raising awareness of male gender role conflict, and we provide process models for approaching these tasks. In the first case illustration, a male supervisor and female supervisee repair a gender-related misunderstanding. In the second illustration, a supervisor helps his male supervisee with a "missed understanding" about vulnerability in relationships.

WOMEN AND POWER IN SUPERVISION

In a study of conversations on an Internet list (Wolfe, Wang, & Bergen, 1999), men seemed to enjoy the sparring that comes from a good argument, almost as a sport. Women, on the other hand, tended to avoid conflict in online conversations, either remaining silent or assuming a facilitative role. The author concluded that men enjoy the argument-alive competition, whereas women may prefer an altruistic style of interacting. In avoiding conflict, however, women deprive themselves of the power and influence that comes from making a persuasive argument (Wolfe et al., 1999). These findings support the theories of Gilligan, Jordan, Miller, Stiver, and others (Jordan, Kaplan, & Miller, 1991), who emphasize the importance of interpersonal connections for women and the observation (Miller, 1991) that women avoid taking a powerful position in discussions when they associate power with disconnection or rejection of others.

Leary (1957) proposed that human personality develops within a bidimensional field of power and affiliation, and that all interpersonal behaviors are located somewhere in the intersection of these two dimensions. Indeed, many scholars believe that power in clinical relationships interacts in a complex way with the affiliative aspects of human discourse (Carson, 1969; Kiesler, 1979; Strong, Hills, Kilmartin, & DeVries, 1988; Tracey, 1994). Writers from the Stone Center for the Study of Women at Wellesley College (cf., Jordan et al., 1991) maintain that women (in particular) develop optimally within systems of affiliation because, from childhood, women are socialized to view personal and interpersonal events in terms of connectedness.

Not surprisingly, the gender issue to receive the most attention by supervision theorists and researchers is relational power (Goodyear, 1990; Granello, Beamish, & Davis, 1997; Munson, 1987; Nelson, 1997; Nelson & Holloway, 1990, 1999; Robyak, Goodyear, & Prange, 1987). In brief, a natural power imbalance exists as a result of the supervisor's advanced standing with regard to the supervisee and is enhanced when the supervisor also serves as an evaluator of the supervisee's clinical work. This unavoidable imbalance of power may be mediated by the gender configuration of a supervision dyad. In most societies, males hold greater interpersonal power, or *agency,* than do females (Williams & Best, 1990). In the case of supervision, the male supervisor theoretically maintains a greater degree of power than any other player, whether the supervision dyad is cross or same gendered. Similarly, a male supervisee may command more power than a female supervisee in group interactions. A female supervisor may behave more deferentially toward male than female supervisees, and female supervisees may behave more deferentially than their male peers, particularly when they work with male supervisors (Nelson & Holloway, 1990; Granello, Beamish, & Davis, 1997).

Most early writers on gender issues in supervision focused on parity for female supervisees (Munson, 1987). To understand how parity is extended to—or withheld from—women in supervisory relationships, researchers became interested in how gender is reflected in clinical conversations, particularly with respect to the inherent power imbalance. Research suggests that supervisors tend to grant more power in session to male than to female supervisees (Nelson & Holloway, 1990) and that, over time, female supervisees tend to relinquish power to their supervisors (Granello, Beamish, & Davis, 1997), giving in to social role conditioning (Eagly, 1987) that requires women to be deferent. These findings echo those from research on psychotherapy, which has documented the greater use of power by male than female therapists, particularly with female clients (Cooke & Kipnis, 1986; Heatherington & Allen, 1984).

More recently, writers in the area of feminist supervision have been more explicit about how to both empower and educate. Supervision from a feminist perspective involves a number of behaviors on the part of the supervisor—analyzing the inherent power imbalance in supervision and in psychotherapy, attending to gender and other multicultural variables in both supervision and therapy relationships, engaging the supervisee in understanding the social construction of gender and gender roles, and actively granting power to the supervisee in session (Brown, 1990; Brown & Brodsky, 1992; Nelson, 1997; Porter & Vasquez, 1997; Szymanski, 2003).

Gender undoubtedly exerts influence on the expression of power in the supervisory process and may either increase or mitigate the inherent power differential. Why is this phenomenon important? One could state that people simply "talk that way" and that supervision is just another form of conversation. From a feminist perspective, however, one could argue that in clinical relationships we need to change the nature of our interactions to be as respectful as possible to our clinical charges. Taking a feminist perspective on any human discourse requires leveling the playing field so that women can exercise a shared degree of power with men.

From an interpersonal perspective, this leveling involves appropriate self-disclosure, as well as avoiding highly directive strategies in clinical relationships. Likewise, through affiliation, supervisors can use their role to empower their female supervisees (Holloway, 1995; Miller, 1991; Nelson, 1997; Nelson & Holloway, 1999). Empowering affiliative behaviors in supervision can include assuming a collegial posture; guiding from a knowledgeable, yet tentative stance; listening actively to a supervisee's concerns; and conveying openness to learn from the supervisee (Nelson, 1997). In a scenario that follows, we will demonstrate a male supervisor's use of affiliative behaviors to work through a gender-related "missed understanding" between himself and a female supervisee.

PROCESS MODEL FOR EMPOWERING FEMALE SUPERVISEES

Marker

In a supervisor–supervisee–client triad, there are numerous possible gender configurations. Supervisor and supervisee may both be female, whereas the client is male. Perhaps more in this circumstance than any other, Markers of the supervisee's difficulty may be explicit comments like, "Maybe this is a male thing, but I just don't understand why my client . . ." or "This is the first time I've worked in an all-male environment," which are direct requests for help in a particular area. These kinds of Markers suggest a missed understanding (i.e., the need for knowledge about issues that seem foreign to the supervisee).

More difficult to recognize are Markers of "misunderstanding" caused by "missed understandings" in cross-gendered therapy or supervisory relationships. A lack of awareness of gender politics is signaled, for example, when a female supervisee fails to recognize her diminished power in relation to a male client, or when a male supervisor is surprised that his comments are seen as sexist by his female supervisees.

Markers that emerge in ongoing interactions can often be identified by linguistic, paralinguistic, or nonverbal behaviors. Observing a female supervisee's work with a male client, for example, the supervisor might notice several qualifiers and tag questions, suggesting deference (e.g., "I'm pretty much worried that you may be . . . , don't you think?"). Of course, the more difficult Markers to spot are those related to gender misunderstandings within supervision itself. Although some supervisees may assert discomfort, it is often the supervisor who is the first to notice and acknowledge a gender-related issue. As one example, a supervisee may become less engaged in the conversation over time. Or a palpable tension might be felt in the interaction. However, because the initial phase of any relationship is typically more polite and less marked by risk taking or confrontation, gender Markers—or Markers of any cultural difference—that occur then tend to be less conflictual than later conversations.

Task Environment and Resolution

When a gender misunderstanding is identified in the therapy relationship, the Task Environment can include some or all of the following sequences: *exploration of feelings, focus on the therapeutic relationship, assess knowledge (gender role socialization)*, and *focus on self-efficacy*. If, however, the supervisory relationship is the site of the difficulty, the sequences are also likely to include a *focus on the supervisory alliance* and a *focus on evaluation*. The event that follows depicts a gender pairing with some of the more common and difficult challenges, a female supervisee with a male client and a male supervisor. In this case, the Task Environment proceeds in a back-and-forth movement between an exploration of feelings and a focus on the supervisory alliance, followed by a focus on evaluation.

When one or both parties becomes aware of a misunderstanding Marker in their interaction, it is first necessary to focus on the relationship to reestablish the connection and clarify the source of discomfort. The discomfort may be related to something going on that is seen as inconsistent with previously established and agreed-on goals and tasks, or due to the power imbalance in supervision, or to some combination of these phenomena. An exploration of feelings by both supervisee and supervisor can help clarify the gender-related concern and build connections through awareness.

As in therapy, exploring feelings about a sticking point in the supervisory relationship involves uncovering perceptions and the implied and inferred meanings that underlie the emotional reactions being experienced. For example, a supervisee who fears disclosing a failure of some sort to her male supervisor may expect harsh criticism, resulting in a loss of self-esteem and further loss of relational power. Knowing what the supervisee's reactions mean to her is critical for the supervisor to challenge erroneous assumptions about his intentions or adopt a different interactional posture that better honors her needs for safety and power.

In some cases, exploring feelings in the here and now can lead to a discussion of the supervisee's transference to the supervisor, if this dynamic is operative and if the relationship is safe enough to handle such a frank discussion. The supervisee may be experiencing a gender-related transference from another relationship with an authority figure or with an intimate partner, or the transference may be based in gender-related socialization.

Resolution

A successful event involves resolving the specific gender-related misunderstanding at hand, not "resolving" the supervisee's personal issues related to gender. In discussing misunderstandings in the therapy relationship *not* mirrored in the supervisory relationship, the *Resolution* is a straightforward indication that the supervisee has integrated what's been learned and can apply it to advantage with a client. When the misunderstanding originates or carries into the supervisory relationship, however, the Resolution is configured differently. No impasse or conflict—gender based or otherwise—can be considered resolved until supervisor and supervisee have discussed how to recognize and manage similar situations when they arise in the future. Thus, to successfully conclude a misunderstanding in supervision, it is necessary to revisit the original point of concern and address the supervisee's comfort level in continuing the relationship with this new awareness.

A SUCCESSFULLY RESOLVED GENDER-RELATED EMPOWERMENT EVENT

In the following illustration, the client, Eli, is a 12-year-old boy who was referred by his school and parents for being truant on several occasions and breaking numerous school rules, including selling cigarettes to his classmates on school grounds. Eli had seen the therapist, Lisa, for several sessions when this event took place. Lisa is a 32-year-old former middle school teacher, working with a 27-year-old male supervisor in an advanced practicum at a school-based mental health clinic.

Earlier in the week, the supervisor had observed a live family session with the therapist, Eli, and his mother through closed-circuit television. Lisa questioned the boy about whether he understood the affect of his behavior on his mother. The supervisor, noting Lisa's critical tone, decided that in the next supervision session, he would ask Lisa to talk about her experiences with the family.

At this point, the supervisor is not aware of a gender-related problem. Rather, he sees Lisa's problem as either countertransference or a skill difficulty (see chap. 2), and his intention is to help her notice the authoritarian "teacher" attitude in her approach to Eli. What begins as a skill difficulty event, however, evolves into a gender-related misunderstanding.

Marker

Supervisor: How did you feel about the session with Eli and his mom? *deliberately vague, to see where Lisa will take her answer*

Lisa: I was doing a second intake session with them on Monday, and she told me that he has been truant several times, but the thing that really bothers her right now is that he has been selling cigarettes to kids on the school grounds. He just seems out of control and very disrespectful of her. She works really hard to put food on the table and he can see that she's hurting, and he does these things anyway. And he's going to fail if he keeps this up, and it just seems like a real waste. Then when I'm in there alone with him, I feel like asking him why he doesn't understand that this is hurting her and him too. I wanted to, but didn't.
strictly cognitive, avoids discussing her feelings

Supervisor: Actually, I saw part of the family session and was wondering what you were feeling there as you were talking about his impact on his mother.
redirects Lisa to her feelings with a more specific question

Lisa: (*quickly*) Well, if you mean did I have some feelings about what he was doing to his mother, of course I did. She seemed to be at a loss about what to do with him.
recognizing that the supervisor has an "agenda," becomes defensive

In her defensiveness, the supervisee has given a clue that she is feeling criticized by her supervisor. At this point, although the source of her discomfort is unclear, her defensive tone alerts the supervisor to her distress. It is still early in the session, and the supervisor decides that, rather than focusing on Lisa's discomfort, he will try to put her at ease by focusing on the case. As shown below, his attempt to work toward comfort meets with little success.

Supervisor: Yeah. She did. I sensed, too, that you were kind of at a loss as well, and that you were feeling, and still may feel, frustrated with him.
reflects Lisa's feelings

Lisa: Oh, for sure! He is a bright kid, and he is just wasting his time on these self-destructive behaviors when he could be using that intelligence in a productive way. It's hard to watch.
feeling understood, is willing to acknowledge her own frustration

Supervisor: It sure is. I wonder, too, if you were feeling kind of like his mother seems to feel.
leading

Lisa: It may also be because of my having been a teacher. I'm so used to needing to crack down on the kids, and I know I need to get the "teacher" out of my style, but it's hard in this case.
understands the supervisor's point and has the same concern herself

Supervisor: I know it. It's tough. I know you have his best interests at heart, and you are learning to be his therapist rather than his teacher. So it will require thinking differently about him. Maybe we could try to understand more about what is driving him. I wonder if what he's experiencing has anything to do with his being an adolescent. Do you know what I mean? What do you understand about adolescent guys?
reassuring, validates Lisa's experience and then wonders whether Lisa's problem is a lack of knowledge

Lisa: Are you asking what I know about male adolescents?
unclear about the supervisor's motives

Supervisor: Sure. Let's talk about that—what types of behaviors can you expect to see from guys in that age group?

Lisa: Well, of course you'll see experimentation and testing of authorities and these kinds of things. Is that what you're getting at?
defensive, feels interrogated

The topic of Lisa's "teacher style" is not a new one, and she readily acknowledged a problem in this area. The supervisor, seeing a Marker for a "missed understanding" (i.e., Lisa's lack of knowledge about adolescent boys) moved their interaction in that direction. Although he sensed Lisa's defensiveness and wanted to make the process more comfortable for her, he was unaware that she was feeling disempowered, both in her status as a supervisee and as a woman being supervised by a younger man.

At this point, the missed understanding is evolving into a misunderstanding. Lisa has no intention of acknowledging her discomfort, however, for fear of a confrontation that she is certain she will lose. Still unaware of the power issue between them, the supervisor decides to change tactics and inquire about Lisa's obvious discomfort in their current interaction.

Exploration of Feelings *and* Focus on the Supervisory Alliance

Supervisor: Sure. Yeah. You know, I was thinking we could talk about the developmental pieces that factor into Eli's behavior. But, you're obviously uncomfortable right now with where we are going.
tries to be transparent

Lisa: Well, I feel like I'm being quizzed. I mean, I haven't read up on adolescent psychology lately, so I can't give you statistics or something like that.
open about her experience of what's taking place

Supervisor: Wow! OK. I'm not trying to quiz you at all. I was trying to provide an opportunity for us to talk about how we can understand Eli's behavior.
taken aback, clarifies his intent

Lisa: Well, I feel like you *are* quizzing me. (*stops making eye contact*)
feeling mistrust

Supervisor: OK. That's important. Something I did is not working for you. Is there a way we can understand what that is?
validates, still unaware of the gender issue between them

Although the supervisor does not understand what he did to result in Lisa's feeling quizzed, he is willing to abandon his previous intention to assess her knowledge and skills in working with adolescent boys. Respecting Lisa's experience, he asks her to help him understand his contribution to her discomfort. As discussed in other chapters, focusing explicitly on the source of tension in the relationship is a critical first step toward resolving any misunderstanding.

As shown in the next sequence, the supervisor's willingness to back off from his agenda and explore Lisa's unease gives her the space to explain how overpowered she feels, albeit not that explicitly.

Lisa: I am really uncomfortable. I'm just not sure what it's about. I need to take a minute.
takes a risk

Supervisor: OK.
waits, confused

Lisa: (*long pause*) I just feel stuck. I feel like I'm being examined.

Supervisor: OK. So, when I asked you the question about male adolescents, you felt examined?
wants to clarify his contribution to Lisa's discomfort

Lisa: Yes. I felt like you were testing me to see if I knew enough to be doing this work with adolescents, and I felt like you already disapproved of what I *do* know.
explains her feeling of disempowerment

Supervisor: That's a lot of disapproval on my part, alright! That must feel lousy.
acknowledges Lisa's emotional experience

Lisa: Oh, I don't really think you disapprove that much. I don't know if you do or not. Some of this is me, my earlier experience. I knew when we started this that it was going to be a stretch for me to work with a male supervisor. I knew I needed to, but it's just hard for me working with men. It really is.
labels her discomfort in working with men

At last, the supervisor realizes the gender-related misunderstanding that is threatening the supervisory alliance. Continuing a focus on their relationship, he allows Lisa to explore her immediate thoughts and feelings. Once he gives her the lead, she describes her experience, with a dual focus on their work together and on her transference toward him. As evident in the next excerpt, the supervisee's responses were only partially related to the supervisor's behavior. His willingness to move toward connection with her and to process their relational impasse allows her to gradually explore her transferential reaction.

Supervisor: Can you tell me more about what is hard for you?
open, offers Lisa the lead

Lisa: I just, I just . . . My father is an extremely critical and demanding man. I could never do enough or be enough to make him happy, and I just feel so uncomfortable around male authority figures. And I know I told you at the beginning that I wasn't going to have a problem with it, but I am. I was just thinking that I know it's good for me to do this because it's something I need to get over, and I thought I needed to work with a male, so I went along with it. But it's hard.
discloses her transference, takes a risk

Supervisor: I can see that. It seems like an incredible struggle for you.
stays with Lisa's immediate feelings

Lisa: Yes.

Supervisor: So, here we are, and I'm a male authority figure, and you're afraid that I might be critical and difficult, too?
seeks to understand Lisa's experience with him

Lisa: Yes. I'm sorry. I'm just so bad at this. I can't seem to get used to working with men and this may just be me and my problem that I need to get on top of, so this is a good opportunity. It really is.
blames herself

Supervisor: Whoa. I'm hearing how hard this really is for you. And you seem to be taking responsibility for this whole thing yourself. You know, I bet I said or did something in this conversation that I could have said or done so that you would be less uncomfortable about being with me.
suggests that he also needs to take responsibility for their misunderstanding

Lisa: Well, it *is* mostly me. I do this a lot. I just can't seem to get on top of it.
embarrassed

Supervisor: Well, as you said, you would like to work on it, and I am willing to work on it with you. So I'm wondering how I can make this easier for you. What is it about my style that most reminds you of your father?
wants to help Lisa understand her transference reaction

Lisa: It just that I felt you were being critical of me back there, like you sensed I was doing something wrong and didn't tell me. Like you were just being silently disapproving. Then I felt challenged when you asked me what I knew about adolescent boys, like you had some things you wanted me to say but you weren't going to let me know what they were, so you were going to set me up to fail.
open

Supervisor: It felt like a trap.
reflects, using a metaphor to create meaning

Lisa: Yes. And that is what my father used to do—quiz me and criticize me for not measuring up.

Supervisor: Oh, what a bind that must have felt like for you! A real no-win. I'm sorry you felt that. I didn't mean to be setting you up. To be perfectly honest, though, I was noticing that you seemed pretty upset with Eli, and I was wondering where that was coming from. Now that I think about it, I think I was aware on some level of your sensitivity to criticism, so maybe I was trying to avoid seeming critical by asking the question about boys. Looks like I didn't succeed.
wanting to be transparent to empower her, labels his countertransference

Lisa: So you are saying that you *were* feeling critical.
interprets his remark as criticism

The supervisor, wanting to be as open as possible to alleviate the tension and work through the misunderstanding, is surprised that despite his transcparence, Lisa still sees him as critical. To ground this occurrence in the supervision context, he addresses the unavoidable aspect of evaluation and his authoritative role in the relationship.

Supervisor: I don't recall feeling critical in the sense that I thought you were doing a poor job. Actually, I was feeling like a supervisor, seeing areas of strength as well as growth edges. That is part of what I feel I need to be doing here—to examine those two things. So in that sense, I may have been being critical—in the sense that it is my job to help you grow by giving you constructive feedback. I'm getting, though, that you may associate constructive feedback with some hurtful criticism you've received in the past.

Lisa: Yes. And I'm just afraid of men because they seem so critical so much of the time, and it's so hard to imagine that they really respect me, you know?
more open

Supervisor: It's hard to distinguish what might be useful feedback from a kind of general, I don't know, disdain maybe, coming from men?
wants to clarify her personal dynamics

Lisa: Yes. That's exactly it. Disdain.

Supervisor: Ouch. I am not a woman, but I know that it's possible to have experienced some incredible disrespect from men *and* boys in your life. I'm sorry that's happened to you.

Lisa: Thank you. (*cries softly*)

Supervisor: (*silent*)

In a very clinical moment, the supervisor addressed the gender difference directly and clarified the distinction between his own intentions and the supervisee's experiences with other male figures. The supervisor's success in empathizing with Lisa's feelings of oppression is evident in both her expression of gratitude and her tears. In an intimate moment between them, the supervisor allows Lisa to stay with her feelings of sadness before moving forward. The silence also allows the supervisee to digest the corrective experience with a male supervisor who, without becoming defensive, withdrawing, or critical, allowed her to express her fears about him and men in general. Although the supervisor could now take the process into a more therapeutic discussion of Lisa's past treatment at the hands of men, doing so would likely make her feel more vulnerable and disempowered. If, however, she moved the conversation in that direction herself, the supervisor would follow.

Lisa: I feel better.

Supervisor: (*smiles*) I'm glad.

Lisa: I can see that you are trying to do the best you can for me, and I want to try to take the feedback without imagining that you are criticizing my whole person.

Supervisor: I'll try to be as gentle as I can, but as honest as I can, too.
expresses commitment to their alliance

Lisa: OK.

Supervisor: I'm beginning to understand the source of your sensitivity, and I want to honor that while helping you to have a useful supervision experience. How could I have handled the situation in a way that would have been more comfortable for you?
invites a more collaborative atmosphere

Lisa: I don't know. But I felt like you expected me to recite specific things about adolescent boys, and it just felt weird.

Supervisor: So when I asked you that, you felt like I expected a certain answer.
clarifies

Lisa: Yup. Exactly. I don't like to be questioned for some reason. You know, it would have been okay to just to ask me what I was feeling.
owns her part of the rupture and offers a suggestion

Supervisor: Aargh. (*grins*) That's a question too. What should I do?
more comfortable, goes "one down"

Lisa: Oh no! Oh my God, I just put you in a bind. (*laughs*) Boy, I must be some confusing case to work with!
can now take an observing perspective on the process but puts herself down

Supervisor: (*smiles*) Hey, you aren't either. We're here to try to find words to understand things, to understand each other. So, OK. You're comfortable with some kinds of questions but not others.
notices the put down, normalizes Lisa's experience and clarifies

Lisa: I guess that's true! I don't like to be quizzed, but I like to be invited to talk.
expresses her needs directly

Supervisor: I'm getting it. So no more "what do you know about" kinds of questions.

Lisa: Yeah. Like if you were wanting to conceptualize about Eli, you could have just asked me what I thought was going on for him or something like that.
takes a risk

Supervisor: That wouldn't have seemed liked it was coming from a critical place.
reflects

Lisa: No. Definitely not. Because I think he is trying to express some real anger toward something or somebody but he just keeps doing self-destructive things to express it.
wants to demonstrate that she does understand her client

Lisa moved the focus back to the therapy relationship, feeling empowered because she recognized her supervisor's honest attempts to put her at ease and not overpower her. The supervisor takes this cue to return to his original concern, Lisa's work with Eli.

Focus on Evaluation

Supervisor: OK. Yeah. I think you're right. Can I give you a little constructive feedback then? Would that be okay today? Or would you like to wait until next session?
asks permission before redirecting

Lisa: Sure. I feel better. I still feel like you are in the driver's seat, which is hard, but I feel like you understand more about me and what I need. Go ahead! (*ducks and smiles*)

Supervisor: OK. It's just that it seemed to me, listening to the tape, that you felt like you were taking sides with mom, as a teacher might do. Do you think there is some validity to that?
more tentative than previously

Lisa: Yes. Absolutely. I'm still trying to remember that I'm a therapist and no longer a teacher and that it's really OK for me to support kids who act out. I know it sounds dumb, but that's what I'm dealing with.
wants to show her competence but is deferential

Supervisor: It's not dumb at all; it's normal for former teachers to go through this transition when they are learning to do therapy.
supportive, challenging her deference

Lisa: Yeah? Cool. Because that's what's up with me for sure. I'm working on giving myself permission to just back him.

Supervisor: Yeah. Good. It's really OK to do that. I know it's hard right now, but you'll lean into it.
expresses confidence in her

Lisa: Yeah.

Resolution

Supervisor: Hey, we're out of time, but I just want to add that if more stuff comes up about me being a guy, I'm open to processing it.

Lisa: It's very scary, but I think I'd like to try.
honest

Supervisor: OK. Are you willing to tell me the next time you feel uncomfortable with something?

Lisa: I'll try.

Supervisor: Good. Because I'd want to be helpful with that, and I want to know what I can do to make this process more positive for you.
reiterates his commitment to her

Lisa: OK. Thanks.

In this case, an interesting complexity was age—the female supervisee was older than the male supervisor. Possibly feeling intimidated by the age difference, it took the supervisor a while to recognize Lisa's gender-based discomfort. Once he did notice it, however, he moved to find its source in their relationship. Continuing to focus on her discomfort, the supervisor helped Lisa identify the gender-related personal and interpersonal issues contributing to her anxiety. In other words, he assumed a personal, affiliative stance to hear her out. He did not argue. Rather, he listened, empathized, and inquired how he might adjust his style to help Lisa's comfort level in their work together.

Perhaps the greatest power imbalance in supervision is between a male supervisor and a female supervisee. The power of the male supervisor derives from two sources, his gender and his status as supervisor. As shown in the preceding example, for some female supervisees, this dynamic can prove extremely daunting.

Of course, female supervisors also need awareness when gender-related misunderstandings arise with their female supervisees. Regardless of the supervisor's sex, when problems occur, affiliative strategies should be used to invite female supervisees to assume power in supervision (Holloway, 1995; Nelson, 1997). In other words, by approaching supervisees' feelings as well as their cognitions, and by expressing understanding about their interpersonal experiences, supervisors can help women find their voices and feel recognized and empowered.

Specifically addressing a female supervisee's feelings of intimidation or powerlessness in relation to himself or to male clients, implies that the male supervisor not only understands gender-based dynamics but also does not fault her for deferential behavior. It can be daunting for some male supervisors to enter into a female supervisee's affective world and join her as she addresses her gender-related fears. Gender role expectations based on what Brooks (1998) called the *male chorus* (p. 104), or internalized traditional male role expectations, may interfere with this recommendation. That is, some male supervisors may reluctantly engage in an intimate conversation with a supervisee or may not be receptive to her feedback about his behavior. A discussion of male gender role conflict (O'Neil, 1981) and its potential influence on the supervisory process is necessary to understand the basis for such reluctance.

MALE GENDER ROLE CONFLICT

The concepts *gender role conflict* (O'Neil, 1981) or *gender role strain* (Pleck, 1981) refer to a state of anxiety reflecting a disconnection between culturally determined male role expectations and the intimacy demands of friendship, marriage, family, and work (O'Neill, Good, & Holmes, 1995).

Restrictive emotionality, a primary characteristic of male gender role conflict, is associated with some men's dissatisfaction with marital and family relationships (Campbell & Snow, 1992) and with health risks related to anger and anxiety (Eisler, Skidmore, & Ward, 1988). Both male gender role conflict and restrictive emotionality occur across cultures, although African American and Hispanic/Latino men tend to report these difficulties to a greater degree than do European American men (Levant et al., 2003).

This area's authors (Levant, 1995; Pollack, 1995) emphasize the intense dilemma many men face between wanting intimacy and fearing the exposure and vulnerability that accompany intimate contact. There is, indeed, a powerful injunction on boys to limit their feelings and become stoic in the face of adversity (Levant, 1995; Pollack, 1995).

Pollack (1998) used the term *boy code* to refer to the culturally determined rules that govern masculine behavior. According to the boy code, men are expected to be independent, self-guiding, nonreliant, and unemotional. A recent episode of *This American Life* on National Public Radio featured the story of a gay man who tried to make it in the straight world by pledging a college fraternity. In the episode, he describes "coming out" to the fraternity brothers. Although shocked, they supported him, but expressed respect for his having managed his pain on his own, without "leaning" on anyone else. In other words, the fraternity, albeit enlightened about the inevitability of discovering a gay presence within its ranks, had yet to become aware of the powerful influence of the boy code. Although able to summon some acceptance for a gay man, the fraternity nonetheless communicated the expectation that, gay or not, he remain true to masculine cultural injunctions to avoid intimacy and be tough.

Both psychotherapy and supervision emphasize a level of intimacy and expression of emotion that can be challenging for men. Socialization does not typically prepare young males to engage in discussions about relationships and feelings (Fivush, 1989; Levant, 1995). For these reasons, many male therapists in training reared with a strict boy code experience a profound double bind. Many boys grow up believing that they must present an image of competence and that expressing feelings and displaying of vulnerability indicate emotional instability. However, in professional training they learn that these types of expressions are required for competent functioning as a psychotherapist. Thus, clinical situations can threaten men in two ways—by requiring them to identify and express feelings and by requiring them to engage in a process that makes him feel incompetent (Wester & Vogel, 2002).

This dilemma can create a profound sense of dissonance for the developing male therapist. Good supervision will assist him to navigate these difficult waters. Working with male supervisees requires an awareness of just how vulnerable they may feel with a powerful other and patience about their level of readiness to express emotion. Male supervisees who are not familiar with the theory and research on gender role conflict may benefit from it, and discussions about their own socialization as men and personal experiences with intimacy expression can also be helpful.

For some men, approaching feelings too rapidly can backfire and threaten the early supervisory alliance (Wester & Vogel, 2002). It may be tempting to avoid personal discussions in supervision, focusing only on client problems (Sells, Goodyear, Lichtenberg, & Polkinghorne, 1997; Wester & Vogel, 2002). Just as therapists need to allow male clients some leeway to speak in terms of thoughts, rather than feelings, especially in the early phases of treatment (Levant, 1995), supervisors should offer the same grace period to male supervisees still developing the full range of their therapeutic skills.

Misunderstandings can develop, however, when a supervisee is pushed beyond his limits, with no awareness of why he feels uncomfortable in the supervisory process. If the supervisor is female, a misunderstanding can occur if she fails to recognize that her male supervisee needs extra time to allow his emotional responses to emerge in both therapy and supervision. If the supervisor is male, he may need to make a special effort to communicate to the supervisee that it is desirable and appropriate for two men to sit together discussing feelings and sensitive topics.

PROCESS MODEL FOR RAISING AWARENESS OF MALE GENDER ROLE CONFLICT

Marker

By its very nature, gender role conflict tends to be out of awareness. Consequently, male supervisees are unlikely to explicitly ask for help with this problem. Rather, a misunderstanding can occur when the supervisee is unaware that gender role conflict is operative. In therapy, Markers can appear when a client seems frustrated by the supervisee's notable lack of attention to her feelings. In supervision, Markers related to this problem can appear when the supervisor tries to focus on the supervisee's experience and he responds with a singular emphasis on the client, the client's difficulties, or what can be done to assist the client.

Allied to the masculine role of problem solver/change agent is the need to avoid experiencing powerlessness or helplessness. Many male supervisees have a tremendous fear of not measuring up to the supervisor's expectations for producing and achieving timely, tangible results with their clients. Markers signaling fear include a reluctance to explore areas of weakness, focusing on goals for supervision, or an intense reaction to constructive criticism work. In extreme situations, what begins as a gender role conflict can result in a full-blown crisis of confidence (see chap. 8).

Task Environment and Resolution

Depending on the unique features of the incident, the Task Environment in this event can include some or all of the following interactional sequences: exploration of feelings, focus on the supervisory alliance, attends to the parallel process, normalizing experience, focus on the therapy relationship, focus on skill, and focus on multicultural awareness. A deft supervisor can help a supervisee move away from the confining male role by first trying to understand the supervisee's unique definition of his role as helper. Exploring supervisees' thoughts and feelings, supervisors help supervisees with performance worries manage their fears and try on new and disconcerting therapeutic roles. Exploring feelings with a supervisee struggling with gender role conflict can involve some tinkering, however. Trial and error may be needed to discover how to discuss feelings in a way that fits. The supervisor may use a creative approach, bringing levity to the discussion through jokes, metaphor, or analogy.

With the level of comfort reestablished, the supervisor may elect to focus on the here-and-now relationship, repairing the misunderstanding through an illustration of the importance of feelings in moving through an impasse. In so doing, the supervisor can explain the parallel process, because—as shown in the following illustration—feeling stuck with a client lends itself well to a conversation about being stalemated in supervision. Not only is the parallel process around "stuckness" simple to understand, but also discussing "feeling stuck" can be far less threatening than discussing other feelings, such as sexual attraction, dependence, incompetence, or anger.

Once the supervisee's feelings are evident, the supervisor can label and discuss the concept of gender role conflict and how it might hamper his therapeutic style. The power of naming an experiential phenomenon can result in a profound normalizing of experience, a natural outcome of this type of discussion. The supervisee becomes aware that he is not alone and that there are indeed words to describe his internal experience.

Next, with a return in focus to the therapeutic relationship, the supervisee's attention can be drawn to his behavioral limitations with clients. Understanding the basis for his restricted therapeutic repertoire, the supervisee begins to conceptualize his clients differently and recognize just how much more there is to understand about them—if only he can relax and feel less pressured to be a change agent.

In the Resolution phase of a gender role conflict event, the repaired misunderstanding (or missed understanding) is evident by the supervisee's greater awareness of how gender influences his work in supervision as well as with his clients, male and female. Again, "resolution" does not mean resolution of the gender role conflict per se, but rather of the specific incident occasioned by the gender role conflict. Down the road, this new understanding should lead to a more flexible and balanced approach to therapy and supervision, as well as personal growth and development.

A SUCCESSFULLY RESOLVED GENDER ROLE CONFLICT EVENT

The following illustration involves Bruce, a 28-year-old beginning practicum student in a county mental health agency, and his 40-year-old male supervisor, psychoanalytically trained, who is on the faculty at a local university. The supervisee is struggling to connect with his male client, Derek, who feels unable to extricate himself from a painful, unhealthy relationship with a woman.

The supervisor is aware that Bruce himself feels stuck and wants to help him experience his feelings of inertia without pushing him too hard. When he realizes that Bruce's stuck feelings mirror those of the client, the supervisor wants to avoid engaging in a parallel process in which he winds up feeling stuck as well. Thus, the supervisor's goal is to stop the process by helping Bruce see his own participation in it. The challenge, however, is to find a way to help Bruce with what he suspects may be Bruce's expectation to perform at a high level without expressing feelings of doubt and uncertainty.

The Marker of a gender-related "missed understanding" unfolds as the supervisee continues to focus exclusively on the client and his attempts to help. In this initial sequence, the supervisor encounters Bruce's frustration with not being able to move his client forward, as well as Bruce's reluctance to address his own emotional state. The supervisor knows that intimacy between men sometimes can be challenging. Moreover, he believes that an individual's resistance needs to be respected as his best effort to protect self-worth. For these reasons, the supervisor refrains from pushing Bruce to express feelings.

Marker

Bruce: I just don't know how to move Derek though. I know there's something I need to do to move him out of this, but I don't know what it would be. I've tried everything, it seems.
implies frustration without labeling it

Supervisor: Tell me more about what's been going on.
[*extended discussion about what's been occurring in the therapy with Derek*]

* * *

Supervisor: So, you seem kind of stuck, trying to figure out how to move him.
reflects Bruce's feelings

Bruce: Yeah, that's for sure. I guess I'm not helping him. (*quickly*) We've tried brainstorming what his life would look like if he told her not to call him. We've

tried talking about his getting another job where he wouldn't have to see her at work. We've tried teaching him to be assertive with her about his needs, which she ignores. He just needs to get out of that relationship!
gets somewhat agitated

Supervisor: So, to you, helping him would be to get him out of this mess as soon as possible.
summarizes Bruce's view of his role

Bruce: Yeah. And I know that's not always possible, but I don't know. We've been at this for several weeks now. I get tired of listening to it.

Supervisor: Sounds frustrating.
labels the feeling

Bruce: I'm tired of listening to him! He needs to MOVE, man!
begins experiencing his feelings more immediately

The Marker is complete, with the supervisor realizing that Bruce clearly experiences a number of feelings, but it is hard for him to acknowledge them. The supervisor also sees that, in defining his role as Derek's liberator, Bruce trapped himself in a set of expectations in which he needs to be the change agent.

The supervisor knows that he needs to spend time helping Bruce examine his role with regard to the client. This examination takes time and attention to feelings, motivations, and fears, which the supervisor expects to be related to Bruce's gender role expectations for himself. The supervisor wants to move gingerly, however, and initiates the Task Environment by testing how close Bruce can get to discuss his feelings in relation to what's happening in the therapy.

Exploration of Feelings *and* Focus on the Therapeutic Relationship

Supervisor: So, you're just kind of stuck trying to figure a way to help him out of this, and you're not sure how to get yourself out of your own feelings of inertia.
ties the supervisee's feelings to the client's dilemma

Bruce: Yeah. That pretty much sums it up. I feel like I'm not being helpful to him.

Supervisor: Well, you are here, talking to me about this, and in that sense, you are working to be helpful to him. Let's see how we can work with this.
reassures and normalizes the supervisee's experience

Bruce: OK. It seems like a challenge.
implies self-doubt

Supervisor: I think it might be helpful to examine your own experience as you work with him so that maybe we can help you too. I sense you feel kind of stuck yourself, stymied, in your relationship with him, like you're in the inertia with him but don't know how to break the two of you out of it.
takes a risk, focusing on the supervisee's lack of success with his client

Bruce: So, why is it so important to know How *I* feel?
uncomfortable and confused

Supervisor: Well, I think it's important in that it may give you some information about him and about how he gets people stuck in the inertia with him. Maybe you can help him see that. I mean, it looks to me like you are really feeling stuck in there with him. And Derek's girlfriend may be as well.
ties the supervisee's feelings to a conceptual understanding of the client

Bruce: I never thought of it that way. That could be, for sure. But I still don't know how to get him out of it. I'm tired of trying to pry him up and out.
more open but still rigidly "stuck"

Supervisor: (*smiles*) So, the more you try to pry or push, the more stuck you feel, huh?
uses humor to reiterate the point

Bruce: Yeah. Yup. It's like having your wheels stuck in a snowdrift. (*laughs*)
feels understood

Supervisor: You just keep spinning and spinning and getting in deeper.
joining, picks up the metaphor

Bruce: Yeah. I need to put a board in front of the wheels so I can drive over it, if I only knew where to find the right board.
enjoys the banter

Though this dialogue serves merely as a "miniversion" of how a male supervisor can move a novice supervisee through his discomfort with feelings and focusing on relationships, it illustrates methods one might use to create a sense of comfort. The supervisor began with empathy and reflective statements to invite the supervisee to focus on feelings, then educated Bruce about the importance of examining his own feelings in his relationship with Derek. The supervisor used humor as a joining tool and honored his supervisee by adopting his metaphor of being stuck in a snowdrift. The supervisee responded well to all of these efforts, feeling more at ease and connected with the supervisor.

Next, encouraged by the supervisee's participation in their dialogue, the supervisor moves the process along by examining the supervisory relationship, emphasizing the parallel process of Bruce feeling stuck in both the therapy and the supervision relationship. As we will see, the supervisor again encounters the supervisee's doubt and fear about discussing their interaction.

Attend to the Parallel Process *and* Focus on the Supervisory Alliance

Supervisor: So you need a board, he needs a board, and we need a board in here—something solid and real that can get us out of this slump. (*pause*) Hmmm. So, yeah. You know, sometimes the only real thing I have to go on is the actual

situation between myself and my client, the moment in the room, what's right in front of our faces, like *our* feeling stuck right now.
continues the metaphor and uses his own experience as an example

Bruce: So how will focusing on that help?
still confused

Supervisor: I'm not positive that it will, but it helps to stop trying to make something happen and examine what it's like to just be together with the feelings in the room. Trying to make something happen can be like spinning your wheels and digging deeper into the snow.
Acknowledging that his knowledge is not perfect, grants permission to the supervisee to be vulnerable

Bruce: I know it, but that feels uncomfortable to me—too, I don't know, too close, I guess.
labels the source of his discomfort

Supervisor: So just to sit and experience the closeness of being stuck together makes you pretty anxious. Yeah. It's hard to do. What fears come up for you?
expresses empathy and inquires about Bruce's fears

Bruce: (*quietly*) Well, I'm afraid something will be expected of me, like to emote or *cry*, I guess.
tries to be open

Supervisor: So sitting in a feeling place with another person makes you feel like you need to get out of there or else you might do or say something awkward?
empathizes

Bruce: Yeah! I mean, it's an uncomfortable space, especially with another guy, you know? It's like "Yo! How's it goin' over there."
identifies the gender piece

Supervisor: Uncomfortable stuff, eh? I feel it sometimes, too.
self-discloses, modeling vulnerability and letting the supervisee know he's not alone

Bruce: Totally uncomfortable stuff.
feels understood

Addressing the supervisory component of the parallel process enabled Bruce to express his concern about revealing feelings with another man. This is a critical moment in the supervisory interaction because both parties have shared their interpersonal discomfort with each other. The supervisor's primary goal at this juncture is to enhance Bruce's sense of safety in the relationship. Though he intends to return to a discussion of the parallel process, the supervisor recognizes that he and his supervisee need to spend time working with the feelings that are current in the room.

Rather than ask the supervisee to examine his fears on his own, the supervisor elects to normalize Bruce's experience and help him feel comfortable by educating him about gender role conflict. This education process, a type of multicultural awareness, enhances the supervisee's knowledge base about gender role socialization and accomplishes three objectives: (a) it allows the supervisee to take a break from discussing feelings and assures him that the supervisor has no intention of holding his feet to the fire; (b) it raises the supervisee's awareness about his own gender role conflict; and (c) it builds on the supervisor's earlier self-disclosure, assuring the supervisee that his feelings are normal, understandable, and to be expected. If this next stage in the event is successful, the supervisee will be able to apply the concept of gender role conflict to his own immediate experience.

Normalizing the Experience *and* Focus on Multicultural Awareness

Supervisor: I'm impressed that you are able to disclose your discomfort with that. That's great. I mean, I sometimes get uncomfortable with that stuff too. It's part of the hard work of being a therapist, I think. You know this gender role strain, or gender role conflict stuff?
expressing faith in the supervisee, discloses his own discomfort with male intimacy

Bruce: Yeah. We talked about it in classes, but I hadn't applied it to myself.

Supervisor: Yeah. I mean, I think it really plays a role in therapy and supervision, you know? Therapy and supervision are intimate interactions. (*smiles*) Yet, being guys, we kind of shy away from that stuff unless we are with certain women, of course. (*laughs*)
uses humor and includes himself to avoid shaming

Bruce: Yeah. Even there it's tough sometimes though! What's up with this stuff, you know? Why do I feel like I'm giving away the store when I get vulnerable with another guy?!
tries to understand his discomfort with closeness

Supervisor: I think culture just does that to us. We are expected to be tough and handle everything. We're taught to associate intimacy with weakness.

Bruce: Yeah, that's a big one for me. I don't like to give in to weakness.
didactic, implies his own self-awareness process

Supervisor: I understand. It's hard to feel as helpless as you do with Derek. I think we like to believe that therapists are always strong, and as guys we also feel pressured to be strong. So it's a lot of pressure. And this can be nerve-wracking stuff to talk about.
validates, continuing to include his own experience

Bruce: So, you think I'm trying to be tough for Derek?
sees the connection

Supervisor: Well, how does it feel to *you?*
deliberately focuses on feelings

Bruce: You know, that's real. I can connect with that. I think I'm trying to be his dad or something, even though we're about the same age. I guess I need to be the man in this and be tough for him. I don't want to let Derek know how defeated I feel by his inaction.

expands on his understanding, yet in a cognitive way

Supervisor: There's the role conflict stuff again. You don't want to let him down or be seen as ineffective in his eyes.

labels the supervisee's experience

Bruce: No. I don't. Maybe that's why I have the need to push him, to unstick him.

insight

Supervisor: Makes sense.

Bruce: (*excited*) And I keep spinning my wheels because it's so important to me to succeed with him. So I get stuck with him.

continues making connections

Supervisor: Hmm. That's a lot of pressure on you.

Bruce: Yeah. It feels like a lot. I think maybe I need to slow down and take a deeper look at what's going on for him.

expresses a feeling, then quickly moves to an action

Supervisor: Stop spinning.

Bruce: Stop spinning.

The supervisor's willingness to focus work on the supervisory alliance by raising Bruce's gender role awareness and normalizing his experience has paid off. The supervisee is now questioning his own participation in the client's drama. To break through the parallel process, the supervisor modeled how to approach feelings, all the while giving Bruce emotional space and showing respect for his experience. The supervisee felt respected in this interaction, and the experience empowers him to take the lead in the supervisory session.

This supervisory dyad spent a good part of the session focusing on many issues other than the client—a break from their initial routine. It is now time to return to a client focus so that the supervisee can apply his new understanding to more effective work with his client.

Focus on the Therapeutic Process

Supervisor: So, when you think about what is going on for Derek, what comes to mind?

deliberately vague, offers Bruce the lead

Bruce: I think he feels weak, man—helpless. I really do. He's like so ashamed of being stuck in this relationship but he doesn't want to give up.

Supervisor: Hmm. Makes sense. Uh huh. You think he's afraid to give up because that would look weak too?

adds the gender piece to the conceptualization

Bruce: Yeah. Definitely. And I've been aiding and abetting by not helping him talk about his feelings of weakness.
takes an observing perspective on his own behavior with the client

The supervisor's acceptance and gentle approach to discussing potentially frightening issues empowered Bruce and motivated him to consider approaching his client differently. Not only did Bruce recognize the need to do something different with his client, but he also demonstrated awareness of his own contribution to the client's dilemma (i.e., by avoiding Derek's feelings of vulnerability or weakness). So as not to let this important awareness go unnoticed, the supervisor concludes the event by emphasizing that supervision is an appropriate place to examine gender role issues in Bruce's professional development.

Resolution

Supervisor: Well, that sounds like a useful hypothesis. How might you use that insight to intervene with him?

Bruce: That's going to be a challenge. How did we do it here? You got me going by talking about being stuck, like spinning wheels in snow.
shows understanding of the parallel process

Supervisor: That was *your* metaphor. Do you think you could use it with him?
gives the supervisee credit for his own creativity

Bruce: Dude, it's worth a try! I can just describe his situation the same way.
excited

Supervisor: How else might you intervene?
encourages divergent thinking

Bruce: Right now I want to more fully understand his feelings of helplessness, what they are about.
continues to follow the supervisor's lead

Supervisor: Yes. You want to take the time to learn more about his inner experience.

Bruce: Yeah. Just listen for a change, like they taught me in school. (*laughs*)
feeling comfortable, pokes fun at himself

Supervisor: (*laughing*) OK. And you won't feel weak about doing that?
gentle teasing

Bruce: Of course I will, but I'll get over it!

Supervisor: I know you can do it. And you don't have to do it alone. We can process it here whenever you need to. OK?
reassures and emphasizes their collaboration

Bruce: Sure.

Supervisor: Supervision is a place where it's okay to address not just the client's feelings, but ours as well. That's a totally appropriate thing to do.
points out that strength involves discussing feelings

Bruce: I appreciate it. I've needed to deal with this for a long time. Thanks a lot.

Supervisor: No problem!

By focusing on relationship issues, first the supervisory relationship, and second, the therapy relationship, the supervisor helped Bruce examine and process his fears. By framing gender role conflict as a cultural issue, the supervisor helped Bruce see that he was not to blame for his trepidation about being in close relationships with other men. Bruce's shame was framed as a natural outcome of cultural pressure to be strong and effective.

Rather than attempting to "break through" the supervisee's reluctance to explore his relationship with his client by insisting that he do so, the supervisor honored the supervisee's resistance (Teyber, 2000), helping him talk through his fears. For a male therapist who is just learning to work with emotion, working with a male supervisor can help him feel comfortable with someone who understands and has personally experienced the same challenges. If done effectively, the male supervisor can assist the supervisee to process his uncertainties and fears and develop skills to feel more competent within the relational domain.

Of course, it may not always be possible to pair a naive male therapist with a knowledgeable male supervisor. Whether male or female, if the supervisor shows discomfort addressing relational or affective matters, the dyad can stalemate at a cognitive, analytic level, avoiding emotional issues altogether. In sum, the male supervisee has two needs regarding gender role conflict: (a) He needs to understand and accept his uncertainty about managing intimate relationships compared to dealing with other aspects of his life; and (b) He does not need to feel disempowered or ashamed because of his conflict, but rather encouraged to develop his capacity to reflect on his experience and discuss it openly in his personal and professional relationships.

SPECIAL CONSIDERATIONS

Adherence to gender-based social roles varies from individual to individual, and gender is more salient for some people than others. The intent of this chapter is not to stereotype men or women. Some men may feel disempowered or threatened in supervisory relationships, just as many women are, and some women may have gender role conflicts (e.g., about confrontation), like many men. Rather, our purpose is to acknowledge that gender-based phenomena exist and to sensitize supervisors to the often covert influence of gender on the supervisory relationship.

In addition to the examples presented here, we recognize that there are many other gender-related issues that arise in supervision. Supervisees may be uncomfortable with an individual client's gender-based concerns. They need to understand and work with their clients' gender-related conflicts in couples and family work, and they may be reluctant to work with a supervisor of the opposite sex and so on. Because we could not address all potential issues, we chose two concerns that often challenge supervisors.

Another consideration is the intersection of gender with other demographic variables, like race or age. As illustrated in our first case example, a supervisee can feel confused by being older than her supervisor, yet "one down" as a female in a subordinate role. Similarly, a supervisee of color can feel doubly disempowered when working with a White supervisee of either sex.

An important dynamic occurs when supervisor and supervisee have different sexual orientations. This circumstance can be particularly challenging because sexual orientation is typically not visible (see the case illustration in chap. 6). Either member of the dyad may choose not to be "out" in the supervisory relationship for any number of reasons. On the other hand, supervisors who are lesbian, gay, bisexual, or transgendered (LGBT) may have gone through a coming-out process in their professional development and become advocates for the empowerment of LGBT people. Thus, it is less likely for supervisors to be closeted than it is for supervisees, who are new to the profession and are vulnerable by virtue of their subordinate status.

Supervision should be as receptive as psychotherapy itself to an individual's need to openly express sexual orientation (Russell & Greenhouse, 1997). If, at the start of a supervisory relationship, either party elects to be "out" to the other, a discussion of potential similarities and differences can ensue, much as it would for cross-gender or other types of cross-cultural dyads. As mentioned earlier, such conversations need to be ongoing, as the issues are not "resolved" when a single misunderstanding event is successfully concluded.

CONCLUSION

Gender issues in relationships are complex and inescapable. In supervision, the potential for gender-based intra- and interpersonal conflicts is high because of the multiple combinations of gender represented in therapy and supervisory relationships. Addressing gender-related fears with supervisees requires patience and a generous helping of empathy. Ideally, supervisors are comfortable with and understand their own gender-related issues and can pass on some of that hard-earned wisdom to supervisees.

Realistically, however, supervisor and supervisee may struggle together to understand and communicate their personal experiences of gender and repair misunderstandings that arise because of gender role expectations. Both wisdom and struggle matter very much when imparting the value of gender equity to supervisees, who in turn may bring this awareness to their clients.

8

ADDRESSING PROBLEMATIC
EMOTIONS, ATTITUDES, AND
BEHAVIORS: COUNSELING IN
VERSUS COUNSELING OUT

You can exert no influence if you're not susceptible to influence.
—Carl Jung, *Modern Man in Search of a Soul*, 1933, p. 49.

With no discernible precipitant, tears course down the cheeks of your supervisee. You know he's stressed from his training program, he has an ill parent and no money for a visit home. But is it just stress or something more serious? Did something in his work with clients trigger an old wound, or is he realizing that he's just not cut out for the profession?

Since the 1980s, mental health agencies have deliberately addressed problematic attitudes and behavior on the part of training professionals. Problem emotions and behaviors exist on a continuum, ranging from interpersonal skill deficits to major psychopathology and are traditionally referred to as *impairment, incompetence,* or *unethical behavior* (Forrest, Elman, Gizara, & Vacha-Haase, 1999).

Distinguishing between incompetent and impaired performance, Forrest et al. (1999) described impaired supervisees as functioning competently as professionals prior to experiencing a psychological instability or breakdown. Incompetent supervisees, on the other hand, never achieved a baseline of competent functioning, typically because of characterological or chronic emotional difficulties that preceded professional training. These two categories are, of course, by no means distinct or mutually exclusive. Muddying the waters further, unethical behaviors—acting out sexually with clients, compromising client welfare in other ways, violating professional boundaries and the like (Fly, van Bark, Weinman, Kitchener, & Lang, 1997)—may result from impairment or incompetence or from aberrations on the part of supervisees who function well otherwise.

Despite the overlap and lack of empirical support for these three categories, their definitions provide frontline supervisors and training directors with guidance about the kinds of problematic behaviors trainees exhibit, the kinds of remediation to be considered, and the basis for discontinuing an individual's professional training (Forrest et al., 1999). Perhaps most important is Forrest et al.'s point that the feelings, attitudes, and behaviors that reflect impairment, incompetence, or unethical behavior develop gradually and should not be construed as static outcomes or considered independently of the unique context in which a specific supervisee is expected to function.

Supervisors typically operate at the hub of an agency's efforts to address problems with therapists in training. Often the first to notice trainee's difficulties, supervisors are responsible for facilitating interventions and following through on the disposition of a problematic case. The depth and complexity of an administrative or supervisory intervention depend on the seriousness of the supervisee's problem (i.e., where on the continuum of difficulty the supervisee's problem lies).

A supervisee's skill deficit can be addressed through focused, educational supervision (see chap. 2), additional study, and more practice. A crisis in confidence, on the other hand, which can result from being overwhelmed by complex clinical material too early in one's professional development, may require adjustments in the supervisee's work load or performance expectations.

More serious problems, however, occur when a supervisee experiences *emotional exhaustion* from the caregiver role or *vicarious traumatization* (Perlman, 1995) from overexposure to client trauma. Many mental health volunteers working on the front lines in New York City and Washington, DC, after the September 11, 2001, terrorist attacks needed help to recover from exposure to the unthinkable misery they witnessed. Likewise, therapists who provide services to crime victims, war veterans, victims of domestic violence, and the like need to be closely monitored for signs of vicarious traumatization or emotional exhaustion.

A more serious problem is posed by supervisees who exhibit major psychopathology, an addiction or a characterological disorder, particularly if they progressed through all the prerequisite training experiences into practicum or internship without this problem coming to the attention of advisors. Characterological or other serious difficulties can surface for the first time under the dual pressure of doing therapy and receiving supervision.

Academic faculty may have considered supervisees with generalized anxiety disorders, as suffering from perfectionism or a high need for achievement, but the disorder may become evident when supervisees are so anxious that they can't focus on or attend to clients needs.

Because characterological difficulties range from personality styles to disorders (Millon, 1996), supervisors find it challenging to discern the extent of their supervisees' problems simply from their behavior. That said, conducting a formal diagnostic assessment of a supervisee would be considered unethical (Forrest et al., 1999). At the mild end, a supervisee who simply finds it hard to respond to a client's presentation can discuss reactions with the supervisor and role-play alternative responses. The supervisee may consider pursuing therapy to address interpersonal discomfort. However, if a supervisee refuses to address the difficulty or denies it, and if the problem persists after it is repeatedly brought to the person's attention, the lack of compliance may pose a risk of harm to clients.

In extreme cases, continued poor performance coupled with denial and noncompliance with supervisory recommendations may signal chemical dependence or a serious mental health problem such as dissociative identity disorder, major depression, or bipolar or posttraumatic stress disorder. Often individuals at risk for mental disorders survive the rigors of professional training until they begin working intensely with clients, when the resulting stress triggers more primitive coping mechanisms than they had previously displayed.

In the following sections, we discuss three distinct challenges posed by supervisees' problematic emotions, attitudes, or behaviors. We conceptualize these challenges on a continuum of supervisees' receptivity to intervention, ranging from mild (crisis of confidence), to moderate (vicarious traumatization and emotional exhaustion), to severe (characterological difficulties). Following the description and illustration of a process model for addressing supervisees' problematic behavior, we discuss due process procedures, disability, and impaired supervisors.

CRISIS IN CONFIDENCE

Learning to be a psychotherapist is by no means a straight road. Critical incidents related to competence are among the most frequent dilemmas discussed in supervision (Chen & Bernstein, 2000), particularly with novices (Rabinowitz, Heppner, & Roehlke, 1986). Because crises in confidence usually reflect temporary impairment rather than incompetence, supervision, in this circumstance, primarily involves normalizing the feelings of being overwhelmed and helping supervisees develop therapeutic strategies to get back on track with their clients. The "cure" for a therapist's confidence crisis is a client's improvement.

According to one early author (Hogan, 1964), a crisis of confidence normally occurs after therapists in training have seen a few clients and are pursuing advanced practical. At this point, realizing the complexity in helping clients with mental health problems, supervisees can easily become overwhelmed and discouraged. Although authors subsequently elaborated on Hogan's model (Fisher, 1989; Reising & Daniels, 1983), Hogan's original point was supported by research (Mallinckrodt & Nelson, 1991) showing that students in their second practicum tend to rate their working alliances with clients significantly lower than beginning practicum students do.

Perhaps the most common source of a confidence crisis is the training setting itself. Often supervisees work with clients who do not want therapy or whose problems are so severe that therapy may have little or no benefit. Not only are some clients' problems intractable, but also the necessities of training (taping and observation, supervision, a large waiting room and receptionist) compromise the sense of privacy so important in therapy. Novice therapists tend to work in the least private therapy settings with the most needy and most difficult to treat clients.

As one example, Lateesha, a beginning practicum student at an outpatient training clinic, began working with a 50-year-old man with severe obsessive–compulsive disorder. The client, who refused evaluation for hospitalization or medication, also refused to discuss himself or his life in any way whatsoever. Because he was only willing to talk about his compulsive washing and checking behaviors, Lateesha developed a detailed behavioral treatment plan, hoping that some progress and a positive thera-peutic relationship would allow her client to consider other options. The client only paid lip service to the treatment plan, however, and repeatedly "forgot" the assigned homework. After three sessions going nowhere, Lateesha attempted to engage the client in a discussion about the thera-peutic process, to which he responded with belligerence. Dropping out, he called to say that he had decided to consult a "behavioral expert." Lateesha lost faith in herself and felt highly anxious and depressed for a few weeks thereafter.

Throughout the therapy, the supervisor had voiced doubts about whether Lateesha's client was treatable due to the severity and longevity of his disorder, his staunch refusal to discuss himself or consider treatment recommendations, and the strong likelihood of secondary gains. Observing the last therapy session, the supervisor became convinced that the client could not be helped, at least in that setting. Lateesha's precipitous loss of confidence, however, was barely affected when the supervisor praised her efforts and commitment. Indeed, the supervisor stated that it was unlikely that he, or anyone else he knew, could have affected a different outcome with this client. Although Lateesha was grateful for this feedback, it was not until she had seen solid gains with other clients that she began to feel her confidence return.

Many trainees enter our field because they have repeatedly been told that they are "good listeners," someone others can lean on. When this dynamic is excessive, however, various clinical situations can trigger a crisis in confidence. If, for example, a therapist finds it difficult to let clients take the lead or work at their own pace, some clients will terminate prematurely, feeling controlled or bullied. Other clients will be stuck ("yes, but . . ."), with the therapist feeling increasingly helpless, hopeless, and incompetent. In other words, supervisees who see themselves as rescuers and play out this fantasy with clients are highly susceptible to a crisis in confidence when clients don't play along.

Of course, feeling incompetent can arise for anyone at any time. The precipitant may be a personal crisis that makes some supervisees wonder if they are suited for the field. One supervisee, Todd, came close to dropping out of internship after his girlfriend attempted suicide. He was blindsided by this event, tremendously guilty for not having seen the signs of her depression.

It is also common for crises in confidence to occur when therapists, comfortable at one skill level, begin working in a new treatment modality, in a new setting, with a new supervisor, or with a new, challenging client. Even experienced therapists, well aware that it is the match—the "click"— between client and therapist that matters most, can be distraught when a client opts to work with someone else. Supervisors have a difficult task in these situations. The first step is to determine whether the supervisee's bad feelings are due to a loss of confidence, to emotional exhaustion, or to an accurate awareness that they are not suited for the profession. As exquisitely described by Hahn (2001), shame can overwhelm the supervisory process. If the supervisee shuts down time and time again and the relationship cannot sustain a frank discussion of what is occurring, a referral for personal therapy may be the only option. If therapy is not the norm in the supervisee's training program, such a recommendation may heighten the supervisee's sense of shame. In our experience, sensitive and perceptive supervisors who normalize their supervisees' embarrassment can often turn it around productively without this course of action.

In many cases, a crisis in confidence is triggered by an event, a situation, or a difficult case that taps into the supervisee's anxiety, sensitivity to criticism, perfectionism, or narcissistic vulnerability (Gill, 2001). Learning psychotherapy is inherently anxiety provoking because supervisees must simultaneously process information at a high level, tolerate ambiguity, and be emotionally in tune with their clients, their supervisor, and themselves. Indeed, the necessity for introspection distinguishes psychotherapy training from that of other professions (Gill, 2001). Personal issues related to mastery are brought to the fore, and it is common for supervisees to feel a striking disconnect between the ideal and the experienced self (Schaefer, 1967) as well as between the self as knowledgeable therapist versus as unknowledgeable supervisee (Gill, 2001). Authors have pointed out that the exposure and exquisite vulnerability supervisees feel can cause covering up, hiding, censoring, or even misrepresenting their therapy relationships (Bernard & Goodyear, 1998; Gill, 2001; Ladany et al., 1996).

The need to master so many disparate skills simultaneously can exacerbate maladaptive perfectionism, wherein supervisees think they "should be able to fix the unfixable, know the unknowable, and love the unlovable" (Gill, 2001, p. 36). Typically, novices seeing their first clients have been exposed to various theoretical formulations and techniques but are unaware of the degree to which their personal and interpersonal frailties will be tested. When the consequences of making a mistake are perceived as monumental, perfectionism can prompt overactivity in a compulsive need to solve the client's problem or to just "make something happen" (Gill, p. 40). Alternately, the perfectionistic supervisee can "freeze" by, for example, being unable to access feelings, make interventions, or even remember what has occurred (Gill, p. 39).

EMOTIONAL EXHAUSTION AND VICARIOUS TRAUMATIZATION

A more serious impairment for the developing therapist is emotional exhaustion, which may or may not involve vicarious traumatization (VT; Pearlman, 1995). When the therapist has experienced extensive exposure to human tragedy or has developed a sense of powerlessness in the face of seemingly unsolvable client problems, emotional exhaustion can result. Worse still, the therapist might eventually suffer from VT, a stress reaction the therapist has incurred as a result of working with traumatizing client material. Therapists are particularly vulnerable to burnout due to emotional exhaustion or VT because the essence of their work is to relieve human suffering.

Because we tend to think of burnout only in relation to experienced, full-time clinicians, we may minimize or fail to observe signs of related phenomena (i.e., emotional exhaustion and vicarious traumatization) among our supervisees. When we do recognize a supervisee's distress, we may not realize the extent to which it has to do with therapy work. There is, however, a high probability for trainees to experience emotional exhaustion or posttraumatic stress disorder related to their work with clients, but most graduate training programs neither inform nor caution students about this work hazard (Fama, 2003).

As depicted in Figure 8.1, stress and anxiety are generic manifestations of work-related psychological distress. Not to be minimized, stress can affect a supervisee's clinical judgment (Friedlander et al., 1986) and overall work satisfaction (Olk & Friedlander, 1992) and can also lead to more serious manifestations of distress. For supervisees, stress is most likely to arise from

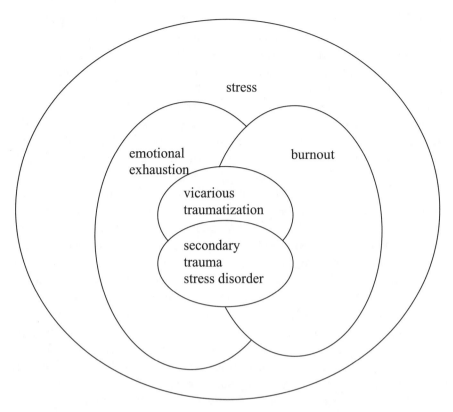

Figure 8.1. Manifestations of work-related psychological distress.

doing the actual work of therapy rather than from other professional concerns, such as agency policies or politics. Research suggests that practicum students and interns tend to find psychotherapeutic work more stressful than supervisors or nonsupervising staff (Rodolfa, Kraft, & Reilley, 1988), but therapists at any level of expertise can be stressed when they experience their work as demanding, challenging, and weighty in terms of responsibility.

In our model, therapy-related stress or anxiety is called emotional exhaustion, which occurs when a therapist feels overloaded, hopeless, or weighed down from listening to painful clinical material. Vicarious traumatization, one manifestation of emotional exhaustion, refers to the negative impact—cognitive as well as emotional—on a therapist's personal sense of security from hearing the horrific stories of trauma survivors. When a therapist also has symptoms associated with posttraumatic stress disorder (e.g., irritability, hyperarousal, flashbacks, avoidance of trigger stimuli, nightmares), this manifestation of VT is referred to as *secondary trauma stress disorder* (STSD; Figley, 1995).

First observed among family members of traumatized individuals, VT was originally termed *secondary catastrophic stress reaction* (Figley, 1995). Recently, therapists and nontherapists alike experienced VT in the aftermath of the September 11, 2001, terrorist attacks on the United States. Profoundly shocked and disturbed by these events, people across the country, as well as internationally—even those not directly victimized—began to describe life post-September 11 as "a new and different world." This change in perceptions about the nature of the world, about being safe in the world, and about being able to control one's destiny is the hallmark of VT (Pearlman, 1995; Pearlman & Saakvitne, 1995).

Although research results are mixed (Fama, 2003), some studies suggest that novice therapists may be more vulnerable to VT than more experienced counterparts (Moore & Knox, 1999; Pearlman & MacIan, 1995). Recently, Fama found a large percentage of pre- and postdoctoral trainees were experiencing one or more symptoms of posttraumatic stress disorder. In another study (Munroe, 1991), VT was unrelated to therapists' age or experience level, but those who worked intensively with traumatized combat veterans reported more intrusive symptoms like avoidance and trauma-related nightmares.

Finally, as shown in Figure 8.1, *burnout* may be unrelated to therapy per se—when a therapist experiences economic and administrative worries, role strain, personal failure, a lack of recognition, or professional isolation (Bermak, 1977)—or it may accompany emotional exhaustion (from any challenging therapeutic work, not only trauma). A cumulative process, burnout can result from VT when a therapist is constantly exposed to traumatic material that cannot be assimilated or worked through (McCann & Pearlman, 1990). Symptoms associated with burnout include cynicism, boredom, depression, and demoralization (Bermak, 1977; Freudenberger & Robbins, 1979). As the term implies, burnout may prompt therapists to leave the field.

When working with psychologically distressed supervisees, supervisors need to differentiate among VT, STSD, and emotional exhaustion and have some understanding of how these conditions arise. Three theoretical explanations for these manifestations of distress have been offered: countertransference, emotional contagion, and constructivism.

Countertransference, as discussed in chapter 5, refers to a therapist's conscious or unconscious emotional reactions to clients and their stories based on personal history. Countertransference can lead to VT when treating clients with trauma histories if a therapist is unaware of emotional responses or loses perspective on the therapist's role, overidentifying or reenacting the client's trauma experience (Pearlman & Saakvitne, 1995). When VT results in clinical errors, misunderstandings, and empathic failures, the therapist's countertransference can increase, which in turn increases a sense of traumatization, thereby creating a self-perpetuating cycle (Pearlman & MacIan, 1995; Schauben & Frazier, 1995).

Emotional contagion, a second theoretical explanation for emotional exhaustion and VT, is a common, empathic response "in which an individual observing another person experiences emotional responses parallel to that person's actual or anticipated emotions" (Miller, Stiff, & Ellis, 1988, p. 254). Research shows that people unconsciously tend to mirror or mimic others in facial expression, posture, movement, and tone of voice (Dimberg, 1982). In extreme circumstances, such as during critical incident debriefing, a therapist can empathize to the point of feeling personally traumatized.

Finally, Constructivist Self-Development Theory (Pearlman & Saakvitne, 1995) was developed to explain therapy-induced VT. As witnesses to horror and trauma, therapists may experience disruptions in their cognitive schemas related to basic psychological needs for safety, trust, esteem, power, intimacy, and independence (Pearlman & MacIan, 1995). Theoretically, it is a person's inability to assimilate the traumatic material into existing schemas that triggers cognitive disruptions. Repeated exposure to more horrific accounts of trauma sustains the disruptions that eventually result in VT.

Little is known about how therapists overcome emotional exhaustion, but research suggests that master therapists (Jennings & Skovholt, 1999) give considerable thought to keeping their stress levels down. A qualitative study (Dlugos & Friedlander, 2001) of committed therapists with 10 or more years in full-time practice suggested several general strategies for sustaining passion in one's work:

> . . . creating boundaries between professional and nonprofessional life, using leisure activities to provide relief, turning obstacles into challenges, finding diverse activities to provide freshness and energy, continually seeking feedback and supervision, taking on social responsibilities, and experiencing a strong sense of spirituality. (p. 298)

Informing supervisees about strategies like these may help them avoid undue stress and its sequelae. Although supervisees in graduate training programs rarely become "burnt out," it is critically important for their supervisors to identify and address the source of their work-related distress. Although each supervisee's phenomenological experience is unique and needs to be treated as such, differential markers of general stress, emotional exhaustion, VT, and STSD follow logically from their conceptual definitions.

Stressed or anxious supervisees demonstrate uncertainty and confusion, some of which may be related to evaluation apprehension. Novices, in particular, may experience confusion or ambiguity about their roles as therapist and supervisee, and some may have difficulty integrating these new roles into their self-concept ("It's hard to see myself as a therapist when I still feel like a kid"). More advanced or experienced supervisees may feel stressed due to role conflicts (see chap. 4) or other strains in the supervisory relationship (Gray et al., 2001; Nelson & Friedlander, 2001).

In a clinical case study, Rothschild (2002) described Ruth, a supervisee who felt exhausted and depressed at the beginning of each day and was so depleted that she feared having to quit work and go on disability. In a group supervision context, Rothschild asked Ruth how long she felt that way and whether she had "any unusually difficult new cases" (p. 61). When Ruth described one especially disturbing case, her trauma was evident—she blanched, her skin became clammy, her hands shook, and an emotional outpouring ensued. Strong group support gave Ruth courage to explore the basis for her reactions (Rothschild, 2002).

Supervisees need information, support, and empathy to overcome traumatic work-related difficulties. The supervisory relationship comes into the foreground when a supervisee's thoughts, feelings, or behaviors signal the presence of emotional exhaustion or VT (Fama, 2003). Merely recounting a traumatic case may not be enough (Rothschild, 2002), and supervisees can be harmed even more if the supervisor attributes their problem solely to countertransference.

To help Ruth, Rothschild (2002) asked her to discuss the case in depth and describe what she was visualizing as she spoke. Together, they recognized that Ruth's ability to vividly imagine events in her clients' lives, in this case, contributed to the problem—she could not separate her client's experience from her own. Next, Ruth was asked to describe her behavior with clients—how and where she sat, how she communicated empathy nonverbally, and so forth—and to consider what experiences in her own life might have been touched by her client's experience. Doing so led Ruth to a childhood memory, being present while a family member was physically attacked. Recounting the incident, Ruth realized that witnessing this trauma prompted her strong desire to become a therapist. This insight helped her see the basis for her vicarious traumatization (Rothschild, 2002).

Empathetic, caring supervisees, like Ruth, tend to suffer in this way. If their distress is solely due to emotional exhaustion and not secondary to a serious, underlying disorder, they should be encouraged to work through it. The supervisor should discourage hasty decisions, such as withdrawal from training or from the field in general, until trying all methods of remediation. With new tools and stronger emotional boundaries, supervisees who have these difficulties can become highly effective clinicians. But addressing the problem before it is too late is crucial. Desperate clients cannot be helped by desperate therapists (Rothschild, 2002).

INTERPERSONAL AND CHARACTEROLOGICAL DIFFICULTIES

Whereas crises in confidence, emotional exhaustion, and vicarious trauma-tization result primarily in problematic thoughts and feelings, supervisees with serious interpersonal and characterological difficulties come to their supervisor's attention because of problematic attitudes and behaviors. Even the most skilled psychotherapist has "baggage" from historical experiences, some trainees' baggage so interferes with their maturity or professional development that their training is severely compromised without help. All too often, students with long-standing psychosocial problems enter mental health professions—consciously or unconsciously—to help themselves when they are not willing, do not see the need, or have been unable to pursue their own treatment.

Wolgien and Coady (1997) found that therapists nominated by peers as among the "best therapists" in their communities saw themselves as wounded healers, learning about the therapeutic journey the hard way, by overcoming their own difficult histories. In other words, psychological challenges do not necessarily hamper one's therapeutic ability. Not having "done one's own work," however, can result in countertransferential problems in both psychotherapy (Hayes, 2002) and supervision.

Both Roberts (2001) and Gill (2001) address the issue of narcissistic vulnerability in supervisees. Before a mental health supervisee actually begins practicing, one cannot anticipate the range of emotional challenges. Feeling vulnerable in supervision is a normal and predictable occurrence when supervisees encounter personal and interpersonal challenges that get triggered in interaction with clients. Supervisees often feel uncertainty and self-doubt related to these challenges, and for most, competency concerns are ever present. For supervisees with difficult family histories and patterned emotional reactions to interpersonal situations that mimic those histories, self-work is necessary so as not to replicate the historical situations in their work with clients, supervisors, and colleagues. Supervisees without enough personal therapy to recognize and work on their own interpersonal patterns represent a special challenge to supervisors. If the patterns are relatively malleable, they represent aspects of personality. When the patterns are intractable, they reflect chronic interpersonal difficulties, characterological problems, or personality disorders (Millon, 1996) and can lead a supervisee to be labeled incompetent (Forrest et al., 1999).

Characterologically narcissistic supervisees pose a unique challenge for supervisors. Gill (2001) discussed three manifestations of narcissistic defenses in supervision: grandiosity, self-sufficiency, and overidentification. The grandiose supervisee expresses superiority by comments like, "The client mentioned that I'm the only one who had ever helped her." In group supervision, the supervisee may repeatedly point out previous clinical experience or offer advice and feedback to others while only describing successes. The self-sufficient supervisee does not feel superior, but, rather, wards off the supervisor's help because it taps into insecurities that the supervisee is fighting to keep at bay. Overly identified supervisees, on the other hand, have difficulty seeing anything in their clients that they have not already discovered in themselves. Over involvement is likely when the supervisee describes diagnostically different clients similarly (Gill, 2001).

Not all personality problems are severe or intractable. Moreover, a supervisee may have a "personality clash" with one supervisor but experience no difficulties with clients, peers, or other supervisors. For this reason, supervisors would be wise to consult with colleagues before concluding that a supervisee's problematic behavior is characterological or reflective of incompetence.

PROCESS MODEL

Marker

Markers of supervisees' emotional, attitudinal, and behavioral problems vary depending on whether the difficulty reflects a crisis of confidence, emotional exhaustion, or a more serious disorder. A crisis in confidence is the most easily worked with in supervision. Supervisees with this problem tend to be able and willing to verbalize what is going on for them. They actively seek the supervisor's help to put what they are experiencing into perspective and regain their confidence. Thus, a Marker for a crisis in confidence might involve a direct expression of supervisees' thoughts and feelings about themselves, such as, "Nothing I do with this client seems to work, and I'm beginning to wonder how I'm actually doing with all my clients" or more acutely, "I'm just not getting it, and I feel so bad that I'm thinking of dropping out." When discussing goals for their clients or professional goals, supervisees in crisis sometimes exhibit a lack of energy or depressed mood. In therapy, they may display frustration with a resistant or difficult client, but supervisees having a confidence crisis are often caring, responsive therapists. Their clients like them and feel helped, even when the supervisee is expressing extreme doubts and painful embarrassment in supervision.

Because emotional exhaustion is more closely related to the actual work of therapy, Markers for this problem can be more subtle. That is, although supervisees may express what they are experiencing, they may not understand how deeply their clients' stories are affecting them. When a supervisor observes a therapist speaking ever more slowly and softly with a depressed client, overidentification should be suspected. Other Markers include seemingly off-hand comments in supervision about feeling very tired or worn out, especially when these comments couple with a disclosure about having had feelings or experiences similar to those of the client.

Emotional exhaustion may also be expressed as shame ("How can I possibly help anyone else when I feel like this myself?"). Supervisors who sense a supervisee's hopelessness or fear of failure should not overlook the possibility of VT, even if the supervisee works with only a single trauma survivor. Because the most critical Marker of VT is cognitive distortion, supervisors should take particular note when a supervisee makes comments about seeing the world differently, feeling less in control, mistrustful, or personally unsafe. STSD, the more serious manifestation of VT, is signaled when a supervisee reports nightmares, flashbacks, or hyperarousal in addition to the cognitive features of VT. As discussed earlier, VT can be understood as a severe form of countertransference. Thus, supervisors need to distinguish between a supervisee's client-specific countertransference, which can be worked through in supervision, and secondary traumatization, which extends well beyond the consulting room and needs to be handled quite differently.

Because of their affective components, crises in confidence and the various manifestations of emotional exhaustion are usually recognized more easily than attitudinal problems or unethical behavior stemming from characterological difficulties. Supervisees with these problems are unlikely to discuss them or easily accept their validity or importance. Furthermore, because characterological problems vary in intensity, their Markers are more difficult to decipher. A supervisee with entrenched personality difficulties may become extraordinarily uncooperative or hostile, may triangulate and "split" various supervisors and advisors by complaining vociferously to one about the other, or may withdraw precipitously from the supervisory relationship. Markers may be evident in group supervision, a staff meeting, or in the broader professional setting (e.g., with support staff, clients in the waiting room, or peers in other common areas).

Of course, characterological difficulties also may surface in a supervisee's work with clients. Indeed, because people with serious relational problems do not recognize these difficulties in themselves, Markers can only be signaled by observation, not by a supervisee's self-report. For this reason, observation across situations (i.e., in therapy, in supervision, with peers, in classes or seminars) is essential. In the absence of consistency across situations, it would be unwise to assume that a supervisee's lack of sensitivity with clients signals a characterological problem rather than an interpersonal skill deficit (see chap. 2).

One common indicator of a supervisee's characterological difficulties is the supervisor's worry. A supervisor may gradually become more and more preoccupied with the realization that something about the supervisee's interactions with others is not quite right. Sometimes characterological disorders are signaled when the supervisor feels emotionally reactive to a supervisee's behavior or communication style. In extreme cases, the supervisors may respond in ways that surprise themselves, such as with sudden anger, confusion, defensiveness, or an unexpected feeling of inadequacy around the supervisee. When this happens, projective identification should be suspected (see the discussion on supervisor countertransference in chap. 5).

Task Environment and Resolution

The task in these kinds of events is to *address* (i.e., not to "resolve") the supervisee's problematic feelings, attitudes, or behaviors. In some situations, the supervisor might only seek to raise a concern about what the supervisee might be experiencing. If the supervisee is stressed or having a crisis of confidence, having the opportunity to self-focus in supervision may be all that's necessary. In these events, the interactional sequences include exploration of feelings, normalizing the experience, a focus on self-efficacy and on the supervisory alliance (e.g., "What can we do to help you?"). If, however, there is emotional exhaustion or VT, the process may also include a focus on countertransference, a focus on skill (conceptual or technical), and a focus on the supervisee's therapy relationships. If there is a concern that the supervisee's problems are significantly interfering with work as a therapist (i.e., when serious problems are suspected), a large part of the event may focus on evaluation.

It is not sufficient to focus on evaluation, however, in the absence of attending to the supervisory alliance. Indeed, it is vitally important that supervisees feel safe enough to disclose what they presently experience and, if relevant, what they have gone through in the past. Aspects of these discussions often resemble a therapy session, but the distinction is a crucial one. The goal of a problematic behavior event is to identify a problem affecting the supervisee's training or professional development, seek the supervisee's acknowledgment of the problem and, if possible, develop a remediation plan. The goal is *not* to work through the supervisee's personal problems as a therapist would.

Although we discuss crises in confidence, emotional exhaustion, and characterological problems in the same chapter, addressing these challenges differs due to variability in their severity and in supervisees' receptivity to intervention. In less-serious circumstances, supervisees tend to be receptive and responsive to their supervisors' feedback and suggestions. In these instances, supervisees feel relief that their supervisors notice, care about what they are going through, and are willing to help. Successful resolutions might involve, for example, making a plan to read about trauma or VT, pursue additional or more intensive supervision, seek out personal therapy, or adjust the supervisee's workload.

By definition, these events are unresolved if the problematic behavior has not been identified and acknowledged. In a single supervisory session, the problematic feelings, thoughts, and behaviors may be successfully identified, but several sessions returning to the issue may be needed before the supervisee acknowledges the problem. More sessions may be needed before the supervisor feels confident that the supervisee's functioning has improved. Recall from the previous discussion that labeling a supervisee's behavior as incompetent or impaired requires an extended evaluation process (Forrest et al., 1999).

In unsuccessful resolutions, the supervisee's resistance to acknowledging the problem can take the form of changing the topic, denying difficulties, shutting down and refusing to disclose, walking out of the session, or acting out in other ways. Often tense, hostile exchanges between supervisor and supervisee that culminate in threats may occur in highly unsuccessful events ("Unless you begin to pay attention to this problem . . .") and counterthreats ("I'll be consulting my attorney").

A SUCCESSFULLY RESOLVED PROBLEMATIC
BEHAVIOR EVENT

In this example, Sarah, a 26-year-old student completing her second couples and family practicum in a community service agency, is working with an experienced male supervisor. Over time, the supervisor noted that Sarah avoided addressing the mothers in the families she was treating. Rather than speak directly with mothers, Sarah focused solely on the fathers and children. In earlier supervision sessions, the supervisor pointed out his observation, and Sarah cavalierly explained that her own mother was highly demanding and domineering.

Marker

Early on in their work together, the supervisor viewed Sarah's difficulty as a workable problem that could be productively addressed in supervision. He suggested that together they identify different ways to work more effectively with the mothers in Sarah's caseload. Over time, however, Sarah's discomfort grew, and the supervisor began thinking that this "sticking point" may go well beyond what could or should be handled in supervision.

Having listened to three excerpts from Sarah's recent therapy sessions, the supervisor starts this session with feedback on one of her tapes. At the outset, the supervisor's intention is to recommend personal therapy for Sarah. This decision was based not only on the supervisor's personal observations of Sarah's behavior but also on her growing reluctance to address the issue with him as well as other input external to the present supervision context. That is, having consulted with Sarah's academic advisor, the supervisor was told that in her first practicum, she had difficulty creating therapeutic connections with individual female clients, and she had not gotten along well with a previous supervisor, also a woman. Essentially, then, the Marker for the event that follows is the accumulated data about Sarah's difficulties with female authority figures.

Focus on Evaluation

Supervisor: I watched your session with the Wilsons. You seemed very confident interacting with the father and the daughter.
supportive

Sarah: Yeah. I think I know where they need to go in terms of finding their power in the family. They both seem pretty cowed by Jayne [*the mother*] and need to find activities that get them in touch with their own needs.
confident

Supervisor: So you see them as needing to kind of break out of a submissive role with regard to her.
clarifies Sarah's conceptualization to demonstrate understanding

Sarah: Yes. Definitely.

Supervisor: It seemed to me, as I watched the tape, that you were less clear about what to do with Jayne. We talked about this last week as well. I am picking up that you are having trouble connecting with her. Feeling pretty uncomfortable?
begins with his observation of Sarah's discomfort, hoping this feedback will prompt her self-exploration of the issue they'd discussed several times before

Sarah: Well, she's pretty overbearing, but I think I can deal with it.
denies discomfort

At this point, two things strike the supervisor—the absence of self-awareness on Sarah's part, given that this has been a common thread in their work together, and the fact that his feedback to her was summarily dismissed. Believing that Sarah's impressions of Jayne are based on projection, the supervisor decides to be as concrete and behavioral as possible in conveying his evaluative feedback about this problem. In his mind, Sarah's response to his next remarks will influence the course of the supervisory session. That is, will she actively work to understand her behavior toward Jayne, or will she continue to deny her discomfort and avoid responding to his feedback?

Supervisor: Hmm. You know, another thing I noticed this week, you seemed to be having trouble making eye contact with her, and I became aware that you barely spoke to her during the session. A couple of times it also seemed to me that you were angry at her and that you made that clear in your tone of voice and body language. It wasn't just the eye contact—you were actually turned physically away from her in session. Were you aware of that? It seemed to me that you were really uncomfortable.

Sarah: (*loudly*) I greeted her when the family came in and asked her how she was doing. I really think, though, that the mother is the problem in this family. She has everyone in a vice grip. I think my job here is to help the father and daughter individuate and shake off her vice grip on them. I think Minuchin would agree with me.
defensive, aligns herself with an authority to justify her behavior

Supervisor: (*slowly*) So, the way you see it now, the bulk of your work will be with the father and the daughter, then.
backtracks, feeling some self-doubt

Sarah: Yes. Definitely.

Sarah's apparent countertransference toward her client seems deeply entrenched, seemingly unshakable. Moreover, she is unreceptive to the supervisor's feedback about her in-session behavior and refuses to consider an alternate conceptualization of the family.

Suddenly uncomfortable, the supervisor experiences a sharp dip in mood, a feeling of lethargy and a sense of incompetence—reactions he is not accustomed to having in supervision. Consequently, he examines his own response to what is going on. As he wonders about his countertransference to Sarah, this thought comes to mind, "Whew, I'm glad *I'm* not a female supervisor! This is bad enough!" Pausing to reflect on his here-and-now experience, he considers whether the problem is more severe than he previously thought. At the same time, he wants to be sure that nothing he does contributes to Sarah's defensiveness.

The supervisor stays focused on the problem to see whether he can help Sarah move off her defensive posture. Because continuing a discussion of Sarah's feelings toward Jayne would undoubtedly result in further defensiveness, the supervisor pursues an educative, less emotion-focused agenda, hoping Sarah will respond well to a different intervention. On the other hand, Sarah's continued defensiveness in light of his flexibility would confirm his growing worries about her problematic attitude and behavior.

Supervisor: This is family therapy, though, too, so I think we need to bring Jayne, who's the mom, after all, into the process somehow, you know? And I'm wondering how we might help you be more comfortable doing that.
mild confrontation, followed by an emphasis on their collaboration

Sarah: I'm not comfortable doing that. She is so controlling, I simply can't run a session with her participating.
rationalizes

Supervisor: You are concerned that if you give her some room in the conversation, she'll just take over?
implies that Sarah may be projecting

Sarah: (*strongly*) I KNOW she will overpower the sessions if I let her go, so I am trying to keep her backed off.
defensive, sensing the challenge to her perception of her client

Supervisor: Yeah. That's an understandable concern at this point. I think, though, that it would help you to understand how the dynamic operates in the family, it'd be a good idea to invite her input more to see how the father and daughter react to it.
empathic but directive

Sarah: (*Silence*)
shut down

Having attempted another approach to no avail, the supervisor becomes increasingly anxious, frustrated, and unsure about how to proceed. Repeated indications of Sarah's defensiveness and rigidity make him suspect that, for some reason, she feels attacked by him. Reflecting again on his behavior, he decides that he has indeed been understanding and flexible. Now, however, he is at the point where frustration could lead him to exert heavy-handed authority. Wanting to avoid a confrontation and restore their working relationship, he decides to focus on the supervisory alliance.

Focus on the Supervisory Alliance

Supervisor: I get the feeling that talking about this case is just really, really hard for you.

Sarah: I don't like this mother and I feel like I don't want to work with her, but they are one of my only family cases right now, and I know I have to.
admits discomfort for the first time

Supervisor: (*gently*) You know, if this is too upsetting, and you aren't feeling up to it, we can find a way to take you off this case. It's not an absolute necessity that you continue with them.
offers to take the pressure off

Sarah: (*tears up*) I just need to believe that I can work through this. I have to. I just have to.

This is a choice point. With Sarah finally showing some receptivity, the supervisor could suggest that they reflect on what's been going on between them since the session began. Although the shift in focus to the supervisory relationship has been productive, the supervisor senses that Sarah couldn't handle such an intimate conversation with him. For this reason, the supervisor decides instead to direct Sarah's attention to her countertransference, emphasizing that this discussion is a natural one to have in supervision.

Focus on Countertransference

Supervisor: Well, why don't we see if we can work with it, then?
emphasizes collaboration

Sarah: OK. Where do we go from here?
receptive

Supervisor: I think we need to talk more about your feelings about Jayne.
directs, feeling in control

Sarah: Well, she just makes me angry, like I want to scream at her.

Supervisor: That's what I mean. It's okay to talk about the fact that she just drives you up a wall.
shows acceptance

Sarah: Yes. I can hardly stand to be in the room with her.

Supervisor: That's really, really tough. I'm sorry that is happening for you. Can you tell me more about what it's like? As we talked about before, your feelings are an important part of what we're doing in supervision.
empathizes and probes

Sarah: I don't know. I just get furious—it's like I can't think.

Supervisor: You know, it seems like whatever is up with this mother, the emotional effect for you is extremely intense, very difficult for you to bear. Can we talk about this?
refers to countertransference, asking permission before stepping further

Sarah: Yes. (*crying softly*)

Supervisor: What is it, Sarah?

Sarah: I just can't do this conversation. I can't. It's too . . . (*silence, crying harder*)

Supervisor: (*softly, after a long pause*) This is also like, just too much?
acknowledges that Sarah has reached her limit

Sarah: Yes. Too much.

Supervisor: OK. This seems like something really, really painful for you. This woman is bringing up something that seems almost unbearable to you to talk about.
shows understanding and acceptance of Sarah's feelings yet implies that the topic does need to be approached

Sarah: I guess it is.

Supervisor: Would you like to take a break for a while and come back, say in 20 minutes or so?
models gentleness

Sarah: Yes. Thanks. That would probably help.

Supervisor: OK. No problem. I'll see you in 20. Get some water and fresh air, OK?

Sarah: OK.

Although the supervisee did not clarify the source of her intense feelings, she has acknowledged them. To respect Sarah's emotional boundaries and avoid pushing her into a regressive state, the supervisor suggests time to regain her composure. Supervision requires ego functioning, and to face her countertransference, Sarah needs all her wits about her.

Recognizing Sarah's strong feelings toward her client and recalling Sarah's difficulties with a female supervisor and other clients, the supervisor continues to speculate about Sarah's relationship with her mother.

Because the countertransferential problem is not toward a single client, the supervisor knows that he will eventually need to address Sarah's experience with female authority figures. This delicate balancing act serves to identify this pattern without implying that Sarah needs to work through her feelings toward her mother in supervision. If Sarah disclosed too much personal information and felt even more vulnerable, the supervisor might draw the line so as not to turn supervision into therapy. But silencing Sarah once she decides to disclose might risk engendering more anger, shame, and defensiveness.

Given Sarah's extreme vulnerability at this moment, it is not the right time to generalize the problem beyond the case currently under discussion. In the service of Sarah's clients, however, the supervisor cannot ignore the problem. Thus, he decides that when Sarah returns to the session, he will continue to address her countertransference again but in a cognitive way, pointing out that it is something she can no longer avoid. Doing so, he keeps an internal eye on his own countertransference to Sarah, recalling how awkward and ineffective he felt in the face of her defensiveness earlier in the session and in previous sessions when her relations with women were discussed.

Sarah: OK. I'm back.

Supervisor: Feeling better?

Sarah: Yeah. Sorry. I'll try not to do that again.

Supervisor: Hey, your reactions are real, and real is a good thing. Ready to continue?
validates her authenticity

Sarah: OK.

Supervisor: OK. I wonder if it would be OK with you if I asked you some personal questions, like data gathering a little bit.
implies the need for collaboration

Sarah: (*laughs defensively*) You want to try to find out how screwed up I am?
sarcastic, covering up

Supervisor: My main curiosity relates to your strong reaction to moms, you know what I mean? I wonder where that reaction comes from, actually.

Uncomfortable that Sarah clearly and correctly perceived his intentions to assess her ego strength, the supervisor unconsciously chooses a loaded word, *curiosity*, to pull away from her. Consciously, however, he sticks to his intent of questioning Sarah about the source of her countertransference. As shown next, the veiled hostility is not lost on Sarah.

Sarah: Funny you should ask that! How could you have known? My mom was a totally controlling, critical, impossible bitch, since you asked. Satisfy your curiosity?
tries to cooperate, but her sarcasm belies her feelings of vulnerability

Supervisor: I see . . . OK. I get it. Wow. Yeah. It makes sense to me! No wonder you just adore controlling mothers!
ignoring Sarah's hostility, tries to engage her

Sarah: No wonder, eh? My favorite people!

Supervisor: So, I'm not going to ask you right now to go into talking about your mom. I think we've had enough of painful discussion for today, and I know this topic is incredibly painful for you. But I'm interested to know if you have ever worked with anyone on this, in your own therapy, I mean.
sets a boundary but keeps a focus

Sarah: I tried once, but it didn't help. The therapist was a woman (*laugh*). I decided my mom needs therapy, not me.
defensive

Supervisor: Hmm. Sounds like she might. But sometimes having had experiences like that with a difficult parent kind of sets you up to react pretty strongly to other folks who remind you of that parent. And when the person you are reacting to is your client, that can be a problem, don't you think?
validates her perception but emphasizes the importance of acknowledging countertransference

Sarah: I guess so. Yeah, I can see that. But why does that mean I need therapy? I mean, I am pretty uncomfortable with that suggestion. My professors told me that you don't necessarily need therapy to do therapy.
brings in other authorities to bolster her resistance

Supervisor: Yeah. Some folks think that way. I think a little differently. See, I think we can be therapists without having worked on our own issues. But I don't think we can be great, or even good, therapists unless we have. And, man, you have some real *hurt* in there. Something hurts so much, you can't even talk about it at this point. That's awful to have to carry around. I feel bad for you. And also, those hurt feelings are bound to come up when you are trying to work with mothers and other women who'll remind you of your past experiences, and you're not real likely to do very good work with them. I think you may be inclined to shut them down or react in some other way to them that will be just like how you reacted to your mom.
to minimize Sarah's growing defensiveness, implies that he, too, has "baggage"

Sarah: Yeah. Well, hmmm. Thanks for your opinion. (*smiles*)
shut down but trying to remain congenial

Clearly this supervisee is self-protective, an understandable reaction to a wounding early experience. The supervisor wonders, however, whether Sarah will ever grow professionally given her apparent defensiveness, a defensiveness that suggests more than a simple countertransference to strong women. Feeling frustrated and suddenly exhausted, the supervisor refocuses on the supervisory alliance, wondering if Sarah can work with him to at least acknowledge her problematic reactions before the session ends. Although her humor has been tinged with hostility, the supervisor senses that Sarah may be comfortable enough now to talk about what's been happening between them. If Sarah can handle a frank, open discussion with him, it just may be her first experience of trust with an authority figure.

Focus on the Supervisory Alliance

Supervisor: (*laughs*) Hey, no problem. You drive a hard bargain, you know?
joins though confronting

Sarah: (*smiles*) I've been told I'm a tough customer.

Supervisor: Whew. (*wiping his brow*) I'm tired! I'm just thinking that you are really good at staving me off. I feel so exquisitely distanced.
models authenticity

Sarah: See? I'm good. (*laughs*)

Supervisor: (*energetically*) You are also quite funny! But I'm so "back here," and you are so "over there!" Even the humor pushes me over here. You must really feel like you can't trust me much!
wants to assess Sarah's ability to observe her own behavior

Sarah: Well, why should I?

Supervisor: Well, why shouldn't you? (*giggles*)

Sarah: (*laughs*) Because you're another big, fat authority figure!

Supervisor: (*laughs*) Ahhhh, now we are getting somewhere!

Sarah: Oh. man, what did you just do? Something inside is going "ka-ching."
takes an observing posture

Supervisor: What's that?

Sarah: I don't know.

Supervisor: All of a sudden, I feel more of a connection with you, and I feel better.
models genuineness

Sarah: I can't say it.

Supervisor: You don't have to, Sarah, but I think you feel it too, at least a little bit. At least you seem more relaxed to me. I don't want to hurt you. I think you are incredibly neat and funny and bright. I'm not here to mess with you. That just doesn't seem like fun to me.
recognizes that Sarah is still hurting and needs some validation

Sarah: Cool . . . very cool . . . (*several seconds of silence*). But that still doesn't mean you're getting me into therapy. (*laughs*)
appreciative but self-protective

Sarah had a small, but important, breakthrough. She responded to the supervisor's interpretation of her countertransference with some insight and communicated a beginning trust in him and appreciation for his hard work with her. The supervisor, feeling both exhausted and hopeful about Sarah's ability to face her demons, is relieved and pleased to have shared a moment of intimacy with her. Knowing that Sarah needs a break from the intensity of the session, he decides not to push her further to seek personal therapy. Rather, he decides to compliment her on her openness and explain that blocks that interfere with one's work as a therapist are normal.

After the normalizing sequence, the Resolution of the event follows with a "checking in" on Sarah's comfort level with the Wilson family. As shown following, the supervisor implies that continued problems in this area cannot be tolerated.

Normalizing Experience

Supervisor: I don't want to pressure you, so we'll just leave it for now, OK? It's normal to have strong reactions to some clients, and for you it may be authority figures, especially female ones. It's something you are definitely going to need to work on. We'll see. We all have certain types of clients who tend to push our buttons, so we all have to work on these kinds of things.

Sarah: OK. Well, yeah. We'll see how it goes. OK?

Resolution

Supervisor: Sure. Do you feel like you can go back into session with the Wilsons?
assesses

Sarah: I'll try this week and see how it goes.
acknowledges her insecurity

Supervisor: Well, before that, I'd like you to review your tape and closely watch how you reacted to Jayne. Take notes on what you see, think about how you were feeling as you watch the session, and we'll take it from there. Do you need me to go over the things I noticed again?
directive and behavioral

Sarah: Yeah, could you?
receptive
[*discussion of the problematic behaviors identified earlier in the event*]

* * *

Supervisor: OK, then. We can go either way, OK? If it looks like you'll be able to work with the Wilsons productively, we can do what people do in supervision, which is keep on talking about your discomfort and see if it helps.
reminds Sarah of the need for openness in supervision

If it doesn't look like you will be able to work with them, then we can take you off the case. It's not the end of the world. This kind of thing happens. We just learn from it. That's all.
implies a consequence for continued poor performance

Sarah: OK.

Supervisor: Good work today, Sarah. You let yourself feel, as hard as it was, and you opened up a little to me and let me do my job. Thanks a lot.
wants to bolster Sarah's self-esteem

Sarah: OK. You're welcome.

During the normalizing sequence and the Resolution of this event, the supervisor offered a great deal of support to a resistant and defensive supervisee, explaining that although her feelings were understandable, her behavior with Jayne Wilson was not acceptable. By addressing their working alliance and expressing appreciation for Sarah's willingness to take risks with him, the supervisor hoped to break through Sarah's isolation, enhance her trust in him, and help reduce her shame and vulnerability about her past. Although Sarah did not agree to seek personal therapy, she did cooperate with a plan to improve her performance.

How was this turn around effected? The supervisor's countertransference to Sarah's defensive style was a prominent feature in this event. Early on he felt defeated in the face of the supervisee's resistance to his carefully worded feedback. Faced with her defensiveness, he did not retaliate, though perhaps tempted. To avoid a harmful escalation, he chose instead to empathize with Sarah's struggle, and she finally opened up. After Sarah's tearful outburst, the supervisor gave them both some space to regroup. Aware of his own volatile feelings throughout the process, the supervisor suspected that a powerful interpersonal drama was being reenacted for Sarah. Because drawing attention to it and labeling it would have been shaming for Sarah, he chose to focus on the threatened rupture to their alliance.

Recall that, for events of this kind, a successful resolution entails identifying and addressing problematic behavior. In the present case, after detailing a plan for improved therapeutic work, the supervisor implied—albeit gently—that in the event of no progress, Sarah would be removed from the case, and there would be a revisiting of her poor performance in this area. Repeated displays of insensitivity toward women clients, coupled with continued resistance to the recommendation of professional help suggests the need for stronger measures. In that circumstance, the supervisor would need to consult with Sarah's academic faculty and with agency administration before proceeding further. Obtaining peer support is essential for working with a highly challenging supervisee like Sarah.

SPECIAL CONSIDERATIONS

Due Process Protections

Over time, as illustrated, a supervisor may determine that a supervisee's relational difficulties are characterological in nature. Typically, such difficulties manifest themselves both in therapy relationships and in supervision, and their presence does not preclude the possibility of competent functioning. Hence supervisors need to make supervisees aware, from the outset of their work together, that openness, receptivity to feedback, willingness to learn and take risks are all important parts of the evaluation criteria.

In problematic situations, it is critical to assess the degree to which a supervisee's behavior is interfering with her functioning. Perhaps the most common intervention recommended by training teams is adjunctive psychotherapy (i.e., "counseling in"). Despite a lack of research on the value of personal therapy for remediating trainees' problematic traits and behaviors, training centers tend to make this recommendation more frequently than any other, for obvious reasons (Forrest et al., 1999). Other forms of remediation include requiring additional coursework and submitting tapes of sessions and case notes to administrative personnel for close monitoring.

In intractable cases, supervisors and training directors may decide to terminate an individual's professional training (i.e., "counseling out"). Regardless of the source of the supervisee's problem, the supervisor's primary concern is to protect the agency's clients. The supervisor's second duty is to support and train the supervisee. Thus, when supervisees are unable to function appropriately and effectively, steps must be taken to protect the client as well as assist the supervisee. Although such assistance may be challenging, a supportive environment can help the supervisee come to terms with difficulties.

In order to ensure fairness, due process must be extended to all staff. Many accredited training programs have adopted a legal term that refers to the individual's constitutional right to a fair hearing, *due process*. In a training context, due process refers to the procedures used to inform trainees about the institutional expectations, the methods of assessment and feedback, and the grievance procedures to follow in contesting their evaluations.

Some training sites provide new staff and trainees with written informed consent documents that contain information about their rights to due process. These documents clearly identify the agency's expectations; the timing and content of assessment procedures; the extent to which supervisees are allowed to respond to regular assessments; a definition of due process, inadequate progress, and impairment; and clearly defined procedures that are followed in the case of inadequate progress or problematic behavior. Procedures for addressing trainees' grievances are also included in the due process document.

Due process measures are intended to protect everyone—the supervisee, the supervisor, and the training site—from misunderstandings about expectations and the basis for evaluating competence. For additional protection, trainees should be provided with a nonsupervising advisor who can advocate for them if a supervisor is in error or causing harm.

At the individual level, it is advisable to give supervisees a written contract that outlines the supervisor's training and background, theoretical orientation, supervision style, expectations for supervision, assessment procedures, and any fees. A template addressing most of these topics (cf. Bernard & Goodyear, 1998) can be adapted to fit the terms agreed on by supervisor and supervisee when they begin working together. Whether or not a due process procedure is in place at the agency, the individual contracting process encourages supervisor and supervisee to discuss mutual expectations at the outset of their relationship and clarify points of confusion before they become harmful misunderstandings.

Impairment, Incompetence, or Disability?

Perhaps the trickiest aspect of addressing supervisees' problematic emotions and behaviors is distinguishing impairment or incompetence from disability. In the United States, the Rehabilitation Act of 1973 and the Americans With Disabilities Act (ADA) of 1990 stipulate that, in sites that receive federal financial assistance, adequate accommodations must be made for persons with disabilities to ensure that they are not discriminated against, provided they request such accommodations. However, these acts also stipulate that disabled individuals must be able to perform the "essential functions" of the position they hold. A supervisee with a borderline personality disorder, for example, may be protected under the ADA as long as the supervisee is able to demonstrate competency in the predefined skills outlined by the training site or academic program in charge of training.

What is not clear, however, is the degree to which mental illness influences a trainee's ability to perform the essential functions of a psychotherapist. A supervisee with schizophrenia who takes psychotropic medication may be able to perform adequately. But what happens if the supervisee stops taking medication? Or what if the supervisee behaves poorly but has not informed the training site of the medical condition prior to being disciplined? Forrest et al. (1999) recommended that training sites clearly articulate which mental illnesses can be accommodated and which are likely to interfere with a supervisee's ability to perform the essential functions expected at the site. It also behooves training directors to clearly define and make available to supervisees the criteria used to assess and evaluate the psychotherapy-related skills deemed salient. When dealing with problematic issues, supervisors should fastidiously document their activities and interactions with supervisees, as well as consultations with colleagues and agency or university legal counsel.

Evaluating the Intangible

How can we as supervisors evaluate an activity like therapy when there is limited empirical evidence about how therapy actually works or about what constitutes effective practice? This dilemma is the crux of the problem we face when trying to identify and evaluate supervisees' psychotherapy skills. In all likelihood, there are as many different evaluation measures as there are training sites (Bernard & Goodyear, 1998)! Moreover, there are no published evaluation measures with demonstrated reliability and validity (Ellis & Ladany, 1997). Hence, in the absence of standardized assessment tools, training sites must develop their own criteria for evaluating supervisees.

To assess evaluation instruments, Ladany and Muse-Burke (2001) developed the following criteria. Adequate evaluation measures should include (a) the mode of therapy to be evaluated (e.g., individual, group, family, or couples); (b) the domain of trainee behaviors under consideration (e.g., therapy or supervision); (c) the competence area (e.g., techniques, conceptualization); (d) the evaluation method (supervisee self-report, case notes, audio or videotape, live supervision, cotherapy, role play, supervision interactions); (e) the proportion of a trainee's caseload to be evaluated (all clients, subgroup of clients, one client); (f) the segment of experience to be assessed (e.g., a part or the entire training experience, a specific session or a session segment); (g) the time period of the assessment (early, middle, or late in the client's treatment as well as early, middle, or late in the training experience); (h) the evaluator (i.e., supervisor, clients, peers, or objective raters); (i) the expected level of proficiency (e.g., demonstrated skill or comparison to the cohort group); (j) the reliability of the instrument (e.g., trustworthiness for qualitative assessments and statistical measurement error for quantitative assessments); (k) the validity of the instrument; and (l) the evaluation format (i.e., quantitative or qualitative, structured or unstructured). Using these criteria, training directors can determine the adequacy of their evaluation measures and change them accordingly to reflect the salient parameters at their own sites.

PROBLEMATIC SUPERVISORS CAN BEGET PROBLEMATIC SUPERVISEES

A challenge not to be left unmentioned is the need for standards of professional behavior for supervisors who, like supervisees, should be held accountable for their work. Although problematic behavior on the part of supervisees is recognized as a critical issue for training sites (e.g., Forrest et al., 1999), supervisor impairment has seemingly been ignored in the literature (Ladany, in press). Yet it is reasonable to expect that incompetent, impaired, or unethical supervisees, if allowed to progress in a training program, will one day become incompetent, impaired, or unethical supervisors.

Moreover, because impairment is a relative state, a supervisor who functioned competently in the past may become impaired due to stress, emotional exhaustion, or burnout. Unfortunately, most of us do not have to look far to identify impaired colleagues or supervisors who have behaved unethically with students or clients. Impaired supervisors create problems for training sites not only when they harm supervisees, but also when they allow problematic supervisees to slip by unnoticed.

Even unimpaired supervisors can cause harm (Ellis, 2001; Gray et al., 2001; Ladany et al., 1999; Nelson & Friedlander, 2001). In a typical scenario, well-meaning supervisors are unaware of the effect of their behavior on a supervisee who is inexperienced, insecure, and somewhat defensive. The supervisor, also overburdened, expects a level of competence that the supervisee has not yet attained. Picking up on the supervisor's impatience and frustration, the supervisee shuts down. Rather than recognizing the supervisee's skill deficits and the response to confrontive behavior, the supervisor starts probing for emotional impairment. The supervisee resists, seeing the probes as intrusive, maybe even hostile. Although the supervisee usually has no problem trusting others, no trust has been established in the supervisory relationship. Pretty soon a negative spiral takes place, and the supervisor declares the supervisee to be impaired or incompetent.

This scenario is, unfortunately, all too common. As we discuss in the last chapter of this book, what looks like impairment or incompetence on the supervisee's part may actually be an iatrogenic outcome of supervision.

CONCLUSION

Clearly, we cannot fully account for all the crises that can arise for therapists in training. We have, however, addressed some of the most commonly encountered problems.

In our model, a strong supervisory relationship is the bedrock for navigating mild to severe crises, and focusing on the working alliance is crucial for breaking through a supervisee's defensiveness. In doing so, supervisors should not lose sight of the fact that, whether the supervisee's difficulties are temporary or chronic, they likely are painful. After all, consider the magnitude of pain a person would feel acknowledging inability to work in a chosen profession. Thus, without neglecting our duty to protect clients, we should not forgo our humanism when confronting supervisees who display problematic feelings, attitudes, or behaviors.

9

FINAL THOUGHTS:
THE LONG AND SHORT OF IT

Life teaches us to be less harsh with ourselves and with others.
—Ipehigenia in Tauris, IV, iv

In this book, we closely examined eight classes of critical events in supervision and presented a theoretically informed model for working through the specific tasks associated with each event. We would like to make additional points regarding the clinical use of our model and implications for future research on change mechanisms in supervision.

THEORETICAL AND PRACTICAL IMPLICATIONS

The Components of the Process Models, Simply Put, Are Not Simply Put

Our process models were created to reflect the complexities of supervision from a relational perspective, yet to be heuristically appealing. In an attempt to simplify the various models for illustrative purposes, we avoided adding variable upon variable and process upon process (i.e., the complexities of real life). That said, some important points must be made.

First, supervisory events, like therapy events, are not discrete entities. Rather, they blend together and overlap in time. Moreover, like characters in a novel, events in supervision occur and reoccur as supervisees move toward a greater understanding of their clients, themselves, and the learning process.

211

As shown in chapter 7, for example, events often fall within events. A role conflict event may occur within a countertransference event when the supervisee takes issue with the shift in focus to his personal background and experience. A skill deficit event can easily turn into a crisis in confidence (chap. 8) if the supervisee displays acute anxiety that requires addressing before returning to the skill deficiency. In these circumstances, the supervisor must juggle two or more tasks simultaneously. When this occurs, successfully resolving an event may require revisiting, reconsidering, and working through over multiple supervisory sessions.

Second, although common Markers for each critical event exist, those described are not the only ones. Markers can also be misunderstood because the same behavior can signal different problems. Repeatedly arriving late or unprepared for a supervisory session, for instance, may signal a role conflict, a crisis in confidence, or even sexual attraction for the supervisor. For this reason, as shown in several of our case examples, the Marker phase of an event can be lengthy. An extensive dialogue may need to occur before the supervisor is certain what he or she is dealing with.

When signals are crossed, the supervisor can inadvertently mislead the supervisee. In the best-case scenario, they double back and refocus. In the spirit of interpersonal sensitivity, supervisors need to remember that meanings in supervision—or in any relationship—are coconstructed and open to negotiation and renegotiation. As illustrated in our cases, a "stop action" is often essential, when the supervisor inquires about the supervisee's experience of what is transpiring in the session and in the relationship (Ladany et al., 1996). This figure/ground reversal, in which the supervisory relationship comes to the fore and recedes into the background, is the hallmark of an interpersonal approach to supervision.

Third, the stages, or interaction sequences, in the Task Environments of each model are not mutually exclusive, nor should they be applied invariably or in the order we presented. Rather, a given sequence may not appear at all or may reoccur on multiple occasions throughout an event. In actual supervisory sessions, the stages are recursive and at times, weave together metaphorically, forming something more akin to a tapestry than building blocks in a tower. There is, nonetheless, a forward movement, as some sequences logically appear earlier in an event (e.g., exploration of feelings) than others (e.g., attend to the parallel process).

Fourth, event Resolutions—unsuccessful ones, in particular—are sometimes unidentifiable. We know, for instance, that supervisees often conceal their negative reactions to supervisors (Ladany et al., 1996), feeling one-down in the process or concerned about the consequences of a poor evaluation (Nelson & Friedlander, 2001). Hence, supervisors must be sensitive to supervisees' covert feelings and not confuse compliance with a successful resolution of a critical incident. Part of the "stop action" involves addressing supervisees' reluctance to share their perceptions about what is occurring and to address reticent verbal and nonverbal behavior. It goes without saying, of course, that supervisors must be committed to working with and through whatever material arises in response to their inquiries.

In sum, supervisors must keep the working alliance in the forefront of their minds, attending to it as closely as they would the therapeutic alliance with their clients. Indeed, the supervisory alliance is arguably more crucial, because supervisors have more power over their supervisees' lives than therapists do over most clients' lives, and a poor supervisory alliance can indirectly harm the supervisee's work with a countless number of present and future clients.

SUPERVISEES' DEVELOPMENTAL ISSUES

Supervisors must approach each critical event with the supervisee's developmental level and needs in mind. As discussed in chapter 2, for example, what may be a skill *difficulty* for a novice can mark a skill *deficit* for an experienced supervisee. And although a crisis of confidence is normal for an entry-level trainee (Hogan, 1964), it can signal serious doubts about continuing in the profession for an intern or postdegreed supervisee (see chap. 8).

Therapist development has been described as a process of increasing complexity and nuance of thought (Skovholt & Rønnestad, 1992; Stoltenberg, McNeill, & Delworth, 1998). Supervisees have different needs as they gain experience (Heppner & Roehlke, 1984; Stoltenberg, McNeill, & Crethar, 1994), and effective supervisors adapt their strategies to accommodate these changing needs over time (Wiley & Ray, 1986). Although our model only alludes to the complexity of supervisees' development as it influences a supervisor's choice of strategies, several important points should be kept in mind. In general, beginners tend to experience a heightened degree of performance and evaluation anxiety, needing more support, encouragement, and reassurance than their advanced counterparts. More experienced supervisors are often distant from their own professional development process. Therefore, it is easy to forget that novices need positive feedback on the most basic of basics—sitting appropriately, listening attentively, showing care and concern, and tracking themes. For this reason, when working with beginners, it is important to normalize their uncertainty and anxiety and provide positive and constructive feedback *in every supervisory session*. After all, being evaluated on one's interpersonal sensitivity is unique to this learning context. Supervisees who have been excellent students throughout their lives can be devastated by any negative feedback.

Some of the interactional sequences in our model, such as examining parallel processes or projective counteridentification (chap. 5), can be less meaningful to novices than to postdegreed supervisees, interns, or advanced practicum students, who may prefer discussing the influence of their personal and interpersonal issues on clients (Heppner & Roehlke, 1984). Less-skilled and less-experienced supervisees need a task-oriented supervisory style (Friedlander & Ward, 1984), with information, explicit feedback, and skill-based interventions, whereas more advanced supervisees often understand and tackle the multiple layers of meaning embedded in parallel processes and countertransference (McNeill & Worthen, 1989; Neufeldt, Iverson, & Juntunen, 1995).

However, we encourage supervisors not to assume that entry-level therapists cannot handle discussions of countertransference or that highly experienced supervisees barely need didactic training or structure. Rather, each supervisee comes with a unique set of needs that only partially reflects on-the-job hours. In our experience, there have been many novices who, in the first month of training, exceeded expectations of their more experienced peers.

The Role of Role Induction

Throughout this book, we recommend that supervisors negotiate expectations at the beginning of the supervisory relationship to avoid a role ambiguity or conflict event (see chap. 4). Not only is this negotiation a vital part of establishing a supervisory alliance, but it also sets the stage for revisiting the parameters of supervision, if ever necessary.

Typically, role induction includes disclosing the supervisor's educational training and background, clinical experience, theoretical approach, and limits of competence. In addition, behavioral norms and the form of evaluation should be discussed, as well as contact and crisis information and taping for training purposes. Supervisees' goals and expectations should be clarified, including ethics, confidentiality limits, and the use of self in supervision. Along with knowing the parameters of supervision, supervisees must understand that their supervisors value and honor their interactions and are committed to building and preserving strong, trusting relationships. Therefore, it is important to explicitly communicate a desire for a supportive and open process in which the supervisee can examine the growing edges and celebrate strengths and successes.

In many settings, supervisors and supervisees sign a contract: a written agreement about the mutual roles, tasks, and expectations of their work together. The contract informs the supervisee in writing of the supervisor's background and competencies and clarifies what the supervisee is expected to prepare for supervision and what kinds of topics may be discussed in the process. Similar to an informed consent or a disclosure statement a therapist or agency might use with clients, some terms of the relationship are negotiable, but some are not. (See Bernard and Goodyear [2004] for an outline of useful and ethical supervisory contracts.)

The extent to which the parameters of supervision are clear and mutually negotiated likely influences the course of many critical events highlighted in this book. When a supervisor focuses on evaluation, for example, the supervisee should understand the meaning of this feedback in the larger scheme of things. Otherwise, this sequence in the event could prompt an irreversible rupture in the working alliance. Consider the example in chapter 4; the supervisee did not view supervision as a place to discuss personal issues because "supervision is not therapy." Such misunderstandings commonly arise during conversations about countertransference, sexual attraction, multicultural awareness, gender differences, and so forth. If the supervisee actively resists the process, the supervisor should consider whether a role conflict exists before peremptorily placing blame on the supervisee's attitude. In other words, clarifying the need for boundaries around discussing personal issues in supervision is essential to avoid occasioning a role conflict, role ambiguity event, or the unsuccessful conclusion of another event.

Supervisors should not be misled by their own expectations for trainees with prior experience in supervision. It is easy to assume that advanced trainees know how supervision works and its appropriate and necessary roles. However, each supervisee brings a unique set of expectations that may not match those of the supervisor or of the work setting. Moreover, because merely changing supervisors can engender role conflict, supervisors need awareness and sensitivity about how their supervisees experience novel or contradictory approaches to supervision.

Conflict as a Normal Occurrence

Though conflict is not characteristic of all supervisory relationships, it is a natural part of supervision (Mueller & Kell, 1972) and therapy (Safran et al., 1990). Because the relationship involves both clinical and evaluative components, it can confuse and bewilder. Supervisees must trust their supervisors, but the evaluative aspect of supervision introduces an element of tension that can readily interfere with this trust. Thus, part of the process is to address the dynamic of trust versus evaluation, repeatedly if necessary.

Due to its complexity, the supervisory relationship is often difficult to navigate. Supervisors assume different roles, and because supervisees can be confused about which roles complement a given supervisor's style, the potential for conflict is high. The success of supervision depends, in part, on the supervisor's ability to create an open context for discussing roles and role confusion, along with trust and evaluation apprehension.

Supervisors also serve as powerful models for managing conflict in relationships. A wise person once said of supervision, "Do unto others as you would have them do unto others." In other words, supervisors who work through challenging events model the skills that supervisees must learn to negotiate conflicts and repair alliances with their clients (see the case illustrations in chaps. 4 and 5). Supervisors who openly and actively listen to supervisees' complaints and disappointments and who can sensitively reverse a process knotted in conflict provide their supervisees with a template for doing the same in therapy relationships.

Supervisors as Professional Gatekeepers

Supervisors are quality control agents, so to speak, in the settings where clients are seen. In this role, supervisors carry out various functions to safeguard the welfare of people receiving services from their supervisees. As mentioned in chapter 1, we do not view the primary objectives of supervision as case review or case management. This is not to say, however, that these aspects of supervision are less important than working through critical events. Rather, challenging incidents can and do arise during a straightforward discussion of a client's progress, the supervisee's approach to clients, or when observing a tape, considering a client's suicide risk, reviewing a report, or deciding on an assessment battery. During case management, which follows or precedes a case review, important strategies for handling the various services provided to a client are discussed. When weighing the need for testing or considering a referral for medical consultation, for example, a skill deficit or multicultural awareness Marker can become evident.

Case review and case management inform supervisors, who serve as both educators and gatekeepers for the profession, of their supervisees' competencies. In executing these two functions, supervisors teach and evaluate their supervisees' skills, ethics, and suitability as therapists. When a supervisee's behavior is problematic, the supervisor may need to forego repairing a threat to the supervisory alliance to first ensure a client's welfare.

As discussed in chapter 8, because differentiating impairment from interpersonal conflict can be extremely difficult, it is best handled through consultation with others. What one supervisor considers impairment, an observer may view as simply a personality clash. If the impairment is confirmed over time and across situations, in the end, supervisors must remain responsible to the public and prevent problematic supervisees from becoming problematic therapists and future problematic supervisors (Ladany, in press).

Applying the Events-Based Model to Other Supervision Formats

Although our purpose was to show the applicability of our model for diverse supervisory situations, our primary focus is the individual supervision of individual psychotherapy. Although we include examples from the supervision of couples and family work, we do not discuss how to work through critical events in peer or group supervision or in the supervision of reflecting teams, assessment, or group therapy.

Although we believe that an events-based paradigm can be created and applied to each of these formats, doing so is outside the scope of this book. However, we encourage readers to consider how similar and different components of the present models could apply to other formats. For example, similar to individual supervision, supervisees in groups can explore their feelings, repair a gender misunderstanding, or attend to parallel processes as they arise. Unique to group supervision, however, are peer interactions and peer feedback, important features that lend themselves to different Markers and different kinds of events.

An events-based paradigm could also be created for handling critical events in the supervision of supervision. In all likelihood, the same interaction sequences occur in this context, although with important differences. Whereas the exploration of feelings and normalizing of experiences might look quite similar, attending to parallel processes requires the additional layer of supervision of supervision. Likewise, the critical events and associated tasks are often identical (e.g., addressing a gender role conflict, attending to parallel processes), but the content discussed during a "sup of sup" event would likely differ (e.g., supervisor countertransference toward a supervisee).

RESEARCH IMPLICATIONS

We see the value of our models in their heuristic appeal for practitioners as well as a starting point for researchers interested in investigating change mechanisms in supervision. If, as we believe, working through emerging critical events successfully in the supervision process results in positive supervision outcomes (i.e., enhanced learning and development, satisfaction, and positive client outcomes), this premise is deserving of empirical attention.

There are two phases in developing and validating task-analytic models (Greenberg, 1984, 1986; Greenberg, Heatherington, & Friedlander, 1996). In the first phase, the investigator identifies an important, frequently reoccurring task—such as repairing a rupture in the alliance (Safran et al., 1990)—with theoretical and empirical support for its importance. Next, based on the available theory, research literature, and clinical experience, a conceptual model is derived. Alternately, a rational–empirical model can be created inductively from a handful of successful events intensively studied to identify important stages in the Task Environment (Greenberg et al., 1996).

In this book, a few of our process models were derived from a scrutiny of transcripts from actual supervision sessions, but most models were based on our cumulative experience as supervisors, informed by relevant literature. Thus, we encourage readers to advance to the next step. Like in task analyses of psychotherapy research, research can be designed to determine which interactional sequences in our supervisory Task Environments are most characteristic of successful resolutions. To do so, in the second, verification phase of a task analysis, qualitative and quantitative research methods are applied to compare and contrast successfully and unsuccessfully resolved events. The result of such an analysis is a refined conceptual model, with components that reflect the best fit for a successful resolution of each event.

As one example, for countertransference events, we proposed several useful interactional sequences, including exploration of feelings, focus on countertransference, focus on the therapy relationship, and attend to the parallel process. The Resolution was a statement, on the part of the supervisee who better understood her problematic reaction to her client, had some ideas about how to work with him more effectively, and felt relieved (first case illustration, chap. 5). Researchers could identify a small sample of successfully resolved countertransference events with this kind of Resolution and analyze them qualitatively for the presence of these four interactional sequences. Next, a comparison of more successful with less successful cases would determine which sequences are essential, if other sequences need to be added to the model, and if there is an optimal order to the sequences. Further testing with a still larger sample, ideally with quantitative measures (e.g., of the supervisee's satisfaction with what occurred in the event or of changes in his or her behavior in subsequent therapy sessions), would provide additional knowledge to effectively address countertransference in supervision.

CONCLUSION

Because our model is relational in nature and emphasizes collaboration, we encourage supervisors to avoid taking an autocratic stance with their supervisees. Moreover, as illustrated in several examples throughout the book (e.g., chaps. 3, 4, and 7), we believe that effective supervisors not only learn from their supervisees but also look inward at their own biases, countertransference reactions, and hurtful expressions of cultural differences.

Relational theorists maintain that one should not undertake relational psychotherapy without understanding the nuances of one's own emotional and behavioral reactions to others (DeYoung, 2003). Conducting supervision from a relational perspective is hampered when a supervisor also fails to undertake the introspection process. Indeed, we believe it is important for supervisors to model lifelong learning, personal growth, and self-reflection, regardless of the avenues selected to further this process.

In brief, our overarching purpose in writing this book was to offer supervisors and supervisors in training a heuristic model that would be theoretically and empirically informed, clinically appealing, and practical. As authors collaborating on this book, we learned a great deal and shared some hard-earned lessons about supervision with each other and the reader. As with any conceptual model, we anticipate ours will evolve and be enhanced as we learn more about its applicability and its limits. To that end, we encourage readers to contact us with comments, questions, reactions, and other feedback about the usefulness of our work for theirs.

REFERENCES

American Association for Marriage and Family Therapy. (2001). *AAMFT code of ethics*. Washington, DC: Author.

American Counseling Association. (1995). *Code of ethics and standards of practice*. Alexandria, VA: Author.

American Psychological Association. (2002). Ethical principles of psychologists and code of conduct. *American Psychologist, 57*, 1060–1073.

American Psychological Association. (2003). Guidelines on multicultural education, training, research, practice, and organizational change for psychologists. *American Psychologist, 58*, 377–402.

Ancis, J., & Ladany, N. (2001). Multicultural supervision. In L. J. Bradley & N. Ladany (Eds.), *Counselor supervision: Principles, process, & practice* (3rd ed., pp. 63–90). Philadelphia: Brunner-Routledge.

Ancis, J. R., & Sanchez-Hucles, J. V. (2000). A preliminary analysis of counseling students' attitudes toward counseling women and women of color: Implications for cultural competency training. *Journal of Multicultural Counseling and Development, 28*, 16–31.

Arkowitz, S. W. (2001). Perfectionism in the supervisee. In S. Gill (Ed.), *The supervisory alliance: Facilitating the psychotherapist's learning experience* (pp. 35–66). Northvale, NJ: Jason Aronson.

Arlow, J. A. (1963). The supervisory situation. *Journal of the American Psychoanalytic Association, 11*, 576–594.

Association for Counselor Education and Supervision. (1995). Ethical guidelines for counseling supervisors. *Counselor Education and Supervision, 34*, 270–276.

Association of State Provincial Psychology Boards. (1991). *ASPPB code of conduct*. Montgomery, AL: Author.

Atwood, M. (1986). *The handmaid's tale*. Boston: Houghton Mifflin.

Avis, J. M., & Sprenkle, D. H. (1990). Outcome research on family therapy training: A substantive and methodological review. *Journal of Marital and Family Therapy, 16*, 241–264.

Bahrick, A. S., Russell, R. K., & Salmi, S. W. (1991). The effects of role induction on trainees' perceptions of supervision. *Journal of Counseling and Development, 69*, 434–438.

Barnat, M. R. (1980). Psychotherapy supervision and the duality of experience. In A. K. Hess (Ed.), *Psychotherapy supervision: Theory, research, and practice* (pp. 51–67). New York: Wiley.

Bartell, P. A., & Rubin, L. J. (1990). Dangerous liaisons: Sexual intimacies in supervision. *Professional Psychology: Research and Practice, 21*, 442–450.

Beehr, T. A., & Newman, J. E. (1978). Job stress, employee health, and organization effectiveness: A facet analysis, model and literature review. *Personnel Psychology, 31*, 665–699.

Bermak, G. E. (1977). Do psychiatrists have special emotional problems? *American Journal of Psychoanalysis, 37,* 141–146.

Bernard, J. M., & Goodyear, R. K. (1998). *Fundamentals of clinical supervision* (2nd ed.). Needham Heights, MA: Allyn & Bacon.

Bernard, J. M., & Goodyear, R. K. (2004). *Fundamentals of clinical supervision* (3rd ed.). Needham Heights, MA: Allyn & Bacon.

Bernsen, A., Tabachnick, B. G., & Pope, K. S. (1994). National survey of social workers' sexual attraction to their clients: Results, implications, and comparison to psychologists. *Ethics & Behavior, 4,* 369–388.

Beutler, L. E., & Clarkin, J. F. (1990). *Systematic treatment selections: Toward targeted therapeutic interventions.* Philadelphia: Brunner/Mazel.

Biddle, B. J. (1979). *Role theory: Expectations, identities, and behaviors.* New York: Academic Press.

Bordin, E. S. (1979). The generalizability of the psychoanalytic concept of the working alliance. *Psychotherapy: Theory, Research, and Practice, 16,* 252–260.

Bordin, E. S. (1983). A working alliance based model of supervision. *The Counseling Psychologist, 11*(1), 35–41.

Bowlby, J. (1979). *The making and breaking of affectional bonds.* London: Tavistock.

Bromberg, P. M. (1982). The supervisory process and parallel process in psychoanalysis. *Contemporary Psychoanalysis, 18,* 92–110.

Brooks, G. R. (1998). *A new psychotherapy for traditional men.* San Francisco: Jossey-Bass.

Brown, L. S. (1990). The meaning of a multicultural perspective for theory building in feminist therapy. In L. S. Brown & M. P. Root (Eds.), *Diversity and complexity in feminist therapy* (pp. 1–21). New York: Harrington Park Press.

Brown, L. S., & Brodsky, A. M. (1992). The future of feminist therapy. *Psychotherapy, 29,* 51–57.

Campbell, J. M., & Snow, B. M. (1992). Gender role conflict and family environment as predictors of men's marital satisfaction. *Journal of Family Psychology, 6,* 84–87.

Caplan, G. (1970). *The theory and practice of mental health consultation.* New York: Basic Books.

Caplan, R. D., & Jones, K. W. (1975). Effects of work load, role ambiguity, and Type A personality on anxiety, depression, and heart rate. *Journal of Applied Psychology, 60,* 713–719.

Carson, R. C. (1969). *Interactions concepts of personality.* Oxford, England: Aldine.

Cass, V. C. (1979). Homosexual identity formation: A theoretical model. *Journal of Homosexuality, 4,* 219–235.

Celenza, A. (1995). Love and hate in the countertransference supervisory concerns. *Psychotherapy: Theory, Research, Practice, and Training, 32,* 301–307.

Chan, C. S. (1989). Issues of identity development among Asian-American lesbians and gay men. *Journal of Counseling & Development, 68,* 16–20.

Chen, E. C., & Bernstein, B. L. (2000). Relations of complementarity and supervisory issues to supervisory working alliance: A comparative analysis of two cases. *Journal of Counseling Psychology, 47*, 485–497.

Clarke, K. M. (1990). Creating of meaning: An emotional processing task in psychotherapy. *Psychotherapy: Theory, Research, & Practice, 26*, 139–148.

Constantine, M. G. (1997). Facilitating multicultural competency in counseling supervision. In D. B. Pope-Davis & H. L. K. Coleman (Eds.), *Multicultural counseling competencies: Assessment, education and training, and supervision* (pp. 310–324). Thousand Oaks, CA: Sage.

Constantine, M. G. (2001). Multicultural research in psychotherapy supervision: Current status and future directions. *Psychotherapy Bulletin, 36*, 20–25.

Constantine, M. G., & Ladany, N. (2000). Self-report multicultural counseling competence instruments and their relation to multicultural case conceptualization ability and social desirability. *Journal of Counseling Psychology, 47*, 155–164.

Constantine, M. G., & Ladany, N. (2001). New visions for assessing multicultural counseling competence. In J. G. Ponterotto, J. M. Casas, L. A. Suzuki, & C. M. Alexander (Eds.), *Handbook of multicultural counseling* (2nd ed., pp. 482–498). Thousand Oaks, CA: Sage.

Constantine, M. G., Ladany, N., Inman, A. G., & Ponterotto, J. G. (1996). Students' perceptions of multicultural training in counseling psychology programs. *Journal of Multicultural Counseling and Development, 24*, 241–253.

Cook, D. A. (1994). Racial identity in supervision. *Counselor Education and Supervision, 34*, 132–139.

Cook, D. A., & Helms, J. E. (1988). Visible racial/ethnic group supervisees' satisfaction with cross-cultural supervision as predicted by relationship characteristics. *Journal of Counseling Psychology, 35*, 268–274.

Cooke, M., & Kipnis, D. (1986). Influence tactics in psychotherapy. *Journal of Consulting & Clinical Psychology, 54*, 22–26.

Cooper, C. L., & Marshall, J. (1976). Occupational sources of stress: A review of the literature relating to coronary heart disease and mental ill health. *Journal of Occupational Psychology 49*, 11–28.

Coulehan, R., Friedlander, M. L., & Heatherington, L. (1998). Transforming narratives: A change event in constructivist family therapy. *Family Process, 37*, 465–481.

Cross, W. E., Jr. (1971). The Negro-to-Black conversion experience. *Black World, 20*, 13–27.

Cross, W. E., Jr. (1995). The psychology of nigrescence: Revising the Cross model. In J. G. Ponterotto, J. M Casas, L. A. Suzuki, & C. M. Alexander (Eds.), *Handbook of multicultural counseling* (pp. 93–122). Thousand Oaks, CA: Sage.

DeYoung, P. A. (2003). *Relational psychotherapy: A primer.* New York: Brunner-Routledge.

Diemer, R. A., Lobell, L. K., Vivino, B. L., & Hill, C. E. (1996). Comparison of dream interpretation, event interpretation, and unstructured sessions in brief therapy. *Journal of Counseling Psychology, 43*, 99–112.

Dimberg, U. (1982). Facial reactions to facial expressions. *Psychophysiology, 19,* 643–647.

Dlugos, R. F., & Friedlander, M. L. (2001). Passionately committed psychotherapists: A qualitative study of their experience. *Professional Psychology: Research & Practice, 32,* 298–304.

Doehrman, M. J. (1976). Parallel processes in supervision and psychotherapy. *Bulletin of the Menninger Clinic, 40,* 9–104.

Downing, N. E., & Roush, K. L. (1985). From passive-acceptance to active commitment: A model of feminist identity development for women. *The Counseling Psychologist, 13*(4), 695–709.

Eagly, A. H. (1987). *Sex differences in social behavior: A social-role interpretation.* Hillsdale, NJ: Lawrence Erlbaum Associates.

Efstation, J. F., Patton, M. J., & Kardash, C. M. (1990). Measuring the working alliance in counselor supervision. *Journal of Counseling Psychology, 37,* 322–329.

Eisler, R. M., Skidmore, J. R., & Ward, C. H. (1988). Masculine gender-role stress: Predictor of anger, anxiety, and health-risk behaviors. *Journal of Personality Assessment, 52,* 133–141.

Ekstein, R., & Wallerstein, R. S. (1958). *The teaching and learning of psychotherapy.* New York: Basic Books.

Ellis, M. V. (1991). Critical incidents in clinical supervision and in supervisor supervision: Assessing supervisory issues. *Journal of Counseling Psychology, 38,* 342–349.

Ellis, M. V. (2001). Harmful supervision, a cause for alarm: Comment on Gray et al. (2001) and Nelson and Friedlander (2001). *Journal of Counseling Psychology, 48,* 401–406.

Ellis, M. V., Chapin, J. L., Dennin, M. K., & Anderson-Hanley, C. (1996, August). *Role induction for clinical supervision: Impact on neophyte supervisees.* Paper presented at the meeting of the American Psychological Association, Toronto, Canada.

Ellis, M. V., & Ladany, N. (1997). Inferences concerning supervisees and clients in clinical supervision: An integrative review. In C. E. Watkins Jr. (Ed.), *Handbook of psychotherapy supervision* (pp. 567–607). New York: Wiley.

Epstein, L., & Feiner, A. H. (Eds.). (1979). *Countertransference.* New York: Jason Aronson.

Fama, L. D. (2003). *Vicarious traumatization: A concern for pre- and post-doctoral level psychology trainees.* Unpublished dissertation, University at Albany, State University of New York.

Fassinger, R. E. (1991). The hidden minority: Issues and challenges in working with lesbian women and gay men. *The Counseling Psychologist, 19,* 157–176.

Figley, C. R. (1995). Compassion fatigue: Toward a new understanding of the costs of caring. In B. H. Stamm (Ed), *Secondary traumatic stress: Self-care issues for clinicians, researchers, and educators* (pp. 3–28). Baltimore: The Sidran Press.

Fisher, B. L. (1989). Differences between supervision of beginning and advanced therapists: Hogan's hypothesis empirically revisited. *Clinical Supervisor, 7*, 57–74.

Fivush, R. (1989). Exploring sex differences in the emotional content of mother-child conversations about the past. *Sex Roles, 20*, 675–691.

Fleming, J., & Benedek, T. F. (1983). *Psychoanalytic supervision: A method of clinical teaching.* New York: International Universities Press.

Fly, B. J., van Bark, W. P., Weinman, L., Kitchener, K. S., & Lang, P. R. (1997). Ethical transgressions of psychology graduate students: Critical incidents with implications for training. *Professional Psychology: Research and Practice, 28*, 492–495.

Forrest, L., Elman, N., Gizara, S., & Vacha-Hasse, T. (1999). Trainee impairment: A review of identification, remediation, dismissal, and legal issues. *Counseling Psychologist, 27*, 627–686.

Fouad, N. A., & Brown, M. T. (2000). Role of race and social class in development: Implications for counseling psychology. In S. D. Brown & R. W. Lent (Eds.), *Handbook of counseling psychology* (3rd ed., pp. 379–408). New York: Wiley.

Frawley-O'Dea, M. G., & Sarnat, J. E. (2001). *The supervisory relationship: A contemporary psychodynamic approach.* New York: Guilford Press.

Freudenberger, H. J., & Robbins, A. (1979). The hazards of being a psychoanalyst. *Psychoanalytic Review, 66*, 275–300.

Friedlander, M. L., Heatherington, L., Johnson, B., & Skowron, E. (1994). Sustaining engagement: A change event in family therapy. *Journal of Counseling Psychology, 41*, 438–448.

Friedlander, M. L., Keller, K. E., Peca-Baker, T. A., & Olk, M. E. (1986). Effects of role conflict on counselor trainees' self-statements, anxiety level, and performance. *Journal of Counseling Psychology, 33*, 73–77.

Friedlander, M. L., Siegel, S. M., & Brenock, K. (1989). Parallel processes in counseling and supervision: A case study. *Journal of Counseling Psychology, 36*, 149–157.

Friedlander, M. L., & Snyder, J. (1983). Trainees' expectations for the supervisory process: Testing a developmental model. *Counselor Education and Supervision, 22*, 342–348.

Friedlander, M. L., & Ward, L. G. (1984). Development and validation of the Supervisory Styles Inventory. *Journal of Counseling Psychology, 31*, 541–557.

Fukuyama, M. A. (1994). Critical incidents in multicultural counseling supervision: A phenomenological approach to supervision research. *Counselor Education and Supervision, 34*, 142–151.

Gabbard, G. O. (1994). Sexual excitement and countertransference love in the analyst. *Journal of the American Psychoanalytic Association, 42*, 1083–1106.

Gabbard, G. O. (1995). The early history of boundary violations in psychoanalysis. *Journal of the American Psychoanalytic Association, 43*, 1115–1136.

Gelso, C. J., & Carter, J. A. (1985). The relationship in counseling and psychotherapy: Components, consequences, and theoretical antecedents. *The Counseling Psychologist, 13,* 155–243.

Gelso, C. J., & Hayes, J. A. (2001). Countertransference management. *Psychotherapy: Theory, Research, Practice, and Training, 38,* 418–422.

Gill, S. (Ed.). (2001). *The supervisory alliance: Facilitating the psychotherapist's learning experience.* Northvale, NJ: Jason Aronson.

Glaser, R. D., & Thorpe, J. S. (1986). Unethical intimacy: A survey of sexual contact and advances between psychology educators and female graduate students. *American Psychologist, 41,* 42–51.

Goin, M. K., & Kline, F. (1976). Countertransference: A neglected subject in clinical supervision. *American Journal of Psychiatry, 133,* 41–44.

Goodyear, R. K. (1990). Gender configurations in supervisory dyads: Their relation to supervisee influence strategies and to skill evaluations of the supervisee. *Clinical Supervisor, 8,* 67–79.

Granello, D. H., Beamish, P. M., & Davis, T. E. (1997). Supervisee empowerment: Does gender make a difference? *Counselor Education and Supervision, 36,* 305–317.

Gray, L. A., Ladany, N., Walker, J. A., & Ancis, J. R. (2001). Psychotherapy trainees' experience of counterproductive events in supervision. *Journal of Counseling Psychology, 48,* 371–383.

Greenberg, L. S. (1983). Toward a task analysis of conflict resolution in gestalt therapy. *Psychotherapy: Theory, Research, and Practice, 20,* 190–201.

Greenberg, L. S. (1984). Task analysis: The general approach. In L. N. Rice & L. S. Greenberg (Eds.), *Patterns of change: Intensive analysis of psychotherapy process* New York: Guilford.

Greenberg, L. S. (1986). Change process research. *Journal of Consulting and Clinical Psychology, 54,* 4–9.

Greenberg, L. S., & Foerster, F. S. (1996). Task analysis exemplified: The process of resolving unfinished business. *Journal of Consulting and Clinical Psychology, 64,* 436–446.

Greenberg, L. S., Heatherington, L., & Friedlander, M. L. (1996). The events-based approach to couple and family therapy research. In D. H. Sprenkle & S. M. Moon (Eds.), *Research methods in family therapy* (pp. 411–428). New York: Guilford Press.

Greenberg, L. S., & Pinsof, W. (1986). Process research: Current trends and future perspectives. In L. S. Greenberg & W. M. Pinsof (Eds.), *The psychotherapeutic process: A research handbook* (pp. 3–20). New York: Guilford.

Grinberg, L. (1979a). Countertransference and projective identification. *Contemporary Psychoanalysis, 15*(2), 226–247.

Grinberg, L. (1979b). Projective counteridentification and countertransference. In L. Epstein & A. H. Feiner (Eds.), *Countertransference* (pp. 169–191). New York: Jason Aronson.

Hahn, W. K. (2001). The experience of shame in psychotherapy supervision. *Psychotherapy: Theory, Research, Practice, and Training, 38,* 272–282.

Hansen, L. S., & Gama, E. M. P. (1996). Gender issues in multicultural counseling. In P. B. Pedersen & J. G. Draguns, et al. (Eds.), *Counseling across cultures* (4th ed., pp. 73–107). Thousand Oaks, CA: Sage.

Hardiman, R. (1982). White identity development: A process-oriented model for describing the racial consciousness of White Americans. *Dissertation Abstracts International, 43,* 104A. (University Microfilms No. 82–10330)

Hassenfeld, I. N., & Sarris, J. G. (1978). Hazards and horizons of psychotherapy supervision. *American Journal of Psychotherapy, 32,* 393–401.

Hayes, J. A. (2002). Playing with fire: Countertransference and clinical epistemology. *Journal of Contemporary Psychotherapy, 32,* 93–100.

Hayes, J. A., McCracken, J. E., McClanahan, M. K., Hill, C. E., Harp, J. S., & Carozzoni, P. (1998). Therapist perspectives on countertransference: Qualitative data in search of a theory. *Journal of Counseling Psychology, 45,* 468–482.

Heatherington, L., & Allen, G. J. (1984). Sex and relational communication patterns in counseling. *Journal of Counseling Psychology, 31,* 287–294.

Hedges, L. E. (1992). *Interpreting the countertransference.* New York: Jason Aronson.

Heller, J. (1961). *Catch-22.* New York: Simon and Schuster.

Helms, J. E. (1990). *Black and White racial identity: Theory, research, and practice.* New York: Greenwood.

Helms, J. E. (1992). *A race is a nice thing to have. A guide to being a White person or understanding the White persons in your life.* Topeka, KS: Content Communications.

Helms, J. E. (1995). An update of Helms' White and people of color racial identity models. In J. G. Ponterotto, J. M Casas, L. A. Suzuki, & C. M. Alexander (Eds.), *Handbook of multicultural counseling* (pp. 181–198). Thousand Oaks, CA: Sage.

Helms, J. E., & Cook, D. A. (1999). *Using race and culture in counseling and psychotherapy: Theory and process.* Boston: Allyn & Bacon.

Heppner, P. P., & Roehlke, H. J. (1984). Differences among supervisees at different levels of training: Implications for a developmental model of supervision. *Journal of Counseling Psychology, 31,* 76–90.

Hill, C. E., & O'Brien, K. M. (1999). *Helping skills: Facilitating exploration, insight, and action.* Washington, DC: American Psychological Association.

Hilton, D. B., Russell, R. K., & Salmi, S. W. (1995). The effects of supervisor's race and level of support on perceptions of supervision. *Journal of Counseling and Development, 73,* 557–563.

Hogan, R. A. (1964). Issues and approaches in supervision. *Psychotherapy: Theory, Research, and Practice, 1*(3), 139–141.

Holloway, E. L. (1984). Outcome evaluation in supervision research. *The Counseling Psychologist, 12,* 167–174.

Holloway, E. L. (1995). *Clinical supervision: A system approach*. Thousand Oaks, CA: Sage.

Hunt, W. (2001). The use of countertransference in supervision. In S. Gill (Ed.), *The supervisory alliance: Facilitating the psychotherapist's learning experience* (pp. 165–179). Northvale, NJ: Jason Aronson.

Ivey, A. E., Fouad, N. A., Arredondo, P., & D'Andrea, M. (1999). *Guidelines for multicultural counseling competencies: Implications for practice, training, and research*. Unpublished manuscript.

Jennings, L., & Skovholt, T. M. (1999). The cognitive, emotional, and relational characteristics of master therapists. *Journal of Counseling Psychology, 46,* 3–11.

Johnson, M. K., Searight, H. R., Handal, P. J., & Gibbons, J. L. (1993). Survey of clinical psychology graduate students' gender attitudes and knowledge: Toward gender-sensitive psychotherapy training. *Journal of Contemporary Psychotherapy, 23,* 233–249.

Jordan, J. V., Kaplan, A. G., & Miller, J. B. (1991). *Women's growth in connection*. New York: Guilford Press.

Jung, C. G. (1933). *Modern man in search of a soul*. Oxford: Harcourt.

Kiesler, D. J. (1979). An interpersonal communication analysis of relationship in psychotherapy. *Psychiatry: Journal for the Study of Interpersonal Processes, 42,* 299–311.

Klein, M. (1975). Notes on some schizoid mechanisms. In *The writings of Melanie Klein* (Vol. 3, pp. 1–24). London: Hogarth Press. (Original work published 1946)

Ladany, N. (in press). Conducting effective clinical supervision. In G. P. Koocher, J. C. Norcross, & S. S. Hill (Eds.), *Psychologists' desk reference* (2nd ed.). New York: Oxford University Press.

Ladany, N., Brittan-Powell, C. S., & Pannu, R. K. (1997). The influence of supervisory racial identity interaction and racial matching on the supervisory working alliance and supervisee multicultural competence. *Counselor Education and Supervision, 36,* 284–304.

Ladany, N., Constantine, M. G., Miller, K., Erickson, C. D., & Muse-Burke, J. L. (2000). Supervisor countertransference: A qualitative investigation into its identification and description. *Journal of Counseling Psychology, 47,* 102–115.

Ladany, N., Ellis, M. V., & Friedlander, M. L. (1999). The supervisory working alliance, trainee self-efficacy, and satisfaction with supervision. *Journal of Counseling & Development, 77,* 447–455.

Ladany, N., & Friedlander, M. L. (1995). The relationship between the supervisory working alliance and trainees' experience of role conflict and role ambiguity. *Counselor Education and Supervision, 34,* 220–231.

Ladany, N., Hill, C. E., Corbett, M. M., & Nutt, E. A. (1996). Nature, extent, and importance of what psychotherapy trainees do not disclose to their supervisors. *Journal of Counseling Psychology, 43,* 10–24.

Ladany, N., Inman, A. G., Constantine, M. G., & Hofheinz, E. (1997). Supervisee multicultural case conceptualization ability and self-reported multicultural competence as functions of supervisee racial identity and supervisor focus. *Journal of Counseling Psychology, 44,* 284–293.

Ladany, N., Lehrman-Waterman, D., Molinaro, M., & Wolgast, B. (1999). Psychotherapy supervisor ethical practices: Adherence to guidelines, the supervisory working alliance, and supervisee satisfaction. *The Counseling Psychologist, 27,* 443–475

Ladany, N., Marotta, S., & Muse-Burke, J. (2001). Supervisee integrative complexity, experience, and preference for supervisor style. *Counselor Education and Supervision, 40,* 203–219.

Ladany, N., & Melincoff, D. S. (1999). The nature of counselor supervisor non-disclosure. *Counselor Education and Supervision, 38,* 161–176.

Ladany, N., & Muse-Burke, J. L. (2001). Understanding and conducting supervision research. In L. J. Bradley & N. Ladany (Eds.), *Counselor supervision: Principles, process, & practice* (3rd ed., pp. 304–329). Philadelphia: Brunner-Routledge.

Ladany, N., O'Brien, K., Hill, C. E., Melincoff, D. S., Knox, S., & Petersen, D. (1997). Sexual attraction toward clients, use of supervision, and prior training: A qualitative study of psychology pre-doctoral interns. *Journal of Counseling Psychology, 44,* 413–424.

Ladany, N., Walker, J., & Melincoff, D. S. (2001). Supervisor style, the supervisory working alliance, and supervisor self-disclosures. *Counselor Education and Supervision, 40,* 263–275.

Lambert, M. J., & Ogles, B. M. (1997). The effectiveness of psychotherapy supervision. In C. E. Watkins Jr. (Ed.), *Handbook of psychotherapy supervision* (pp. 421–446). New York: Wiley.

Leary, T. (1957). *Interpersonal diagnosis of personality; a functional theory and methodology for personality evaluation.* Oxford, England: Ronald Press.

Lehrman-Waterman, D. E., & Ladany, N. (2001). Development and validation of the evaluation process within supervision inventory. *Journal of Counseling Psychology, 48,* 168–177.

Leong, F. T. L., & Wagner, N. S. (1994). Cross-cultural counseling supervision: What do we know? What do we need to know? *Counselor Education and Supervision, 34,* 117–131.

Levant, R. F. (1995). The new psychology of men. *Professional Psychology: Research and Practice, 27,* 259–265.

Levant, R. F., Richmond, K., Majors, R. G., Inclan, J. E., Rossello, J. M., Heesacker, M., et al. (2003). A multicultural investigation of masculinity ideology and alexithymia. *Psychology of Men and Masculinity, 4,* 91–99.

Ligiero, D. P., & Gelso, C. J. (2002). Countertransference, attachment, and the working alliance: The therapist's contributions. *Psychotherapy: Theory, Research, Practice, and Training, 39,* 3–11.

Linehan, M. M. (1980). Supervision of behavior therapy. In A. K. Hess (Ed.), *Psychotherapy supervision: Theory, research, and practice* (pp. 148–180). New York: Wiley.

Linehan, M. (1993). *Cognitive-behavioral treatment of borderline personality disorder.* New York: Guilford Press.

Little, M. (1951). Countertransference and the patient's response to it. *International Journal of Psychoanalysis, 32,* 32–40.

Liu, W. M. (2002). The social class-related experiences of men: Integrating theory and practice. *Professional Psychology: Research and Practice, 33,* 355–360.

Liu, W. M., Ali, S. B., Solek, G., Hopps, J., Dunston, K., & Pickett, T. (2004). Using social class in counseling psychology research. *Journal of Counseling Psychology, 51,* 3–18.

Loganbill, C., Hardy, E., & Delworth, U. (1982). Supervision: A conceptual model. *The Counseling Psychologist, 10*(1), 3–42.

Lower, R. B. (1972). Countertransference resistances in the supervisory situation. *American Journal of Psychiatry, 129,* 156–160.

Mallinckrodt, B., & Nelson, M. L. (1991). Counselor training level and the formation of the psychotherapeutic working alliance. *Journal of Counseling Psychology, 38,* 133–138.

Mann, T. (1939). *The beloved returns. (Lotte in Weimar).* Stockholm: Bermann-Fischer.

Martin, J. S., Goodyear, R. K., & Newton, F. B. (1987). Clinical supervision: An intensive case study. *Professional Psychology: Research and Practice, 18,* 225–235.

McCann, L. I., & Pearlman, L. A. (1990). Vicarious traumatization: A framework for understanding the psychological effects of working with victims. *Journal of Traumatic Stress, 3,* 131–149.

McElroy, L. P., & McElroy, R. A., Jr. (1991). Countertransference issues in the treatment of incest families. *Psychotherapy: Theory, Research, Practice, and Training, 28,* 48–54.

McKinney, M. (2000). Relational perspective and the supervisory triad. *Psychoanalytic Psychology, 17,* 565–584.

McNamara, K., & Rickard, K. M. (1989). Feminist identity development: Implications for feminist therapy with women. *Journal of Counseling and Development, 68,* 184–189.

McNeill, B. W., & Worthen, V. (1989). The parallel process in psychotherapy supervision. *Professional Psychology: Research and Practice, 20,* 329–333.

Melincoff, D. S. (2001). Counselor trainees' sexual attraction toward their supervisors: A qualitative study. *Dissertation Abstracts International, 62*(4-B), 2069.

Melincoff, D. S., Ladany, N., Walker, J. A., Tyson, A., & Muse-Burke, J. (2003). *Trainees' sexual attraction toward their supervisors.* Manuscript submitted for publication.

Miller, J. B. (1991). The development of women's sense of self. In J. V. Jordan, A. G. Kaplan, J. B. Miller, I. P. Stiver, & J. L. Surrey (Eds.), *Women's growth in connection* (pp. 11–26). New York: Guilford Press.

Miller, K. I., Stiff, J. B., & Ellis, B. H. (1988). Communication and empathy as precursors to burnout among human service workers. *Communication Monographs, 55,* 250–265.

Millon, T. (1996). *Personality and psychopathology: Building a clinical science: Selected papers of Theodore Millon.* Oxford, England: Wiley.

Minuchin, S. (1974). *Families and family therapy.* Cambridge, MA: Harvard University Press.

Mitchell, S. A. (1988). *Relational concepts in psychoanalysis: An integration.* Cambridge, MA: Harvard University Press.

Moore, D. L., & Knox, P. L. (1999, August). *Secondary traumatic stress symptoms in therapists.* Paper presented at the 107th meeting of the American Psychological Association, Boston, MA.

Moskowitz, S. A., & Rupert, P. A. (1983). Conflict resolution within the supervisory relationship. *Professional Psychology, 14,* 632–641.

Mueller, W. J., & Kell, B. L. (1972). *Coping with conflict: Supervising counselors and psychotherapists.* New York: Appleton-Century-Crofts.

Munroe, J. F. (1991). Therapist traumatization from exposure to clients with combat-related posttraumatic stress disorder: Implications for administration and supervision. *Dissertation Abstracts International, 52,* B1731.

Munson, C. E. (1987). Sex roles and power relationships in supervision. *Professional Psychology: Research and Practice, 18*(3), 236–243.

Munson, C. E. (1997). Gender and psychotherapy supervision: The partnership model. In C. E. Watkins (Ed.), *Handbook of psychotherapy supervision* (pp. 549–569). New York: Wiley.

Munson, C. E. (2002). *Handbook of clinical social work supervision* (3rd ed.). New York: Haworth Press.

Nash, V. C. (1975). The clinical supervision of psychotherapy. *Dissertation Abstracts International, 36,* 2480B–2481B. (University Microfilms No. 75-24, 581)

National Association of Social Workers. (1999). *National Association of Social Workers code of ethics.* Washington, DC: Author.

Nelson, M. L. (1997). An interactional model for the empowerment of women in supervision. *Counselor Education and Supervision, 37*(2), 125–139.

Nelson, M. L., Englar-Carlson, M., Tierney, S., & Hau, J. (2004). *Class jumping into academia: The social class experiences of counseling academics.* Unpublished manuscript, University of Wisconsin, Madison.

Nelson, M. L., & Friedlander, M. L. (2001). A close look at conflictual supervisory relationships: The trainee's perspective. *Journal of Counseling Psychology, 48,* 384–395.

Nelson, M. L., & Holloway, E. L. (1990). Relation of gender to power and involvement in supervision. *Journal of Counseling Psychology, 37*, 473–481.

Nelson, M. L., & Holloway, E. L. (1999). Supervision and gender issues. In M. Carroll & E. L. Holloway (Eds.), *Clinical supervision in context* (pp. 23–35). London: Sage.

Neufeldt, S. A. (1999). *Supervision strategies for the first practicum* (2nd ed.). Alexandria, VA: American Counseling Association.

Neufeldt, S. A., Beutler, L. E., & Banchero, R. (1997). Research on supervisor variables in psychotherapy supervision. In C. E. Watkins Jr. (Ed.), *Handbook of psychotherapy supervision* (pp. 508–524). New York: Wiley.

Neufeldt, S. A., Iversen, J. N., & Juntunen, C. L. (1995). *Supervision strategies for the first practicum.* Alexandria, VA: American Counseling Association.

Newman, J. E., & Beehr, T. A. (1979). Personal and organizational strategies for handling job stress: A review of research and opinion. *Personnel Psychology, 32*, 1–43.

Norcross, J. C. (2001). Purposes, process, and products of the task force on empirically supported therapy relationships. *Psychotherapy: Theory, Research, Practice, and Training, 38*, 345–356.

Ogden, T. H. (1982). *Projective identification and psychoanalytic technique.* New York: Jason Aaronson.

Olk, M., & Friedlander, M. L. (1992). Role conflict and ambiguity in the supervisory experiences of counselor trainees. *Journal of Counseling Psychology, 39*, 389–397.

O'Neil, J. M. (1981). Male sex role conflicts, sexism, and masculinity: Psychological implications for men, women, and the counseling psychologist. *Counseling Psychologist, 9*, 61–80.

O'Neil, J. M., Good, G. E., & Holmes, S. (1995). Fifteen years of theory and research on men's gender role conflict: New paradigms for empirical research. In R. F. Levant & W. S. Pollack (Eds.), *A new psychology of men* (pp. 164–206). New York: Basic Books.

Orange, D. M. (1995). *Emotional understanding: Studies in psychiatric epistemology.* New York: Guilford Press.

Osipow, S. H., & Spokane, A. R. (1984). Measuring occupational stress, strain, and coping. *Applied Social Psychology Annual, 5*, 67–86

Ossana, S. M., Helms, J. E., & Leonard, M. M. (1992). Do "womanist" identity attitudes influence college women's self-esteem and perceptions of environmental bias? *Journal of Counseling & Development, 70*, 402–408.

Paul, G. L. (1967). Strategy in outcome research in psychotherapy. *Journal of Consulting Psychology, 31*, 109–118.

Pearlman, L. A. (1995). Self-care for trauma therapists: Ameliorating vicarious traumatization. In B. H. Stamm (Ed.), *Secondary traumatic stress: Self-care issues for clinicians, researchers, and educators* (pp. 51–64). Baltimore: The Sidran Press.

Pearlman, L. A., & MacIan, P. S. (1995). Vicarious traumatization: An empirical study of the effects of trauma work on trauma therapists. *Professional Psychology: Research & Practice, 26*, 558–565.

Pearlman, L. A., & Saakvitne, K. W. (1995). *Trauma and the therapist: Countertransference and vicarious traumatization in psychotherapy with incest survivors*. New York: Norton.

Petty, M. M., & Odewahn, C. A. (1983). Supervisory behavior and sex role stereotypes in human service organizations. *The Clinical Supervisor, 1*, 13–20.

Phinney, J. S. (1989). Stages of ethnic identity development in minority group adolescents. *Journal of Early Adolescence, 6*, 34–49.

Pleck, J. H. (1981). *The myth of masculinity*. Cambridge, MA: MIT Press.

Pollack, W. S. (1995). No man is an island: Toward a new psychoanalytic psychology of men. In R. F. Levant & W. S. Pollack (Eds.), *A new psychology of men* (pp. 33–67). New York: Basic Books.

Pollack, W. S. (1998). *Real boys: Rescuing our sons from the myths of boyhood*. New York: Henry Holt & Company.

Ponterotto, J. G. (1988). Racial consciousness development among White counselor trainees: A stage model. *Journal of Multicultural Counseling and Development, 16*, 146–156.

Ponterotto, J. G., Casas, J. M., Suzuki, L. A., & Alexander, C. M. (2001). *Handbook of multicultural counseling* (2nd ed.). Thousand Oaks, CA: Sage.

Ponterotto, J. G., Fuertes, J. N., & Chen, E. C. (2000). Models of multicultural counseling. In S. D. Brown & R. W. Lent (Eds.). *Handbook of counseling psychology* (3rd ed., pp. 639–669) New York: Wiley.

Pope, K. S., Keith-Spiegel, P., & Tabachnick, B. G. (1986). Sexual attraction to clients: The human therapist and the (sometimes) inhuman training system. *American Psychologist, 41*, 147–158.

Pope, K. S., Schover, L. R., & Levenson, H. (1980). Sexual behavior between clinical supervisors and supervisees: Implications for professional standards. *Professional Psychology, 10*, 157–162.

Pope, K. S., Sonne, J. L., & Holroyd, J. (1993). *Sexual feelings in psychotherapy: Explorations for therapists and therapists-in-training*. Washington, DC: American Psychological Association.

Porter, N. (1995). Supervision of psychotherapists: Integrating anti-racist, feminist, and multicultural perspectives. In H. Landrine (Ed.), *Bringing cultural diversity to feminist psychology* (pp. 163–175) Washington, DC: American Psychological Association.

Porter, N., & Vasquez, M. (1997). Covision: Feminist supervision, process, and collaboration. In J. Worrell & N. Johnson (Eds.), *Shaping the future of feminist psychology: Education, research, and practice* (pp. 155–171). Washington, DC: American Psychological Association.

Rabinowitz, F. E., Heppner, P. P., & Roehlke, H. J. (1986). Descriptive study of process and outcome variables of supervision over time. *Journal of Counseling Psychology, 33*(3), 292–300.

Rarick, S. L. (2000). *The relationship of supervisor and trainee gender match and gender attitude match to supervisory style and the supervisory working alliance*. Unpublished doctoral dissertation, Lehigh University, Bethlehem, PA.

Reid, P. T. (2002). Multicultural psychology: Bringing together gender and ethnicity. *Cultural Diversity and Ethnic Minority Psychology, 8,* 103–114.

Reising, G. N., & Daniels, M. H. (1983). A study of Hogan's model of counselor development and supervision. *Journal of Counseling Psychology, 30,* 235–244.

Rhodes, R. H., Hill, C. E., Thompson, B. J., & Elliott, R. (1994). Client retrospective recall of resolved and unresolved misunderstanding events. *Journal of Counseling Psychology, 41,* 473–483.

Rice, L. N., & Greenberg, L. (Eds.). (1984). *Patterns of change: Intensive analysis of psychotherapy process.* New York: Guilford Press.

Rice, L. N., & Saperia, E. P. (1984). Task analysis of the resolution of problematic reactions. In L. N. Rice & L. S. Greenberg (Eds.), *Patterns of change: Intensive analysis of psychotherapy process* (pp. 29–66). New York: Guilford Press.

Ridley, C. R., Mendoza, D. W., Kanitz, B. E., Angermeier, L., & Zenk, R. (1994). Cultural sensitivity in multicultural counseling: A perceptual schema model. *Journal of Counseling Psychology, 41*(2), 125–136.

Roberts, J. L. (2001). Stage fright in the supervision process. In S. Gill (Ed.), *The supervisory alliance* (pp. 81–89). Northvale, NJ: Jason Aaronson.

Robiner, W. N. (1982). Role diffusion in the supervisory relationship. *Professional Psychology, 13,* 258–267.

Robyak, J. E., Goodyear, R. K., & Prange, M. (1987). Effects of supervisors' sex, focus, and experience on preferences for interpersonal power bases. *Counselor Education and Supervision, 26,* 299–309.

Rodolfa, E., Hall, T., Holms, V., Davena, A., Komatz, D., Antunez, M., et al. (1994). The management of sexual feelings in therapy. *Professional Psychology: Research and Practice, 25,* 168–172.

Rodolfa, E., Kraft, W. A., & Reilley, R. R. (1988). Stressors of professionals and trainees at APA-approved counseling and VA medical center internship sites. *Professional Psychology: Research and Practice, 19,* 43–49.

Rodolfa, E., Rowen, H., Steier, D., Nicassio, T., & Gordon, J. (1994). Sexual dilemmas in internship training: What's a good training director to do? *APPIC Newsletter, 19*(2), 1, 22–24.

Rosenberger, E. W., & Hayes, J. A. (2002). Therapist as subject: A review of empirical countertransference literature. *Journal of Counseling & Development, 80,* 264–270.

Rosenblatt, A., & Mayer, J. E. (1975). Objectionable supervisory styles: Students' views. *Social Work, 20,* 184–189.

Rothschild, B. (2002). The dangers of empathy: Understanding the keys to vicarious traumatization. *Psychotherapy Networker, 26*(4), 61–69.

Russell, G. M., & Greenhouse, E. M. (1997). Homophobia in the supervisory relationship: An invisible intruder. *Psychoanalytic Review, 84,* 27–42.

Rust, P. C. (1993). "Coming out" in the age of social constructionism: Sexual identity formation among lesbian and bisexual women. *Gender & Society, 7,* 50–77.

Safran, J. D., Crocker, P., McMain, S., & Murray, P. (1990). Therapeutic alliance rupture as a therapy event for empirical investigation. *Psychotherapy: Theory, Research, Practice, and Training, 27,* 154–165.

Safran, J. D., & Muran, J. D. (1996). The resolution of ruptures in the therapeutic alliance. *Journal of Consulting and Clinical Psychology, 64,* 447–458.

Sansbury, D. L. (1982). Developmental supervision from a skills perspective. *The Counseling Psychologist, 10*(1), 53–57.

Schaefer, R. (1967). Ideals, the ego ideal, and the ideal self. *Psychological Issues, 5,* 131–174.

Schauben, L. J., & Frazier, P. A. (1995). Vicarious trauma: The effects on female counselors of working with sexual violence survivors. *Psychology of Women Quarterly, 19,* 49–64.

Schiavone, C. D., & Jessell, J. C. (1988). Influence of attributed expertness and gender in counselor supervision. *Counselor Education and Supervision, 28,* 29–42.

Searles, H. F. (1955). The informational value of supervisors' emotional experiences. *Psychiatry, 18,* 135–146.

Searles, H. F. (1979). The analyst's experience with jealousy. In L. Epstein & A. H. Feiner (Eds.), *Countertransference* (pp. 305–327). New York: Jason Aronson.

Sells, J. N., Goodyear, R. K., Lichtenberg, J. W., & Polkinghorne, D. E. (1997). Relation of supervisor and trainee gender to in-session verbal behavior and ratings of trainee skills. *Journal of Counseling Psychology, 44,* 406–412.

Skovholt, T., & Rønnestad, H. (1992). *The evolving professional self: Stages and themes in therapist and counselor development.* New York: Wiley.

Sluzki, C. E. (1992). Transformations: A blueprint for narrative changes in therapy. *Family Process, 31,* 217–230.

Sodowsky, G. R., Kwan, K. L. K., & Pannu, R. (1995). Ethnic identity of Asians in the United States: Conceptualization and illustrations. In J. G. Ponterotto, J. M. Casas, L. A. Suzuki, & C. M. Alexander (Eds.), *Handbook of multicultural counseling* (pp. 123–154). Newbury Park, CA: Sage.

Somers, A. (1982). Sexual harassment in academe: Legal issues and definitions. *Journal of Social Issues, 38,* 23–32.

Steering Committee. (2001). Empirically supported therapy relationships: Conclusions and recommendations of the Division 29 Task Force. *Psychotherapy: Theory, Research, Practice, and Training, 38,* 495–497.

Stenack, R. J., & Dye, H. A. (1983). Practicum supervision roles: Effects on supervisee statements. *Counselor Education and Supervision, 23,* 157–168.

Stoltenberg, C. D., McNeill, B. W., & Crethar, H. C. (1994). Changes in supervision as counselors and therapists gain experience: A review. *Professional Psychology: Research and Practice, 25,* 416–449.

Stoltenberg, C. D., McNeill, B. W., & Delworth, U. (1998). *IDM supervision: An integrated developmental model for supervising counselors and therapists.* San Franciso: Jossey-Bass.

Strong, S. R., Hills, H. I., Kilmartin, C. T., & DeVries, H. (1988). The dynamic relations among interpersonal behaviors: A test of complementarity and anti-complementarity. *Journal of Personality and Social Psychology, 54*, 798–810.

Sue, D. W., Arredondo, P., & McDavis, R. J. (1992). Multicultural counseling competencies and standards: A call to the profession. *Journal of Counseling and Development, 70*, 477–486.

Sue, D. W., Carter, R. T., Casas, J. M., Fouad, N. A., Ivey, A. E., Jensen, M., et al. (1998). *Multicultural counseling competencies: Individual and organizational development.* Thousand Oaks, CA: Sage.

Sue, D. W., & Sue, D. (1999). *Counseling the culturally different: Theory and practice* (3rd ed.). New York: Wiley.

Sullivan, H. S. (1953). *The interpersonal theory of psychiatry.* New York: Norton.

Szymanski, D. W. (2003). The feminist supervision scale: A rational/theoretical approach. *Psychology of Women Quarterly, 27*, 221–232.

Teyber, E. (2000). *Interpersonal process in psychotherapy: A relational approach* (4th ed.). New York: Wadsworth.

Thompson, C. E., & Jenal, S. T. (1994). Interracial and intraracial quasi-counseling interactions when counselors avoid discussing race. *Journal of Counseling Psychology, 41*, 484–491.

Tracey, T. J. (1994). An examination of the complementarity of interpersonal behavior. *Journal of Personality and Social Psychology, 67*, 864–878.

Troiden, R. R. (1989). The formation of homosexual identities. *Journal of Homosexuality, 17*, 43–73.

Twohey, D., & Volker, J. (1993). Listening for the voices of care and justice in counselor supervision. *Counselor Education and Supervision, 32*, 189–197.

Vander Kolk, C. J. (1974). The relationship of personality, values, and race to anticipation of the supervisory relationship. *Rehabilitation Counseling Bulletin, 18*, 41–46.

Van Sell, M., Brief, A. P., & Schuler, R. S. (1981). Role conflict and role ambiguity: Integration of the literature and directions for future research. *Human Relations, 34*, 43–71.

Walker, J. A. (2003). *Countertransference in therapy and supervision: Proximal parallel process.* Unpublished doctoral dissertation, Lehigh University, Bethlehem, PA.

Walker, J. A., Ladany, N., & Pate-Carolan, L. (2003). *Gender-related events in psychotherapy supervision in relation to the supervisory working alliance and trainee self-disclosure.* Manuscript submitted for publication.

Wampold, B. E. (2001). *The great psychotherapy debate: Models, methods, and findings.* Mahwah, NJ: Lawrence Erlbaum.

Ward, L. G., Friedlander, M. L., Schoen, L. G., & Klein, J. G. (1985). Strategic self-presentation in supervision. *Journal of Counseling Psychology, 32*, 111–118.

Watkins, C. E. (1990). The separation-individuation process in psychotherapy supervision. *Psychotherapy, 27*, 202–209.

Watkins, C. E. (1995). Pathological attachment styles in supervision. *Psychotherapy: Theory, Research, Practice, and Training, 32*, 333–340.

Wester, S. R., & Vogel, D. L. (2002). Working with the masculine mystique: Male gender role conflict, counseling self-efficacy, and the training of male psychologists. *Professional Psychology: Research and Practice, 33*(4), 370–376.

Wiley, M. O., & Ray, P. B. (1986). Counseling supervision by developmental level. *Journal of Counseling Psychology, 33,* 439–445.

Williams, J. E., & Best, D. A. (1990). *Sex and psyche: Gender and self viewed cross-culturally.* Thousand Oaks, CA: Sage.

Wolberg, L. R. (1988). *The technique of psychotherapy* (Part 2). New York: Grune & Stratton.

Wolfe, C. R., Wang, A., & Bergen, D. (1999). Assessing the winning teams program of interactive satellite-based training. *Behavior research methods, instruments, and Computers, 31,* 275–280.

Wolgien, C. S., & Coady, N. F. (1997). Good therapists' beliefs about the development of their helping ability: The wounded healer paradigm revisited. *Clinical Supervisor, 15*(2), 19–35.

Worthington, E. L., Jr., & Stern, A. (1985). Effects of supervisor and supervisee degree level and gender on the supervisory relationship. *Journal of Counseling Psychology, 32,* 252–262.

Yarris, E., & Allgeier, E. R. (1988). Sexual socialization for therapists: Applications for the counseling/psychotherapy of women. *Women & Therapy, 7,* 57–75.

AUTHOR INDEX

SUBJECT INDEX

ABOUT THE AUTHORS

Nicholas Ladany, PhD, is an associate professor and program coordinator and director of doctoral training in the Counseling Psychology Program in the Department of Education and Human Services at Lehigh University in Bethlehem, Pennsylvania. Prior to this, he was assistant professor at Temple University and a visiting faculty member at the University of Maryland. He received his PhD at the University at Albany, State University of New York in 1992. He has published numerous articles and presented nationally and internationally in the area of psychotherapy supervision and training. In addition, his primary research interest and activity include the interrelationships between supervision process and outcome and psychotherapy process and outcome, including such issues as the working alliance, self-disclosures and nondisclosures, multicultural training, and ethics. In 2001, he received the Outstanding Early Career Achievement Award from the Society for Psychotherapy Research. He is the associate editor of *Psychotherapy: Theory, Research, Practice, and Training* and coedited the book *Counselor Supervision: Principles, Process, and Practice.* He is a licensed psychologist in Pennsylvania.

Myrna L. Friedlander, PhD, is a professor and director of doctoral training in the Division of Counseling Psychology in the Department of Educational and Counseling Psychology at the University at Albany, State University of New York. She received her PhD from The Ohio State University in 1980. A licensed psychologist in New York, she has served as clinician, educator, supervisor, and consultant in a variety of schools, counseling centers, hospitals, and community agencies. She is the 2001–2002 recipient of the Distinguished Psychologist Award from the Psychological Association of Northeastern New York, and in 1999, she received the University at Albany President's Award for Excellence in Research. Dr. Friedlander's theory and research on supervision and the process of psychotherapy have appeared in book chapters and many different refereed journals. A supervisor for over 25 years, she coauthored three instruments on training and supervision, the Self-Efficacy Inventory (Friedlander & Snyder, 1983), the Supervisory Styles Inventory (Friedlander & Ward, 1984), and the Role Conflict and Role Ambiguity Inventory (Olk & Friedlander, 1992). She is a fellow of the American Psychological Association, the American Psychological Society, and the American Association of Applied and Preventive Psychology; she is a member of the Society for Psychotherapy Research and is an adjunct clinical assistant professor in the Department of Psychiatry at Albany Medical College. She is currently an editorial board member of the *Journal of Marital and Family Therapy, Psychotherapy: Theory, Research, Practice, and Training,* and *Psychotherapy Research.* She is a licensed psychologist in New York.

Mary Lee Nelson, PhD, is an associate professor in counseling psychology at the University of Wisconsin—Madison. She received her PhD in counseling psychology at the University of Oregon in 1989. She worked as a staff psychologist and trainer in student counseling centers at both the University of Oregon and the University of Washington, where she served as coordinator of training. She is a licensed psychologist in Washington State and conducted a psychotherapy and supervision practice in Seattle for 11 years. She was also on the counseling faculty of educational psychology at the University of Washington for 12 years. She has taken coursework at the Center for Object Relations in Seattle and was a member of the Northwest Alliance for Psychoanalytic Study.

Dr. Nelson conducts process research on gender, power, and conflict in clinical relationships, particularly supervision. She has published numerous articles and chapters on these topics and others, including methods of training mental health practitioners. She has reviewed for several counseling and psychotherapy journals and currently serves on the editorial board of *The Counseling Psychologist* and *Psychotherapy Research.* She is a licensed psychologist in Wisconsin.

DATE DUE

PRINTED IN U.S.A.